To Brian &
family - The entire
family is in the book
Hope you enjoy it
Love & xxx
Mom

AN INTELLIGENT TORY

Henry Worms, Lord Pirbright
(1840–1903)

Partner in the financial House of Worms,
Conservative Junior Minister
and the first Jewish Privy Councillor

James Grimshaw

Book Guild Publishing
Sussex, England

First published in Great Britain in 2014 by
The Book Guild Ltd
The Werks
45 Church Road
Hove, BN3 2BE

Copyright © James Grimshaw 2014

The right of James Grimshaw to be identified as the author of
this work has been asserted by him in accordance with the
Copyright, Designs and Patents Act 1988.

All rights reserved. No part of this publication may be reproduced, transmitted, or stored in a retrieval system, in any form or by any means, without permission in writing from the publisher, nor be otherwise circulated in any form of binding or cover other than that in which it is published and without a similar condition being imposed on the subsequent purchaser.

Typesetting in Garamond by
YHT Ltd, London

Printed and bound in Great Britain by
CPI Group (UK) Ltd, Croydon, CR0 4YY

A catalogue record for this book is available from
The British Library.

ISBN 978 1 909984 41 7

Contents

List of Illustrations		ix
Preface		xi
Introduction		1
1	**Frankfurt to London**	5
	Germany	5
	Britain	8
	Jewish Emancipation	12
	Rise of the House of Worms	13
2	**Tea and Coffee**	15
3	**Science, Law or Politics?**	19
4	**The Anglo-Jewish Association – Apprenticeship for Politics**	27
	Introduction to Jewish Affairs	27
	Prominence in Jewish Affairs	29
	Dissent	35
5	**Banking and Marriage – the Austrian Connections**	41
	The Bankers	41
	Marriages in Austria	42
	Banking and Trade	43
	A Grand Ceremony	45

CONTENTS

	Politics in Austria	48
	Return to London	54
	A Criminal Conversation	57
	Marriages in London	60
6	**House of Commons: House of Lords**	65
	Into Parliament	65
	In Opposition	69
	Intelligent Toryism	75
	The Primrose League	79
	Imperial Interests	81
	Reform and Litigation	86
	In Government	90
	Sugar and Spice	93
	Trade and Industry	99
	Imperial Obsessions	101
	Opposition Again	105
	House of Lords	110
7	***La Belle Époque***	115
	Prélude	115
	Fin de Siècle	118
8	**Baron Pirbright of Pirbright**	129
	Two Village Lords	129
	Two Village Priests	136
	Apology for Empire	140
	A New Sovereign	147

9 Epilogue	151
Genealogical Tables	161
The Worms Family	161
The House of Rothschild	162
The Cousinhood of Financiers	163
Todesco, Gomperz and Oppenheimer Families of Vienna	164
Worms–Samuel Family Relationships	165
Samuel–Phillips Family Relationships	166
Worms–Phillips–Levy Relationships	167
Bibliography	169
Notes	175
Index	193

List of Illustrations

1   Park Crescent, London (2012)
2   Palais Todesco, Vienna (ca. 1880)
3   The Grand Salon, Palais Todesco (2012)
4   Salon Paris, Palais Todesco (2012)
5   Ceiling painting *The Judgement of Paris* (2012)
6   Henry Worms (1864)
7   Franziska (Fanny) von Todesco (1863)
8   Eduard von Todesco (ca. 1860)
9   Sophie von Todesco (ca. 1860)
10 Worms–Todesco wedding photograph (1864)
11 Friedrich Ferdinand von Beust (1868)
12 Schloss Trauttmansdorff, Meran (1859)
13 Moritz von Léon (ca. 1890)
14 Alice McLaren Morrison (née Worms)
15 Alice de Worms (1884)
16 Constance de Worms (1894)
17 Grosvenor Place, London (2014)
18 Henley Park, Surrey (ca. 1905)
19 Henry Joseph Tenison Halsey (ca. 1920)
20 Henry Lord Pirbright (1897)
21 The Gardens, Pirbright (2009)

LIST OF ILLUSTRATIONS

22   Wall plaques, Pirbright (2010)

23   Reverend Arthur Krauss

24   Reverend John Dunn

25   The Little Girl Statue with Lord and Lady Pirbright (1897)

26   Lord Pirbright's Hall (1899)

27   Bronze Coronation Medal

28   Commemorative plaque, Lord Pirbright's Hall (2012)

29   Lady Pirbright's Guild of Needlework Badge

30   Princess Christian Homes, Bisley (1911)

31   Henry Lord Pirbright (ca. 1900)

32   Sarah Lady Pirbright (ca. 1885)

33   Freifrau Fanny von Worms-Todesco (1895)

34   Pirbright tomb, St. Mark's Church Wyke, Surrey (2011)

Illustration Acknowledgements

Permission for use of the following illustrations is gratefully acknowledged:

Österreichische Nationalbibliothek, 2, 6–10, 16, 33; Gerstner Beletage, Vienna, 3–5; Tiroler Landesmuseum, Innsbruck, 12; Archiv der Tiroler Adelsmatrikel, Innsbruck, 13; Konrad Heumann, Frankfurter Goethe-Haus, 15; Lyn Wilton, 19; The V&A Museum, London, 20; Pirbright Parish Council, 25, 31–2; Pirbright Historians, 23–4, 26, 27, 29; Normandy Historians, 18. The name of the photographer, if known, is recorded under the caption.

Preface

During my working career as a university scientist and professor of chemistry I wrote many papers and contributions to textbooks, as well as a textbook on my own speciality. On retirement I came to live in Pirbright, where you hear many stories about Lord Pirbright and see the monuments he created around the village, though there is no complete account of his life. I have always been interested in history and so was motivated to write a biography of this Victorian gentleman. Any author steps out of his comfort zone with trepidation; my justification is that in my career I wrote the biographies of chemical compounds. Writing a human biography is only a small step away from this.

There are positive memorials to Lord Pirbright's life seen in the buildings he erected, but also some surprising omissions for one so well known in the village. He is buried in the adjacent parish, not in the village church, and his memorial plaque was erected in Pirbright village hall. Pirbright church contains memorial plaques to another family, the Halseys, where they are described as Lay Rectors, for they had purchased the medieval title of Lord of the Manor. The epitaph inscribed on Lord Pirbright's tomb is fulsome in praise of his intelligence, his kindly character and his achievements in politics. Not mentioned is the fact that he was born into a prominent Jewish family.

So a modern-day Pirbright resident is presented with a number of mysteries to solve. What were Lord Pirbright's political achievements, how did he come to Pirbright and how did he relate to the other village powers, the church and the Lord of the Manor? I feel quite at home collecting evidence from letters, speeches and the character references left by other prominent Victorians, contributions towards the solution of these mysteries. The approach is the same as for a scientific investigation: collect the evidence and then make deductions. The exception to this parallel is that I cannot carry out experiments to confirm my work.

As well as illuminating a man's deeds, a biography must also throw light on his character and the forces which throughout life caused his opinions to develop. I have devoted a chapter to each of the main themes in the life of Lord Pirbright rather than presenting all in chronological order. The obvious disadvantage to this scheme is that events closely related in time are separated into different chapters, but overall I believe this scheme better shows the process of character development. I hope this biography throws light on Lord Pirbright's motivations and his gradual movement towards a Christian burial.

In today's world the Internet makes it possible to search and examine many documents with relative ease. I wish to thank the staff at the Surrey libraries, the British Library and its newspaper section, the University of Southampton, the National Archive and the Sigmund Freud Museum for their tireless help in providing original materials, also Pirbright Parish Council for access to the early minute books. Paul Rösch at Schloss Trauttmansdorff, Mgr. Mathias Böhm at Österreichische Nationalbibliothek, the Tiroler Landesmuseum and the Archiv der Tiroler Adelsmatrikel provided information on Henry Worms' life in Austria. The publications of Professor Reinhard Müller of the University of Graz provided information about the Todesco family in Vienna, while Gerstner Beletage provided details of the Palais Todesco in Vienna. Jonathan and Joan Foster (the Pirbright historians) made available invaluable information about the village. For all of these contributions I am most grateful.

My son, Edwin, provided expertise with photography and corrected much of my prose. He and my daughter, Amelia, read the manuscript. Thank you also to my wife for putting up with Lord and Lady P.

J.G., Pirbright

Introduction

> **Boatswain** (referring to the Captain):
> *But in spite of all temptations*
> *To belong to other nations*
> *He remains an Englishman!*
>
> Gilbert and Sullivan, HMS *Pinafore*, Act II (1878)

The picturesque village of Pirbright lies on the southern edge of the ancient Royal Forest of Windsor. It developed from a Saxon hamlet with a small chapel on a patch of poor-quality arable land, surrounded by heath suitable only for rough grazing. The village became a Royal Manor in the twelfth century and the Lordship was gifted to nobles of high rank, for this was prime hunting territory close to London. It has had a sizeable village church since medieval times, dedicated to St Michael and All Angels, with the first incumbent recorded in 1214. In medieval times the main road across the north of Surrey between Chertsey and Frimley passed through the village.

The last princely Lord of the Manor was Catherine of Aragon. She retained the manor after her divorce from Henry VIII until her death, when it reverted to Henry and was sold, finally being acquired in the eighteenth century by the Halsey family. There were no big farms here – the Manor Farm was the largest with 120 acres, while the other farms were more like smallholdings carved out of the heathland. The church boasted a tower but by around 1770 the nave was in a ruinous state and collapsed. Villagers had to petition George III for a countrywide collection to be made to pay for the renovations.

By the early nineteenth century the village became a little more prosperous and had two water-driven mills, a village pond, a village green with a cricket pitch, several timber-framed brick-filled farmhouses and a hostelry, the White Hart. There was one modest mansion built by a retired vice-admiral, John Byron (1723–1786), and a local family, the Faggetters, erected a few brick-built labourers' cottages.

When Henry Worms was about to retire from a successful business career

AN INTELLIGENT TORY

he took the lease of nearby Henley Park, an agreeable oasis and a delightful contrast to the desolation of the Pirbright heath, which spreads to the north. He adopted the village and later took the title of Lord Pirbright for services rendered when he was a member of Lord Salisbury's government. He bought out the local builder together with his stock of land, acquired more patches of land and had houses, shops, post offices and a village hall constructed. These were for let and the village was expanded considerably. Henry Worms became the *de facto* village squire when Henry J.T. Halsey, the inheritor of that medieval position, chose to ignore his duties. As Lord Pirbright he was elected chairman of the newly formed Parish Council in 1895.[1]

The solid red brick houses Henry Worms had constructed still dominate the village centre today and speak of his considerable wealth — as did the gossip surrounding his later years. This English lord was born in London but the origins of the Worms family were in Germany, where they were established as small traders in the Jewish ghetto of Frankfurt. Henry Worms' grandfather lived in the same house as the Rothschilds and married one of the Rothschild daughters. Their son Solomon migrated to London and operated in the money markets.

Solomon had one daughter and three sons; the two eldest sons became partners in the financial House of Worms, which had a special interest in Anglo-Austrian trade. As the youngest son, Henry was allowed to develop as he wished and became attracted to politics and the Conservative Party. When one of his brothers died, Henry was drafted into the family firm and on several occasions acted as their representative in Vienna. Through ability combined with a chance conversation at the time of the Franco-Prussian War he greatly enhanced the family's financial assets, setting himself and his brother on the road to becoming English country gentlemen.

How could a Jew build a political career with the Conservative Party when almost every English Jew was Liberal? Henry Worms' friends would not have been able to introduce him to Conservative circles. He married a rich Viennese lady, a marriage which, as well as supporting the family business, quite unexpectedly gave him an entry into British Conservative circles. His new mother-in-law was a prominent Viennese socialite and through her friends, Henry came to know Count Beust, Imperial Chancellor of Austria. It was through Beust's encouragement and letters of introduction that Henry entered and began to climb the Conservative ranks. His ability was recognised by Lord Salisbury, who made him a junior minister, but further advancement was denied, probably due to prejudice against Jews among members of the Cabinet. When in 1895 Salisbury formed a Conservative–

INTRODUCTION

Liberal government coalition, Liberals demanded positions in government, so Henry Worms was pushed out of any government post and moved to the House of Lords as Lord Pirbright.

Henry Worms was very tolerant of the views of his daughters, though the marriages of two of them outside the Jewish faith, which he supported, caused much friction in Jewish circles. He had been prominent in Jewish affairs but in later years became more and more estranged from his co-religionists. His wife proved a doubtful asset, preferring Austria to London, and separated from her husband. She was found to be involved in an adulterous relationship and there was a lurid divorce case. Henry then made a second marriage to the daughter of a prominent London merchant.

This second marriage was ideal. Henry's new wife provided social support when he was an aspiring junior minister, and gradually he developed as a 'swell', spending lavishly on jewellery for his wife and on entertainment. He was lucky to receive a huge inheritance from an uncle who had approved of the free hand Henry had allowed his daughters. With a London house, a country mansion and a wife as his excellent social secretary, Henry Worms was transformed into a gentleman. Now a lord, he retired from the political scene.

Henry was described by many newspaper reporters as a good public speaker and was much in demand at Conservative rallies around the country. Some of his rise to power in the Conservative Party can be attributed to the early years when he was elected president of the Anglo-Jewish Association. Then he was often required to petition government ministers and impressed them with his eloquence. Henry Worms was no shrinking violet, and in Parliament he had several verbal confrontations with the Liberal Party leader, Gladstone. He is accurately described as thrusting, always taking the best advantage from any situation, whether political or personal.

The Worms family was closely related to the Chief Rabbi, so it came as a great shock to the London Jewish community when in his will Henry stipulated a Christian burial. His funeral was well attended and Lady Pirbright received tokens of condolence from all the living children of Queen Victoria. However, the London Jewish community, except for two Rothschild relatives, ignored the event. In the end, his many connections with Austria and with the Jewish community were forgotten and he had become a truly English gentleman.

Note: Two points of spelling from the nineteenth century have been modernised; Frankfort becomes Frankfurt and Rumania becomes Romania. Remember when reading of the fortunes acquired by persons here that the value of money has increased by approximately a factor of one hundred between the turn of the nineteenth century and today.[2]

1

Frankfurt to London

> **Chor Der Gefangenen**
> *O welche Lust, in freier Luft*
> *Den Atem leicht zu heben!*
> *Nur hier, nur hier ist Leben!*
> *Der Kerker eine Gruft.*
>
> **[Prisoner's Chorus**
> Oh what joy, in the open air
> Freely to breathe again!
> Up here alone is life!
> The dungeon is a grave.]
>
> L. van Beethoven, *Fidelio Act I* (1805)

Germany

On a cold January morning in 1903 mourners assembled at Waterloo Station to take the special train via Guildford to Wanborough, continuing their journey by coach to St Mark's Church for the funeral of Lord Pirbright. The deceased was born in London as Henry Worms, the son of an immigrant from Frankfurt and descended from prominent Jewish families. He entered Parliament as a Conservative, which was unusual for a member of the Hebrew faith at that time, and was raised to the peerage for his services in government. It was a surprise to his co-religionists that he chose to be buried in the Anglican church close to his country residence. So what happened in Henry Worms' life that led him to abandon the faith into which he had been born and adopt the life of an English country gentleman?

Jews had spread out around Europe for over one thousand years with little hindrance, reaching the German districts of the Holy Roman Empire from around the tenth century. They were an alien race with no feudal connection to the local rulers, so they could not own land, and since membership of manufacturing guilds was not open to their race, they were forced into trading, money lending and money exchange in order to earn a living. Thus, out of necessity, Jews found a niche in banking and trade.

The Holy Roman Empire was fragmented into many states, both large and small, so the Jewish families supplied an important service facilitating commerce. By the thirteenth century demonstrations against this exclusive race had become common and the Emperor took them under his special protection and control. Jews handled money and so could be taxed, and they thus became a source of revenue for the ruler in whichever district they lived. Their rights of residence in specified places became privileges to be sold by the Emperor – a privilege that was in demand because as the Jewish community grew it became an important tax base. The Jews could not object to any taxes imposed on them, for they were dependent on the local administration to uphold the Emperor's protection of them.[1]

The first record of the Worms family is from the city of Worms, an important Jewish centre from the tenth century and a city directly subject to the Emperor. At some time in 1618 during the religious wars of that period one of the family members migrated from that city when it was controlled by a Calvinist anti-Jewish faction, to the free city of Frankfurt, a safer haven for Jews.[2] Later, as Jews were required to adopt a family surname, this group took the name Worms. Their move brought greater possibilities for trade, for Frankfurt was the nominal capital of the Holy Roman Empire, directly subject to the Emperor, and where the election and coronation of each new emperor took place by a college of twelve hereditary princes. The second city of the Empire was Vienna in Austria. The Emperor lived there from 1440, and that city became home to another important group of Jewish merchants and bankers. The connections by race between all the Jewish communities in the Empire and the disinclination of the aristocracy to be involved in trade gave Jews an important advantage in business.

Frankfurt had bought the rights of residence for its Jews from the Emperor in 1349 and arrangements devolved so that an individual Jew had a residence permit for three years only. After this time the permit was renewed for a further three years on payment of a sum of money. Jews were only allowed to settle in one small area of the city, a single long street called the *Judengasse*. Permission was required to leave the district and a fee for re-entry was levied. The *Judengasse* had housed only a few hundred families when it was first established, but as the families expanded and settlers were allowed in, the street became a very overcrowded ghetto. People lived in tall three-storeyed houses built close to each other with two or three families to a house. The area was noisy, smelly and had grossly inadequate water and sewage facilities. Rickets was a common disease because the street received so little sunlight.³

The Rothschild family lived in the *Judengasse* and their family name derives from a red shield, which was the symbol of their house, dwellings being distinguished by decorated signs rather than by numbers. The story of the Worms and Rothschild families and their migration from Frankfurt to London begins with Benedict Moses Worms (1769–1824) and Mayer Amschel Rothschild (1744–1812). Both families were involved in the cotton cloth trade and they lived in sections of the same house on the *Judengasse.*

Mayer Amschel Rothschild also operated a money-exchanging business and he developed a deep interest in the antique coins passing through the Frankfurt market. In Hanover, where he had other business interests, he made the acquaintance of another coin collector, General von Estorff. The latter subsequently moved to Hesse and introduced Mayer Amschel to the ruling prince of that district. Mayer Amschel Rothschild began business with this prince and obtained the equivalent warrant of 'By Special Appointment' to the court of Hesse. This title on his business cards opened the door to more princely houses, so that he became well known as a coin dealer.

After France had invaded Holland in 1795 and suppressed the Amsterdam Bourse, a type of stock exchange, the activities of this centre transferred to Frankfurt, causing a great increase in business there, and all the city's bankers began to realise enormous profits. The titular head of Germany was the Holy Roman Emperor, who was elected for life, and during the election of the last Holy Roman Emperor, Mayer Amschel Rothschild obtained the title of 'Imperial Agent' by Letters Patent of 29 January 1800. This opened all doors in Germany and beyond for his business, which by now included banking. Mayer Amschel Rothschild's business expanded from Germany into Austria, and then as far as London, at first only facilitating currency exchange, but later looking at bonds for investment.

The intimate business and social connections between Mayer Amschel Rothschild and Benedict Moses Worms led to the marriage of Mayer Amschel's eldest daughter, Jeannette, to Benedict Moses. On his marriage, Benedict received a dowry of 5,000 gulden, and a legacy of 10,000 gulden (about £900)⁴ on the death of his father-in-law. Three sons and a daughter were born from this marriage, and all later migrated to either London or Vienna. Mayer Amschel also had two other daughters married to business associates in Frankfurt, clearly wishing to keep these associates on a tight rein. In his will of 1812 he excluded daughters and sons-in-law from shares in the firm of Mayer Amschel Rothschild & Sons that he had established, putting his business on a firmly patriarchal basis.⁵

Benedict Moses and his wife never left Frankfurt, and after Benedict died, his widow, Jeanette, was persuaded by her Rothschild relations in 1824 to remarry. The new husband was an impecunious stockbroker from the *Judengasse* who gambled away the dowry, and eventually the Rothschild brothers-in-law had to support their impoverished sister.

Britain

The connection of the Worms and the Rothschild families with Britain began as a result of the changing patterns of trade and the upheavals caused by the political revolution in France. By the eighteenth century, overseas trading had begun to make a strong contribution to the British economy and naval warfare with Holland had greatly weakened competition from that country. Later in that century British engineers developed the water-powered cotton spinning mills which made the production of cotton cloth very cheap in Lancashire and the Scottish lowlands. Several Frankfurt firms, including the Rothschilds' started importing British cotton. On the political front, the wars that followed the French Revolution had already closed the Amsterdam Bourse (Stock Exchange) and the Napoleonic period ended the Holy Roman Empire. The last emperor resigned in 1806. Many of the petty German States were coerced into a Confederation of the Rhine and Napoleon removed the restrictions on residence and travel for Jews. Enterprising individuals were then able freely to leave the overcrowded Frankfurt ghetto. Napoleon's influence did not, however, extend to Austria, where Jewish emancipation came much later.

After the fall of Napoleon in 1814, a loose Confederation of German States was set up at the Congress of Vienna binding the smaller states, Prussia and Austria. Collectively they agreed to respect each other's integrity but then proceeded to set up tariff barriers and passed their own local laws. The rulers occasionally met in Frankfurt, with Austria in charge as the most powerful state. Frankfurt had become an independent city-state within the Confederation and its Senate began in 1816 to erode Jewish freedoms granted earlier in the century. A law of 1824 confirmed the private rights of Jewish citizens but excluded them from all political life. Frankfurt's Jews did not receive full legal equality until 1864.[6]

England was attracting Jewish merchants during the second half of the eighteenth century even though Jews had not always been kindly treated there. In the reign of King John from 1199 to 1216, Jews were openly arrested, imprisoned and tortured to make them give up their wealth; they could set up business only under the King's sufferance and he regularly raided their profits through taxation.[7] This raiding of profits continued under the reign of Henry III so that by the reign (1272–1307) of Edward I the Jews were mostly bankrupt. They were forbidden to lend money even when they were only charging a reasonable interest, and since this had been their livelihood, they were forced to sell mortgages at a discount in order to live. Rich Christians bought up these mortgages in order to foreclose and to acquire the land, a practice that caused much resentment among the general population. Finally a statute of Edward I expelled the Jews from England in 1290.[8]

Over the centuries some Jews migrated from Spain and Portugal back to England, where they maintained a precarious and secret existence. By 1656, Oliver Cromwell ruled that the Edict of Expulsion only applied to Jews living in England before 1290, so those who migrated later could come out of hiding to form an open but mostly poor community. After closure of the Amsterdam market the magnet of trade in a safe environment made London a natural destination from Holland for Jews with business skills. The younger sons of the Rothschild and Worms families followed from Frankfurt and other entrepreneurs came from East Prussia. By the beginning of the nineteenth century London housed a community of rich Jewish merchants who began to intermarry.

Nathan Rothschild (1777–1836) was the third son of Mayer Amschel Rothschild who, as a young man, felt that he was not given sufficient scope in the Frankfurt business. After talking to one English commercial traveller visiting Frankfurt, Nathan suggested expansion of the family business to Britain. He proposed that he would represent the family firm of M.A. Rothschild & Sons, trading in cotton and exotic goods bought in Manchester, Glasgow and other British cities, and then shipping these into the Continent using the contacts and associates set up by his father. This he achieved, establishing himself in Brown Street, Manchester in 1797, and by 1802, having realised a fortune of £200,000, he moved to London and founded a house in St Helen's Place in association with his father's gradually increasing business. The venture was successful but it was soon threatened by the manoeuvres of Napoleon aimed at the invasion and defeat of Britain.[9]

Napoleon's wish to invade Britain had been frustrated by the defeat and virtual annihilation of the French and Spanish fleets on 21 October 1805 at the Battle of Trafalgar. Napoleon then abandoned the idea of invading Britain and instead adopted an indirect strategy – that of economic warfare. The Berlin Decrees of November 1806 and the Milan Decrees of December 1807 together established the Continental System – a blockade that was designed to close continental ports and deny Britain its markets in Europe for exports and re-exports, so ruining the British economy.

With a flourishing business in Britain, Nathan Rothschild had to become a smuggler to take his goods into the Continent. He made it appear that the goods did not come from Britain and used obscure shipping routes and ports where the customs officials were not efficient. As a result of the blockade, profits on goods shipped over to the Continent became even greater, and the British government assisted their transportation by establishing a commercial depot on the island of Heligoland off the coast of Germany near the mouth of the Elbe – an island which, from 1807, had been under British control. Through this trade Nathan Rothschild increased his capital and eventually moved into banking. Before 1826 the number of Jewish brokers in the City was limited to twelve and they had to buy this privilege for between £1,000 and £2,000. The Rothschild office and counting house at 2 New Court, St. Swithin's Lane opened in 1811. New Court was then a group of three-storeyed houses in a prosperous neighbourhood. Today it has become an office block south of the Bank of England building and is still in the possession of the Rothschild family.[10]

Solomon Benedict Worms (1801–1882), eldest son of Benedict Moses Worms, the business associate of Nathan's father and also Nathan Rothschild's nephew, arrived in London in 1814 shortly after the Battle of Waterloo. He was probably invited over by his uncle, with the agreement of his father, to learn a trade, and Nathan was the master of merchant banking. William Humboldt, the Prussian ambassador, reported back in 1818 to his government in Berlin: 'Rothschild is now easily the most enterprising business man in this country.'[11] Initially Solomon worked in the Rothschild house in New Court, living with Nathan Rothschild at nearby Angel Court.

A number of wealthy trading families lived in this neighbourhood, including the Cohens. The head of this family, Levi Barent Cohen (1740–1808), was born in Holland and had established himself in London by 1770. Nathan Rothschild married Hanna Cohen, daughter of Levi Barent Cohen, and gradually built up the Rothschild banking business, while Louis Cohen, son of Levi Barent Cohen, built up the firm of Louis Cohen & Sons, stockbrokers and bankers. Ester, a second daughter of Levi Barent Cohen, married Samuel Moses Samuel (1773–1873), a rich merchant, and Henrietta, the daughter of this pair, married Solomon Worms. Two further daughters of Levi Barent Cohen married into wealthy Jewish families: Judith to Moses Montefiore (1784–1885) and Amelia to Denis Moses Samuel (1784–1860), a brother of Samuel Moses Samuel. The Samuel family members were prosperous traders, and Behrend George Samuel (1804–1893), a son of Samuel

Moses Samuel, was later to inherit much of the family fortune. Also related to the Samuel family were the Phillips family, immigrants from Bohemia and rich merchants. Thus a 'cousinhood' of wealthy financiers was formed in London, centred on Levi Barent Cohen as the arch-ancestor. Their interrelationships are given in the appendix.[12]

Solomon Worms inherited money in 1824 on the death of his father, who had remained in Frankfurt. His marriage to Henrietta Samuel in 1827 was celebrated at the Rothschild's recently acquired suburban house at Stamford Hill, near Stoke Newington, overlooking the Lea Valley.[13] From the late eighteenth century the rich had begun to purchase properties in Hackney on the eastern edge of the London conurbation to escape the overcrowding and atmospheric pollution further in, for it was possible to commute on horseback from Stoke Newington and Hackney to the City.[14] Solomon took out denization papers in 1833, which gave him the right of residence in Britain though he remained a citizen of Frankfurt. Naturalisation became possible only after 1835, and Solomon did not apply for this until 1874.

Solomon's wedding must have brought with it a substantial dowry, since the Samuel family was rich from trading in Brazil. The firm of Samuel, Phillips and Co. had settled there during the period after 1808 when Napoleon had invaded Portugal to bolster his Continental System. The Portuguese royal family moved to Brazil and that country became a free-trade area where several Samuel brothers, along with Alfred Phillips, made substantial profits.[15]

There were four children from Solomon's marriage, George (1829–1912), Anthony (1830–1864), Ellen Henrietta (1836–1894) and Henry (1840–1903). Their mother died when the youngest, Henry, was only five years old. In the early nineteenth century, rich Jewish families lived in close proximity to the City of London and most with German origins worshipped in the Great German Synagogue, constructed in 1790 at Dukes Place, City of London, and destroyed by bombing in 1941.[16] As they grew in wealth, these families abandoned the City as a place of residence and soon it became the fashion to live in the West End of London; later they began to acquire houses in the countryside not too far from London. After his marriage, Solomon Worms followed this fashion and set up house at 27 Park Crescent, south of London's Regents Park. Solomon remained at that address until, very late in life, he moved to Brighton. Nash had developed Park Crescent between 1810 and 1830 and this area, along with Belgravia in West London, soon attracted many of the rich, including the Rothschilds, the Cohens and the Phillipses.

After 1826 Solomon was able to set up as a broker without the need to apply for a licence. As his business interests prospered and the children grew up, Solomon planned the firm of G. & A. Worms. This was named after his two eldest sons, George and Anthony, who were its principal brokers. He also traded extensively with Ceylon.

Jewish Emancipation

Life for Jews in early-nineteenth-century Britain was certainly easier than it was in Frankfurt, but, along with Nonconformists and Roman Catholics, Jews suffered many civil disabilities. They were prevented from taking office in city corporations and from sitting in Parliament through the Test and Corporations Acts, passed in 1661 and 1673, shortly after immigration had been permitted by Cromwell. These acts required all aspirants for office to take communion in the form of the Church of England. Similar restrictions made it impossible for Jews, Nonconformists and Roman Catholics to enter Oxford or Cambridge. Another statute, dating from the reign of Edward I, forbade Jews from holding land as freehold, and in its strict application, which was by this time no longer in force, it required them to wear distinctive clothing.

Over the lifetime of Solomon Worms the situation for all non-Anglicans was gradually ameliorated. The efforts of Lord John Russell (1792–1878), Whig and later Liberal politician, ensured that the Test and Corporation Acts were repealed by 1828, though the Anglican bishops in conference at Lambeth became concerned over any unexpected consequences. On their behalf the Bishop of Llandaff (1796–1849, consecrated 1827), in the House of Lords and decidedly a Tory, introduced an amendment obliging anyone accepting public office 'solemnly and sincerely to testify and declare upon the true faith of a Christian'.[17] This new procedure was acceptable to Nonconformists and Roman Catholics but not to Jews. Between 1841 and 1848, two further Jewish relief bills were put forward, passed by the Commons but again rejected by the Lords.

Two men in particular battled hard for a Jewish relief bill. David Salomons (1797–1873), a prominent London financier, was repeatedly elected to the Court of Aldermen of the City of London but then rejected for his inability to swear the required declaration. He was allowed to take this seat after 1845 when a Jewish Disabilities Removal Act opened up municipal offices. Lionel Nathan Rothschild (1808–1879), Nathan's son and a Liberal who supported the then Prime Minister, Lord John Russell, was elected as one of the four MPs for the City of London in 1847 but could not take his seat. At that time many districts elected more than one MP. He resigned so that a vacancy could be declared and stood successfully for re-election in 1848, a procedure that was repeated in 1852 as a means of exerting pressure for a Jewish relief bill. David Salomons, meanwhile, was elected to the House of Commons in 1851 after a by-election for Greenwich; he swore the oath omitting the offensive words and took his seat. After taking part in three parliamentary divisions and being fined on each occasion for not having taken the prescribed oath, he withdrew from Parliament. Lionel Nathan Rothschild was again elected in 1857 and this time remained in waiting at the bar of the House until a compromise was reached and he could take the oath. He remained an MP until 1874. Robert Cecil, later to become the Marquis of Salisbury and Conservative prime minister, voted against this compromise bill.[18]

It was the Liberal Party that pushed for adoption of these measures, and as a consequence, all Jews who entered mainstream politics joined the Liberals. Henry Worms was the first influential Jewish politician who joined the Conservatives. Under the compromise of 1857 between Lords and Commons, each House adopted its own form of oath. In the Commons, Jews could swear on the Old Testament wearing their cap and without reference to the Christian faith. The Lords retained their Christian oath until 1885, after which Lionel Nathan's son Nathaniel Mayer Rothschild (1840–1915) became a peer.[19]

Gradually, other laws restricting the civil rights of members of the Jewish faith were repealed. After 1835 they could be naturalised and by 1847 marriage in the Jewish faith became legal. Jews were allowed to take degrees at Cambridge University by 1856 and at Oxford by 1871. The address given to Queen Victoria on the occasion of her Jubilee in 1887 expressed feelings on the progress made: 'The British Jews have special cause to rejoice at your Majesty's Jubilee, for during your Majesty's reign the disabilities under which they laboured have one by one been removed, and they now fully participate in the civil and political rights enjoyed by the rest of your Majesty's subjects.'[20]

Rise of the House of Worms

Nathan Rothschild's five sons entered the banking business and were eventually set up as heads of the House of Rothschild in London, Frankfurt, Paris, Vienna and Naples. The rise and reign of the House of Rothschild is well discussed by many authors, and more detailed accounts are referenced in the bibliography. Nathan enjoined his sons always to work together and they built up a powerful position as negotiators of government loans around Europe.

The firm of G. & A. Worms was built up by Solomon Worms as a brokerage business specialising in connections with Austria. Solomon built up alliances with Austrian bankers in the manner of a medieval prince: two of his sons were married to daughters of the richest merchant bankers in Vienna, while his daughter married another banker from Vienna. George and Anthony Worms were the original directors of this firm, but after Anthony died Henry took his place. The House of Worms initially helped to broker loans to the Austrian government organised through the House of Rothschild, for which they received a percentage and also had to distribute the interest, transmitted in bulk from Vienna. More lucrative was dealing in Bills of Exchange, claims for payment in the future made on the buyer by a seller of goods. These IOUs could be discounted with banks, or endorsed and passed on as money.[21] There was clear need for a specialist dealing with Bills of Exchange between Britain and Austria, and the House of Worms in London, allied to some of the great banking houses in Vienna, filled this gap, thus becoming extremely powerful.

2

Tea and Coffee

> *No capitalists in the colony have contributed more to its advancement by judgement and moderation in time of excitement, and by firmness and perseverance in periods of difficulty.*
>
> James Emerson Tennent, *Ceylon* (1859)

When Solomon Worms left Frankfurt to seek his fortune he left behind two younger brothers, Gabriel (1801–1881) and Maurice (1805–1867), who soon followed in his footsteps. Maurice came to London and operated on the Stock Exchange while Gabriel, who first acted as a merchant in Paris, joined his brother at the London Exchange in 1830 after the July revolution in Paris. Maurice showed an adventurous spirit, he became a naturalised British subject and in 1841 set sail for the Far East, prospecting for business opportunities. He stopped first in Bombay, then travelled on to Colombo where he made extensive journeys by horse into the interior of Ceylon. Later he moved on to Calcutta and to China. After surveying these areas he decided on Ceylon as a place of opportunity and bought land at Pussellawa in the hill country 24 miles south of Kandy. Gabriel obtained denization rights in Britain during 1841 with the intention of migrating to the colonies and was invited by Maurice to join him in Ceylon, where they set up as G. & M.B. Worms, with their factory at Pussellawa and offices in Colombo. Some of the capital for this venture came from Solomon, who spent time in Ceylon between 1845 and 1851 helping to set up the business, but the overall management of the firm was in the hands of Gabriel and Maurice, both of whom remained bachelors. Solomon returned to Britain to arrange the marriages of his children, one in London and three in Vienna, and to set up the financial house of G. & A. Worms.[1]

Coffee was then the major export crop of Ceylon, with cinchona bark for the extraction of quinine a close second. Pussellawa was given up for the growing of coffee and became both the largest and the most modern plantation and production house on the island. It was, and still is, called the Rothschild Estate, probably after Jeanette Rothschild, mother of the three

Worms brothers. The business was very well regarded and Edward Stanley (1826–1893, from 1869, 15th Earl of Derby) entertained the Worms family in Ceylon during his tour of the British dominions.[2] Prepared coffee beans were sent to Colombo by cart and later by train. They were then exported to Britain. The estate also started a small-scale production of tea, possibly being the first to introduce this commodity to Ceylon. Maurice seems to have brought the tea plants from China, even though at the time this was forbidden by the Chinese government, and nurtured them at Pussellawa, where he employed one Chinese labourer to produce acceptable tea. Presents of small amounts of tea were sent to his relatives in London.[3] However, production could not be scaled up, as the local population had no knowledge of the process that was involved.

By 1862 the brothers had decided to retire to England, and they sold their coffee estates as going concerns for a total of £157,000. Some ten years later coffee plants in Ceylon became infected with the fungal disease coffee rust, which became a problem worldwide. The coffee vines were removed in the 1880s and the estate planted instead with tea bushes using expertise brought in from Assam. It still produces tea to this day. Maurice retired to The Lodge, Egham, and on his death in 1867 this property passed to Solomon Worms. Gabriel retired to lodgings in London, first in Bond Street and then in Dorset Square, and after his death in 1881 the residue of his estate passed to his brother Solomon.[4]

It was Maurice Worms who introduced the family to Egham in Surrey, easily reached from London by train. Henry's brother George was attracted to this area and purchased part of the Milton Park estate in October 1870. He later purchased an adjacent piece of land and from then on maintained the London house together with Milton Park as his country seat. About the same time, Henry purchased a lease on South Gate, a large house along Knightsbridge in London. George and later his descendants lived at Milton Park until 1948, when it was sold to become the headquarters of the British Leather Manufacturing Research Association. The S.C. Johnson wax company bought the property in 1978 for use as its European headquarters, then sold it in 2008 to a property development company that replaced the house with an elegant modern building.[5]

In the 1861 census both George and Anthony Worms gave their occupation as East India merchants and were probably involved in marketing produce from the Worms' venture in Ceylon. By the early 1860s Solomon and his sons were persuaded to invest in Indian commerce. Agricultural products then imported from India included indigo, cinchona bark, opium and tea. The early-nineteenth-century explorers had noted tea bushes flourishing in the tribal areas of Assam and saw that the local population was skilled at producing a very acceptable tea. By the 1860s the problem for this nascent tea industry was one of providing capital to organise production and to develop the estates.

A group of London financiers, who included Messrs. G. & A. Worms, addressed this problem of capital by floating the Land Mortgage Bank of India[6] and so started the development of India as one of the major tea-producing countries of the world. The Land Bank was incorporated on 5 October 1863 with a subscribed capital of £2,000,000 in £20 shares bearing the signature of A.M. Worms as a director. The head office was in London and there were agents in Bombay, Calcutta and Madras.[7] Initially shareholders were asked to subscribe twenty percent of the capital and there were never any further calls on them. The description of this proposed business suggested that lending money on land security in India would be very profitable as this money was needed for industrial development and there was always the security of the land. The company proposed to attract custom by charging lower rates of interest than did the local Indian moneylenders. Anthony died in 1864 and Henry joined this mortgage bank in November of that year to replace him on the board.[8] After four years Henry retired from the board but continued to be associated with the company, acting as a trustee for a few years, though later members of the Worms family were associated only as shareholders.[9]

Debentures were floated for an issue of £500,000 to supply the working capital in India, and these were to be redeemed after thirty years.[10] From the start, however, business was not as profitable as had been predicted. A rise in interest rates in London also made take-up of the debentures slow, though after a year the full sum had been subscribed. The company had also to weather a financial disaster – the 'Black Friday' of 10 May 1866, when the London discount house of Overend, Gurney & Company failed, causing a run on banks. 'At last I became as rich as the Gurneys' was a topical line from one of the Gilbert and Sullivan satirical operettas.[11]

Business ventures of the firm in Bombay were disastrous, but in Calcutta development of the tea industry proved very advantageous and in a short time it began to make a good profit in Indian currency.[12] A problem that the financiers did not foresee arose because, while the value of sterling from 1816 had been tied to gold, the value of the rupee had been tied to silver since 1818 and by 1853 gold was demonetised in India. The rupee began to fall in value between 1871 and 1873 because the newly unified Germany demonetised silver to adopt the gold standard, and the USA did the same. World demand for silver fell, so its price relative to gold also fell. The value of silver was further reduced by the discovery of vast sources of gold and silver in the western United States. The gold was taken up by central banks as a currency reserve but the silver became a drag on the market. So the silver rupee continued to depreciate against the gold sovereign during the last quarter of the century. Albert Simpson, writing in 1897, noted: 'the rupee and the florin [now the 10p piece] both contain the same weight of silver, both are stamped with the same royal head, and it is manifestly absurd that one should buy two shillings [10p] worth of labour and the other only fourteen pennies [now about 6p] worth'.[13]

If, over the working life of a mortgage, the value of silver depreciated, then the recovered Indian capital was of less value in sterling than the original sum. This was a common problem for many British investors in India and it creeps into writings of the period. Oscar Wilde advised one of his characters thus: 'Cecily, you will read your Political Economy in my absence. The chapter on the fall of the Rupee you may omit.'[14] Prudence forced a change in the business plan of the Land Mortgage Company of India. By 1873 the company began to buy working tea estates and run them as going concerns, rather than acting simply as a mortgage company. It also obtained estates after the owners defaulted on the mortgage. Its profits in rupees were invested in India and it acquired a director with a sound knowledge of tea cultivation in India. The company was transformed into a tea-growing and -marketing concern.[15]

As a result of these changes, business began to improve and the tea produced was shipped to England to be sold for sterling. The company had to weather a period of depression around 1880, which saw a flood of cheap tea from China. Its directors remarked at that time: 'We produce tea at a higher cost and of finer quality but the public tends to buy cheaper teas and to be seduced by the gifts given with some inferior teas.'[16] It was able to pay the interest on debentures and to redeem some of them, but shareholders complained of very poor dividends during these times. By 1894 the directors could begin redemption of all debentures at par and this exercise was completed by 1897, when the company was finally liquidated.[17] The Glasgow-based Amalgamated Tea Estates Company Ltd acquired the company's tea estates in India, paying with sterling in London.[18] Shareholders received a return of twenty percent of their share value – that is, the amount they supplied when the company started. The company never defaulted on interest payments to debenture holders, but yearly dividends were not always paid on shares.[19]

3

Science, Law or Politics?

> *A man whose rare gifts of intellect cultivated to the highest were combined with a warmth and largeness of heart*
>
> Sarah Pirbright (1903)[1]

Henry Worms was born in London in 1840, the youngest of four children. He is described as a scholar at home, educated by private tutors, and by his teens he had a sound classical education. In common with most Jewish children of the mercantile class, he spoke fluent French and German and on one occasion in 1854, when Solomon travelled on business to Vienna, he took Henry along with him to improve his German.[2] The speeches Henry made in later years are peppered with classical quotations, and while on an official visit to the seamen's hospital in Greenwich, he astounded his colleagues by conversing with patients in seven different languages. At the age of sixteen it was time for him to decide between a business career or taking a course of further education. His two elder brothers had entered the family brokerage business as soon as they were old enough, but he was looking for some other occupation. Two colleges of further education were open to Jews in the middle of the nineteenth century. The first college to be founded, in 1826, as nondenominational was University College London, situated on Gower Street. The second was King's College London, founded in 1828 as a Church of England alternative to the 'godless hordes of Gower Street' and situated on The Strand. This college soon abolished its restrictions on religion for students, but for many years it required staff to adhere to the Anglican faith. Henry Worms entered the Department of Science and Engineering at King's College in 1856 as a day student. This college also offered evening classes in some subjects, and George Worms attended such classes in economic science from January 1859.

This choice of university seems strange since Jewish students had long favoured University College, but the Worms family lived on Park Crescent, and a few doors along this terrace of houses lived Charles Wheatstone

(1802–1875), Professor of Experimental Philosophy (i.e. Physics) at King's College. Wheatstone was one of the country's foremost experimentalists and had made huge contributions to telegraphy. He was at the height of his career and entirely engrossed in research, having ceased to give lectures to students. It was probably an acquaintance with this great man of science that decided Henry to enter King's College. Its Department of Science and Engineering was also in the fore of the public mind because the government had requested that it supply engineers during the Crimean War of 1852–1856. The number of full-time students was around 60 when Henry Worms attended the Science Department.

From the outset Henry Worms was very self-assured and active in student life. He became a member of the Engineering Society on 18 November 1857. The Society dated from 1847, and W.S. Gilbert (1836–1911), when he was a student, attempted to transform this into a Reading Society. It reverted to its original function soon after Gilbert left the college. At the first meeting of the reformed society, Henry Worms stood for a vacant position on the committee. He came second on a vote by show of hands but promised 'to assist the Society as much as possible, although they objected to have him as an officer or committee member.'[3] During the round of elections for March 1858, Worms was appointed as one of two auditors and gained a place on the committee after a competitive election.

There was much rivalry in the Engineering Society between Henry Worms and George F. Chambers (1841–1915) – they were of a similar age and had entered college at the same time. Chambers later pursued a career as a barrister but retained a lifelong interest in astronomy.[4] When the next round of elections for Society officers arrived in June 1858, both stood for president. Henry Worms won with 17 votes to Chambers' 14 and resigned as auditor. There was a similar competition in December 1858, with 17 votes for Worms against 7 for Chambers, and again in June 1859, when Worms won again. After this date Henry Worms was elected president without opposition until June 1861, when there was a ballot, with Worms receiving 11 votes, Chambers 4 and Cass 3.[5]

The general student body at King's College held set debates almost weekly and usually on political subjects. Henry Worms, true to the sentiments of his Jewish relations in Parliament, assumed leadership of the college's Liberal Party. However, his political allegiance changed over time and he became a strong Conservative as a consequence of his friendship with a contemporary evening-class student of literature who was a Conservative. This student left King's in 1859, eventually moving into Lincoln's Inn to read law. He became a successful barrister, entered Parliament as Sir Edward Clarke QC (1841–

1931), and became Solicitor General for the Salisbury administration in which Henry Worms also served.[6]

The Engineering Society required students to present papers on a scientific topic, and abstracts of these were published in *The Transactions*, which was only available to members of the Society. Volume 1, covering early 1858, was preserved by the then Society President, but no others are known still to exist. Chambers became editor of this journal and in February 1860 the President, Henry Worms, had to call attention to mistakes and omissions in the latest copy. A committee decided unanimously to refuse to accept the work as published. Chambers was 'requested to make good at his own expence the loss incurred by the printing of these Transactions,' payment demanded by 7 February otherwise he would be expelled from the Society. It seems that he did not pay because at the next general meeting on 7 February Chambers is referred to as the late editor. This meeting accepted Chambers' explanation and Henry Worms' proposal that Chambers should not be expelled and a motion 'that a vote of censure be passed on Mr. Chambers and that the vote be recorded in the Transactions' was carried.[7] Chambers extracted his revenge during May of the following year, when he proposed a rule to the effect that if any officer absent himself for more than three consecutive meetings he shall be fined. This rule was passed and a fine of two shillings and six pence imposed (now 12½p but then the cost of a good dinner). It was clearly aimed at Henry Worms, who, by January 1861, was beginning to absent himself from meetings.[8]

Papers read to the Society covered a wide range of topics. Henry Worms contributed to the discussion on the *Leviathan* (later known as the Great Eastern Steamship) on 12 February 1858. The subject was very topical for this ship had only been launched three weeks before. She was by far the largest ship ever built with a capacity to carry 4,000 passengers from England to Australia in comfort without refuelling. He ventured the opinion that 'had she been ready for sea last summer, on the arrival of the news of the outbreak in India [the Indian Mutiny], who can tell how many valuable lives might have been saved at Cawnpore, Lucknow and elsewhere, by the timely arrival of the 10,000 troops she could have carried [presumably in cramped quarters]'. Four weeks later Henry gave a lecture on the progress of engineering science in the last hundred years. He concentrated on the steam engine, tracing progress from engines devised for draining water from Cornish mines in the nineteenth century to the railway locomotive designed by Stevenson in 1829.[9] The following year, Henry read a paper on 'The Manufacture of Iron', after which a resolution was passed that 'this meeting is opined that Mr. Bessemer ... is deservedly entitled to the thanks of the scientific world'. Henry Bessemer (1813–1898) devised a furnace to blow air through crude pig iron, burning off impurities to leave the malleable wrought iron. This made possible the production of cheap, high strength steel.

At a subsequent meeting a paper was read by another student on 'The Suez Canal', after which Henry Worms laid before the meeting the different arguments against and for this undertaking from engineering, commercial and political points of view. He then put forward the resolution 'that this meeting is of the opinion that the Suez Canal would neither be possible in an engineering point of view nor desirable for political reasons'; the resolution was carried. In spite of this discussion, the canal was begun and completed in 1869. A paper on the proposals for mains drainage in London was followed by comments from Henry Worms on the manner of drainage in Paris and Vienna, which would have been quite faraway places to students at that time. His presidential address in October 1860, delivered in front of the college principal, concerned practical engineering and concluded, 'it was necessary that the theoretical and practical parts of engineering should be united.'[10]

The most ambitious project of the Engineering Society was a soirée arranged for 30 November 1859 and announced at a Society meeting by Chambers, when Henry Worms, as president, requested a good attendance, as 'many leading men of science were expected to be present'. Worms intended to repeat the experiment, which Foucault devised in 1851, to demonstrate the earth's rotation. An audience of scientists and laymen assembled in the large lecture theatre of King's College, where a heavy pendulum bob had been suspended by a wire from the ceiling in front of the lecture bench. The pendulum was held away from the vertical by a fine wire trapped between two horizontal screws. A display of scientific instruments was arranged in an adjacent room, while a buffet supper was to be found in the library, completing the entertainment.

The college principal, Dr Jelf, presided while Henry Worms (aged 19) gave his lecture on the experiment of Foucault. During the talk Henry released the retaining screws and set the pendulum in motion. A shadow from the pendulum bob was projected onto a graduated glass plate so that the audience could see that the plane of swing slowly rotated. As the experiment proceeded the pendulum, as planned, first knocked over two pegs set on the floor and later contacted a platinum wire placed on the floor. This closed an electrical circuit, which fired a small cannon. During the course of the experiment the lecturer explained that inertia fixed the plane of swing of the pendulum in space, but it appeared to move because the earth under the pendulum was rotating. The audience 'warmly testified their appreciation of the demonstration given by Worms' and then adjourned for refreshments.[11]

This was a repeat of an experiment conducted under the dome of the Panthéon in Paris. King's College aimed to bring this elegant demonstration of the earth's rotation to the notice of laymen in London, and Henry Worms dressed it in a true showman's style. Professor Wheatstone had been interested in Foucault's work from the beginning and devised a related experiment to demonstrate the rotation of the earth. Henry was elected as a Fellow of the Royal Astronomical Society in 1861 as a consequence of his interest in the earth's motion. He wrote up his lecture in a book, *The Earth and its Mechanism*, published in 1862 and covering the history of the subject from the ancient Greek theories to the time of Foucault. His experiment at King's College is therein described in detail, with a sophisticated mathematical treatment of the apparent motion of the pendulum's axis. Other demonstrations of the earth's rotation are discussed. Henry Worms dedicated his book to Professor Wheatstone, 'with feelings of deepest respect and in admiration of that fertile genius'. Henry's interest in gadgets continued, and he was granted a provisional patent[12] for the invention of 'improvements in apparatus for elevating guns'.

Henry joined the sporting life at King's College, becoming proficient in fencing and boxing. His prowess in boxing served him in good stead during his first parliamentary election in 1869, when he accepted a challenge in this sport from one of the Liberal voters in Deal, and won. He also joined the King's College Company of the Westminster Rifle Volunteer Corps, serving for some ten years, and he was promoted in February 1860 to the rank of captain.[13]

Members of a corps had their own uniform, drilling and practising like members of regular Army regiments. They provided their own arms and equipment and covered all expenses involved in attending the corps, except in time of war. Arms had to be of the standardised calibre and members had to attend eight days of drill in each four-monthly period. These volunteer rifle corps were similar to the modern Territorial Army, and indeed after 1908 they were combined as that organisation. When first formed they were also to some degree sporting clubs, and Henry's love of the sport of revolver and rifle shooting continued throughout his life. As Lord Pirbright he became chairman of the Guildford Rifle Club and donated a challenge cup to the Bisley Rifle Club.[14]

These volunteer rifle corps were set up around the country after 1859 by the Liberal government of Palmerston (1784–1865; prime minister 1855–

1865) to counter a perceived threat of a French invasion, using legislation passed during the earlier Napoleonic wars. National alarm arose when Napoleon III allied with Sardinia to drive the Austrians out of northern Italy and began reunification of that country. The Worms family must have felt patriotic fervour towards Austria because much of their business was with that country. Henry Worms' brother Anthony had just at that time married an Austrian lady and lived with her at the family house in London.

Henry Worms' attention to scientific studies began to wane late in 1860 when he was finding a new direction to his life. He was re-elected president of the Engineering Society in June of 1861 but on 19 November of that year he tendered a letter of resignation and a vote of thanks was unanimously recorded for him for his past services. However, at an extraordinary meeting on 22 November a motion was carried that Worms be allowed to withdraw his resignation. At the next round of elections on 3 December he was nominated as president without opposition. On 2 April 1862 the officers resigned as usual at the start of a new term and Worms did not stand for re-election. He received a unanimous vote of thanks for the services he had rendered to the society and Chambers was elected president. Soon after this the society began to fall apart, and it dissolved itself on 11 June 1862. It functioned intermittently for five years and was reinstated on 21 October 1867.

Henry now decided he wished to enter politics. To do so, he would require a sufficient income since at that time MPs neither received a salary nor had their expenses paid. His first inclination had been towards medicine, but this changed in favour of law – a profession that would give him a suitable income and much better opportunities to fulfil his ambitions. He entered the Inner Temple on 27 October 1860 and his work on the rotation of the earth was published from that institution, not from King's College. During the next year he divided his time between these two institutions and was frequently absent from meetings of the Engineering Society. The college made him an honorary Fellow in 1863 and his popularity remained such that when the college president, the Reverend Dr Jelf, retired in 1868, Henry Worms was made joint treasurer of the presentation fund set up by the Bishop of London.[15]

Law students paid a fee and had to attend lectures for three years but there were no examinations to pass. In the third year they became the pupil of an established barrister for which a fee was extracted. Montague Williams QC (1835–1892), one of Henry's contemporaries at the Inner Temple, noted in his memoirs that Henry was fond of good company. These two, along with Francis Burnand (1836–1917), attended lectures and dined together.

The three would joke and Henry laughed so loudly at Burnand's jokes that on several occasions they came close to being expelled from the lecture room. Burnand practised as an attorney for a short time, but eventually became a comedy dramatist and editor of *Punch* magazine in 1880. Henry Worms was called to the bar on 6 June 1863 and practised as a barrister for about three years. This could have been a lucrative career, had fate not intervened.

The early death of his brother Anthony caused a change in the direction of Henry's life. The family brokerage business set up for George and Anthony needed contacts in Vienna, which Anthony had provided. In 1864 Henry was married in Vienna to the daughter of a wealthy banker, so when his brother died shortly afterwards he was the natural replacement in the brokerage firm. This position could be expected to provide an adequate income for an MP, but to become something more than just a backbencher, Henry had to raise his profile within the Conservative Party. He did so by writing on two of the important foreign affairs problems of the day.

The disintegration of the Turkish Empire was allowing the continuing expansion of Russia through the Balkans. Russia was also expanding into Persia and Afghanistan, moves which threatened British India. These were topics on which one could write a thesis, and several were indeed produced, including one by Gladstone.[16] Henry's thesis, published in 1877, was entitled *England's Policy in the East*. It ran through several editions, later with statistics on both the Turkish and the Russian Empire. Through this work he became a Fellow of the Royal Statistical Society in 1877, and he was beginning to be noticed. However, this particular work was scurrilously attacked by Tollemanche Sinclair (1825–1912), Liberal MP for Caithness, in his book on the same subject, *A Defence of Russia*. Sinclair devoted one chapter in an appendix to violent anti-Semitism, vilifying Henry Worms' book and his opinions.[17]

A second topic of interest to Henry was the political situation in Austria, which at that time was just developing into the dual Austro-Hungarian monarchy. Henry had become very friendly with Count Beust, the Austrian Chancellor, while in Vienna during 1869–70 and was granted access to state papers. He used this opportunity to write a history of the development of the dual monarchy in German. In 1877 he published an English translation under the title *A Political Sketch of the Austria Hungarian Empire*. This was another best-seller, running through several editions. Gladstone often quoted the Austro-Hungarian story as a model for a new relationship between Britain and Ireland.

Henry entered politics through membership of the National Union of Conservative Associations, founded in 1867 as a forum for discussions.

Individual associations had to subscribe and were entitled to send representatives to the general meetings. There was a central council of 24 members, together with an elected chairman. Henry was proposed as a council member in 1878 but not elected. However, he persisted and was elected the following year to the council.[18] Undoubtedly the most significant move Henry made to gain notice in the Conservative ranks was to become president of the Anglo-Jewish Association in 1872, a position which gave him opportunities to address senior members of whichever government was then in office, whether Conservative or Liberal. His ambition to enter Parliament was realised in 1880.

4

The Anglo-Jewish Association – Apprenticeship for Politics

> *Thou shalt not avenge, nor bear any grudge against the children of thy people, but thou shalt love thy neighbour as thyself.*
>
> Leviticus 19: 18

The political scene of the early Victorian period was dominated by land-owning families, and most of those who aspired to government were educated at Oxford or Cambridge. Benjamin Disraeli (1804–1881; from 1876 Lord Beaconsfield) was the principal exception, since he raised an income and came to general notice by writing successful novels. He was also helped by a good financial marriage. Disraeli came from Jewish parents, but when his father quarrelled with the local synagogue he had Benjamin baptised in the Anglican Church. Disraeli became a Conservative prime minister and was the idol of Henry Worms. Henry Worms had two great disadvantages for an aspiring politician: he was educated at King's College, London, and he was without the backing of a land-owning family. He had a niche in banking from which to make money, but he also needed a vehicle through which to project himself onto the political establishment. An opportunity presented itself with the formation of the Anglo-Jewish Association.

Introduction to Jewish Affairs

Solomon Worms, like most of the Jewish people who migrated from Germany, lived first in the City of London and attended the Great German Synagogue. He was one of the officers of the synagogue in 1840. As Jewish families prospered they rented more fashionable accommodation in the West End of London and soon found the Great Synagogue an inconvenient place to reach, so in 1848 they resolved to open a place of worship nearer to the

West End. The committee that was elected to oversee this project included Solomon as co-treasurer, and the new Central Synagogue in Great Portland Street was opened in 1855, adapted from a former warehouse. It was a branch of the Great Synagogue and Solomon was a regular attendee. When the lease for this building expired, it was decided to move into new premises. A lease was taken on another site in Great Portland Street and a building and finance committee for this projected new synagogue was elected. The committee included Henry Worms, recently married and now living near Hyde Park Corner, together with Benjamin Samuel Phillips, who much later became Henry's father-in-law, by a second marriage. Houses were demolished on the site to make way for a grand new building and Lionel Rothschild laid the foundation stone of this Central Synagogue in 1869. It housed a congregation that was independent of the Great Synagogue. (The building was destroyed by enemy action in 1942 and rebuilt on the same site in 1958.)

Until the mid-nineteenth century, there was little co-operation between the different Jewish communities in London. Nathan Adler (1803–1890) was one of the prime movers in creating an overall United Synagogue to regulate those communities who wished to join.[1] An act of Parliament to bring the unity into effect was passed in 1870, the Great and the Central Synagogues being among those subscribing, with Nathan Adler filling the post of Chief Rabbi of the British Empire.

Nathan Adler was born in Hanover and became a rabbi there when that country was ruled by a member of the British royal family. The Duke of Cambridge, regent of Hanover, recommended him for a post in London associated with the Great German Synagogue. Solomon Worms and Nathan Adler were related by marriage, Solomon's cousin Henrietta Worms (1803–1879) having married Nathan. Their son Herman Adler (1839–1911), who was about the same age as Henry, later succeeded as Chief Rabbi.[2] With such prominent Jewish relations as the Adlers, the Rothschilds, the Cohens and the Samuels, it is no surprise that Henry Worms took an interest in Jewish causes. He was treasurer of the United Synagogue from 1879 until he resigned in 1881 due to pressure of work as an MP.[3]

During the second half of the nineteenth century, Jews in Western Europe became concerned over the fate of their co-religionists in the East. The *Alliance Israélite Universelle* was formed in Paris in 1860 to promote progress towards the emancipation of Jews and to take effective action to improve their situation, especially in Eastern Europe and the Turkish Empire.[4] The Board of Deputies represented English Jews, and the two institutions cooperated. When the influence of the French group became weak after the Franco-Prussian war of 1870–1871, many from the Jewish community in

London felt that a more open forum than the Board of Deputies was needed to represent their views. A body similar to the *Alliance*, but independent of it, was formed with membership open to subscription. Its objectives were the promotion of social, moral and intellectual progress among the Jews and lobbying for the protection of those who suffered as a consequence of being Jewish. At a provisional meeting Jacob Waley (1818–1873), a professor at University College, was proposed as president, with a list of three others should he decline.[5] The Anglo-Jewish Association was then formally constituted at a public meeting held on 2 July 1871, Jacob Waley being duly elected president, with David Salomons (1797–1873; Liberal MP for Greenwich) as treasurer.[6] When after one year Waley retired due to ill health,[7] the executive committee passed over its shortlist of three others, reporting that instead, they were 'fortunate enough to obtain as successor Baron Henry de Worms, a gentleman in every way qualified to fill the place of Professor Waley'. The reasons for this choice are not further explained, but Henry Worms was known in business and political circles and was no shrinking violet.[8]

Prominence in Jewish Affairs

Henry Worms had returned from a stay in Vienna during 1869–1870 and the following year was raised to the peerage of Austria, becoming Baron Henry de Worms. The choice of him as president of the Anglo-Jewish Association was a good one because he was an effective public speaker, his skill having been honed at King's College. Henry was also engaging in schemes to enhance his political charisma, and this position as president gave him opportunities to do so through interviews with the highest members of the government.

The first political move of the Anglo-Jewish Association in 1873 was to present an address to the Shah of Persia on the treatment of their co-religionists in his country. The Shah was visiting London, staying at Buckingham Palace, and he gave an audience to various bodies, including the association, at which Julian Goldsmid presented this address. Henry is not recorded as being at the meeting, although as president he transmitted its contents to *The Times*.[9] Two Jewish deputations met the Shah, the Anglo-Jewish Association and, independently, the Board of Deputies led by Moses Montefiori.

Henry also became President of the Council overseeing the Borough Jewish Schools and gave their prizes on several occasions. At first these

London schools were supported privately by Baroness Mayer de Rothschild and the Anglo-Jewish Association. In 1870, the government decided to introduce compulsory elementary education and to supplement private schools with a state nondenominational system. On one occasion at the distribution of prizes by the Chief Rabbi, Henry, who was presiding, indicated that he was in favour of compulsory education and cited the benefits of this system in Prussia. It would be difficult, though, he thought, for Jews to benefit from nondenominational schools and he suggested that the state should assist religious training rather than feel itself called upon to educate atheists. He suggested that certificates of proficiency in religious knowledge should be regarded as indispensable in the filling of appointments. Henry and the Chief Rabbi agreed that Jews could not accept a state grant that would be at the expense of their religion, as they were concerned that two or three hours per week of religious education, as required by the grant, was not enough to pass on their Jewish heritage. At another prize-giving ceremony, Henry addressed the students, saying that while he wanted 'the Jews always to maintain intact the peculiarities of their great nationality', he did not 'wish them to be isolated from the great body of Englishmen and from the nation to which they belonged'. He emphasised the patriotism of the Jews as loyal British subjects further in another speech to the association.[10]

The association organised funds in support of Jewish schools in the East, including a school in Tunis and an Agricultural School in Jaffa, and it collaborated with its partner organisation in Paris to establish other schools in Palestine. A teacher of English was supported at the Jewish school in Baghdad. Henry was one of the members of the committee set up by the association to look into the provision of these schools. A report from the sub-committee on education in 1882 listed schools in fourteen towns in the East supported by the association in conjunction with the *Alliance Israélite* of Paris.[11]

The rise in anti-Semitism within the Christian states emerging in Eastern Europe on the collapse of Ottoman rule became the dominant concern of the Anglo-Jewish Association for many years, starting in 1876. Serjeant Simon (1818–1897; Liberal MP for Dewsbury) and a vice-president of the association, was particularly active in Parliament as a spokesperson for this cause.[12] Henry helped the association to mobilise diplomatic pressure on the problem, organising an international meeting in Paris during 1876 and drafting letters to the Constantinople and Berlin peace conferences.

In their great days, the Ottoman Turks had conquered Eastern Europe from the Black Sea to Hungary and the borders of Austria, laying siege to Vienna in 1529 and again in 1683. By the eighteenth century, Austria had recovered Hungary and stabilised her frontier. As the power of Turkey declined, Serbia and Montenegro became autonomous regions of its empire, *de facto* independent principalities, while Russia desired territorial expansion at the expense of Turkey and aimed to unite the Orthodox Christians. These tensions gave rise to the Crimean War of 1853–1856, where Britain, France and Sardinia supported Turkey against Russia and her attempts at territorial expansion. Peace negotiations after this conflict during the Congress of Paris of 1856 resulted in freedom for the Danubian Provinces (modern Romania) under control of the Great Powers, together with the agreed neutrality of the Black Sea.[13]

In the 1870s the Anglo-Jewish Association turned its attention to the plight of Jews in the Balkans. The immediate cause of unrest was the actions of Bulgarian Orthodox patriots who in 1875 fomented an uprising against Ottoman rule. They showed much brutality towards Muslims and were suppressed with equal brutality by Turkish auxiliary troops. Jews in the Balkans suffered from both sides of the conflict. Widespread sympathy for the Bulgarian cause in Russia led to an upsurge of patriotism and rekindled the idea of uniting all Orthodox nations, with Russia at the helm. In June 1876 Serbia and Montenegro declared war on the Ottoman Empire and later that year Russia mobilised troops in support. As this insurgency was brewing, the association, along with the *Alliance Israélite*, received a flood of letters complaining of harassment of Jews in Romania and in Serbia. While Russian troops were advancing through Turkey a meeting of the council, with Baron Henry de Worms in the chair, moved to request the *Alliance* to convene a meeting in Paris, to include delegates from Vienna and the USA, to discuss the effects of this uprising on the local Jewish population. The meeting was arranged for 11–15 December 1876, and Henry attended along with the secretary of the association, Dr Löwy.[14] The Great Powers moved even faster to agree a truce and organised a conference in Constantinople in the hope of resolving this crisis without further military intervention.[15]

M. Crémieux of the *Alliance* presided over the Paris conference, which now had to consider how its views should be presented in Constantinople. Speeches were made in French and German and Henry proved to be an outstanding asset since he was fluent in both languages. He was appointed to the committee to frame a memorial to the Constantinople conference. At the final meeting in Paris, M. Crémieux moved and M. Seligman of New York seconded 'that Baron Henry de Worms be deputed to proceed to Constantinople as a representative of the European and American delegates assembled, in order to place copies of the memorial in the hands of the individual representatives of the Great Powers'.[16]

The memorial asked for a revision of the European Convention of 1858 regulating the international status of Romania. Romania had been requested to extend political rights to other denominations than just Christians but had not done so. It complained also that Serbia had expelled Jews from every part of the country except Belgrade. The meeting planned for Henry to go in person to Constantinople and attend the conference, but this visit was soon abandoned as it was considered contrary to diplomatic protocol. On his return to London from Paris, Henry chaired a meeting of the association's council held on 21 December to report on the proceedings of the Paris conference. He reported on a meeting the previous day with Lord Derby (the 15th Earl) at which the earl had promised to forward the memorial to the British plenipotentiary in Constantinople, the Marquis of Salisbury, and warmly support it. In the event, all these efforts had no impact. The Constantinople conference had opened on 11 December 1876, Turkey refused to accept any of the Great Power's watered-down terms, so the delegates left Constantinople on 22 January. Most of them would have been unaware of this memorial.[17]

After barely four months the truce broke down, and Russia declared war on the Ottoman Empire on 24 April 1877. Russian armies passed through Romania and crossed the Danube into what is now Bulgaria. Serbia and Montenegro joined forces with Russia soon afterwards and the war proceeded badly for Turkey. Alarmed at this, the Great Powers called for a truce, but the Russian Army continued to advance on Constantinople. Disraeli, the British prime minister, was in a dilemma, as Britain had guaranteed the territorial integrity of Turkey in the treaty agreed after the Crimean War, but she could not condone the Bulgarian atrocities. When the British fleet in the area threatened to bombard Russian troops, the invasion was halted at San Stefano (now Yesilköy), close to Constantinople, and Russia entered into a settlement under the Treaty of San Stefano on 3 March 1878. A Peace Congress followed in Berlin, under the chairmanship of Bismarck, beginning on 13 June 1878, with the prime minister, Lord Beaconsfield (Disraeli), and the foreign secretary, the Marquis of Salisbury, as the British delegates.[18]

The Anglo-Jewish Association now mounted a further effort to bring the cause of the Jews of the Balkans to the notice of the Great Powers. Henry de Worms met with the London Committee of the Jewish Board of Deputies under its chairman, Moses Montefiore (1784–1885), Henry's uncle by marriage, this time to draft a joint memorial which was forwarded in good time on 12 June to the delegates in Berlin.[19] It appealed to the British officials 'to obtain all public rights for the Jews in Rumania, Serbia and

Bulgaria, and the other provinces which may be affected by the issues of war'. The *Alliance Israélite* sent its own delegation to Berlin, but the Jewish problems took low priority over the need to broker peace and prevent further Russian moves southward. The biggest influence in terms of providing a resolution to these Jewish questions was brought to bear by Gerson Bleichröder (1822–1893), a Jewish banker from Berlin. Bleichröder had strong personal and political ties with Bismarck and had a controlling interest in the development of Romania's railways; in addition, the firm of G. & A. Worms was his broker in London. Most of the demands in the memorial were met through Bleichröder's influence.[20] The Treaty of Berlin was signed on 13 July and one minor clause, which was to have disastrous consequences later, assigned Bosnia and Herzegovina to Austrian protection. At the conclusion of the conference, Henry de Worms and Moses Montefiore were among the delegation invited to Charing Cross station to meet Beaconsfield and Salisbury on their return from Berlin.[21]

Under Clause 44 of the Treaty of Berlin, Romania was obliged to give civil rights of property and naturalisation to its Jewish population. Its government had always regarded persons born in Romania of Jewish parents as aliens, as they had not embraced Christianity. To conform to the Treaty of Berlin it was proposed by the Romanian legislature that in the course of a year after such a person had obtained his majority he could acquire citizenship, but only after a vote of the legislature. Thus, all applications had to be made individually and the time scale of the whole process was completely impractical. The Anglo-Jewish Association bombarded the press with complaints on this matter, while Ion Ghica (1816–1897), a member of the Romanian Senate and twice prime minister, defended his country, saying that Jews were happy in the Romanian state and quoting a common Italian proverb (attributed to the poet Metsatasio [1698–1782]): *Chi sta bene non si muove* [Let him who stands well, stand still].

Never at a loss for a quotation, Henry de Worms ended a long letter to *The Times* on the Romanian question with a line from Dante: 'I [Henry de Worms] will only add that if the Great Powers who signed the Treaty of Berlin will not compel the execution of that unanimous verdict, which made the independence of Rumania conditional upon her granting civil and religious liberty to all her subjects irrespective of creed, it will not be the lines of Metsatasio which should be inscribed over the Rumanian frontier, but rather those of Dante in the 3rd canto of the Divina Commedia:- *Lasciate ogni speranza voi che antrate* [All hope abandon, you who enter in!].'[22] Dante (*c*.1265–1321) placed this inscription over the entrance to hell.

Henry wrote to the foreign secretary, the Marquis of Salisbury, expressing the views of the association on the behaviour of the Romanian government, and on 2 March 1879 received a strong commitment on the part of Britain to the full provisions of the Treaty of Berlin.[23] To the annoyance of the association, the government of Romania merely continued with delaying tactics, so Henry again led a deputation to Lord Salisbury to press for enactment of the treaty.[24] The problem rumbled on for many years, with Baron Henry de Worms, later in Parliament, asking questions of the Liberal government's foreign secretary. By August 1884 he had obtained many letters of complaint from Jews in Romania, where they were forbidden to act as brokers in trade and from the hawking of goods, a trade on which most poor Jews relied for a living. Since the Romanian government refused to alter its ways, Henry felt there was 'no other course remaining than the one which I have ventured to adopt – that of gibbeting her misdeeds [exposing her misdeeds to the public]'. This fuss caught the attention of the Romanian newspapers, where all the allegations were of course denied, and many further years had to pass before these complaints were fully addressed; meanwhile, another problem came under the Association's scrutiny.[25]

When the liberal Czar Alexander II was assassinated by a group of radical terrorists in St Petersburg in 1881, rumours soon implicated the Jews. His successor Alexander III, who had long regarded the Jews as a social cancer, began a vigorous regime of suppression. News of riots against the Jewish population in Russia began to seep out and it appeared the Russian government was doing little to prevent mayhem. Serjeant Simon and Henry de Worms took up the cause of these people. Soon after Henry entered Parliament in 1880 as MP for Greenwich he began to agitate on their behalf, asking numerous questions of the foreign secretary during 1881 and 1882 about the treatment of Jews in Russia. The business was taken further when a deputation from the Anglo-Jewish Association headed by Henry de Worms, and including the liberal politicians Serjeant Simon and Arthur Cohen, had an interview with Lord Granville at the Foreign Office. They requested that the government take whatever steps were possible to prevent the recurrence of the past terrible outrages.[26]

The Lord Mayor of London organised a collection for the relief of suffering in Russia, while public meetings were held around the country to discuss the Russian affair, in spite of the government's feeling that such meetings were not desirable at that time. During February 1882 Henry de Worms, Serjeant Simon and others addressed one such meeting organised by the Anglo-Jewish Association's Manchester branch and later moved on to Liverpool to observe a public meeting. Henry wanted good men to come to the front 'and not let it go forth to the world that they were afraid to fight their own battles'. Simon agreed with this, but soon the two men began to differ in their opinion on how to approach the situation, and this divergence of views continued into Parliament.[27]

Dissent

John Simon (1818–1897; MP for Dewsbury from 1868) was active in the Anglo-Jewish Association and took interest in Jewish affairs in Europe. He was a serjeant-at-law, a position which took in some of the functions of a judge, and he is usually referred to as Serjeant Simon. He put a question to the prime minister in Parliament on 10 February and was told that the government preferred to act unofficially so as not further to inflame the plight of Jews in Russia. But this did not satisfy Henry de Worms, and after a number of attempts, de Worms succeeded in putting a resolution on the persecution of the Jews in Russia up for debate on 3 March 1882. In a long parliamentary speech that came from the heart he compared the situation in Russia to that of the Jews in Bulgaria during the atrocities and ended by moving 'that this House, deeply deploring the persecutions and outrages to which the Jews in Russia have been subjected in portions of the Russian Empire, trusts that H.M. Government will find the means either alone or in conjunction with the other Great Powers, of using their good offices with the Government of His majesty the Czar, to prevent the recurrence of similar acts of violence'.

Serjeant Simon spoke to Parliament in opposition to this motion, not because he disagreed with the sentiments of Henry de Worms, but because he believed the motion would put the Jews in greater peril while the government could in no way help them: 'Suppose the Russian government were asked to use their good offices to prevent the atrocities that were going on in certain parts of her Majesties dominions, what would the English people say.' The prime minister, Gladstone, also spoke firmly opposing any resolution, indicating that such a measure could be counterproductive, and Henry withdrew his motion without a vote being taken. His words, however, were appreciated by the House, for Robert Fowler (MP for City of London) remarked that 'the hon. Member [for Greenwich] had done very great service, not only to the community of which he was an honoured member, but to the cause of humanity at large, in bringing this matter before the House'. Although protests continued to be made, the government could do little about the matter. The Russian ambassador flatly refused to accept a letter on behalf of the Russian Jews which the association wished to have delivered to the Czar.[28]

The friction between Serjeant Simon, a Liberal, and Henry de Worms, a Conservative, began in Parliament and continued into the association. It was fed from two sources. First, Serjeant Simon was an old-established MP, a successful barrister and vice-president of the association, while Henry de Worms, its president, had only recently entered Parliament, and thus it was a question of the old guard versus a young pretender. Second, since the Treaty of Berlin, regulating the position of Jews in Romania, had been ratified, the political situation in Britain had changed. In 1878 Henry was an aspiring Conservative politician pushing the Conservative government to do more, even though this might have affected his political future. In this he was well supported by two Liberal MPs, Serjeant Simon and Arthur Cohen. After 1880, however, Henry was in Parliament and a Liberal government under Gladstone was in power. Serjeant Simon and Arthur Cohen, the latter now president of the Board of Deputies of British Jews, were both Liberals and they followed their party line. Henry de Worms was the only Conservative Jewish MP, and the Liberal Jewish MPs resented his opposition to their views.

A meeting of the association's council unanimously resolved in 1882 to give cordial thanks to Baron Henry de Worms for bringing the question of the persecution of the Jews prominently before Parliament. In his reply Henry wrote 'I shall throughout life consider this vote of thanks as a lasting testimony of the confidence reposed in me by my co-religionists at one of the most dangerous and trying epochs of our national history.'[29] A number of people, both Jew and Gentile, felt, however, that to press the government into an untenable position over the Russian question would be a mistake and would damage the Jewish cause. At the meeting which passed the vote of thanks, Serjeant Simon dissented, saying that such a vote of thanks implied a vote of censure on his own actions in the House of Commons in the same affair. As he did not wish to disturb the harmony of the proceedings of the council, he resigned his position as vice-president of the association, so at this price the vote of thanks was unanimous.[30]

During this period of turbulence in Eastern Europe, anti-Semitic views were also beginning to emerge in Germany. After the financial crash of 1873, caused by rampant speculation following German unification, Jews became the scapegoats of all that was wrong with the modern world. The court chaplain Adolf Stöcker fanned the flames of resentment and religious prejudice with his explicitly anti-Jewish Christian Socialist Party. In 1883 Herr Stöcker attempted to give an anti-Semitic lecture in London. He was refused the Mansion House as a venue and eventually found one at the Carlton Club, of which Henry de Worms was a member. Henry was in Austria at the time and on hearing of the nature of the talk wrote to tender his resignation from the club. However, it was soon demonstrated that the club committee had not sanctioned or even known about the talk beforehand. When explanations had been given, Henry withdrew his resignation, writing of the committee's view: 'It is in accordance with those broad views of religious liberty and toleration which in England are not confined to one political party in the State, but are common to all.'[31]

Two years after the unfortunate incident with Serjeant Simon, the association's council was continuing to support Henry de Worms as president and requested him to bring again the civil rights of Romanian Jews before the House of Commons.[32] He was rising through the ranks of the Conservatives and by the time of the association's Annual General Meeting in 1885, the Liberal administration had been defeated and a Conservative government formed. Henry entered the government as secretary to the Board of Trade and when pressure of work caused him to withdraw from Jewish affairs, he had to apologise for his absence at the Anglo-Jewish Associations's AGM.[33]

A serious problem now arose in the association over the wedding of its president's eldest daughter, Alice de Worms, on 18 April 1886, held in the Anglican St James's Church, Piccadilly. At the meeting of the council on 2 May, Mr. E.A. Franklin referred to the fact that the president had taken an active part in the recent celebration of his daughter's marriage at one of the churches in the metropolis. He had given the girl away and hosted an elaborate wedding breakfast. After discussion, the council agreed to convene a special meeting to consider what effect this would have on the present relations between the association and its president.

In the memory of the council were two recent marriages of Rothschild daughters out of the Jewish faith. Anthony's daughter Constance married Cyril Flower, later Lord Battersea, on 21 November 1877 in a civil ceremony at Aylesbury registry office followed by a Jewish religious ceremony in London. Her father had recently died, but other members of the family were present and accepted the marriage. Likewise, Mayer's daughter Hanna married the Earl of Rosebery on 20 March 1878 at a civil ceremony followed immediately by a plain Anglican service at Christ Church, Mayfair. Both her parents were dead and the Earl of Beaconsfield, Disraeli, gave her away. Her family seems to have disapproved of this wedding; none of them witnessed the ceremony, nor spoke at the wedding breakfast, the toast of bride and groom being given by the Prince of Wales. An editorial in the *Jewish World* for

1882 noted that 'we have been startled by several mixed marriages in high places'. It indicated that what had been Jewish practice in this matter – marriage only within the faith – is laid down in Exodus and Deuteronomy beyond the possibility of doubt, and the editor strongly disapproved of marriage out of the faith.[34]

On hearing that the association's council was to convene a special meeting to discuss his participation in the marriage of his daughter, Henry replied immediately: 'Mr. Waley has been good enough to communicate to me the conversation initiated by Mr. Franklin at today's meeting of the Anglo-Jewish Association. I much regret that the spirit of toleration, which is the binding spirit of our Association ... should have been so strangely violated by the gentleman in question. As I cannot and will not consent to submit my actions in my private capacity to the censorship of any person or persons what so ever, ... I resign my post as President.'[35]

The Council met and a resolution that the president's resignation be not accepted was carried by 9 votes to 7, but this did not satisfy Henry, who wrote that he could not regard a majority of 2 as entitling him to any degree of confidence from the association. He adhered to his resignation. There was a movement to re-elect him as president but Henry wrote to the association on 8 June 1886 refusing to be nominated and withdrew his subscription. Sir Julian Goldsmid (1838–1896) was elected President on 19 July 1886 and the thirteen years of Henry de Worms' work with the association ended.[36]

At least one of Henry's relatives, his mother's brother Behrend George Samuel (1804–1893), seems to have approved of his actions over the marriage. In a will dated 21 September 1887, signed after the wedding of Henry's daughter, George bequeathed around £400,000, the major part of his fortune, to Henry, together with his art collection. This George Samuel never married; at a young age he had fallen in love with a Christian woman and his father absolutely refused to allow them to marry. There was one illegitimate daughter, Georgina, who predeceased him and who is buried at the Anglican Church of St Michael and St Mary Magdalene, Easthampstead, Berkshire. George Samuel is buried in the same enclosure and his will provided money for upkeep of the grave.[37]

Henry de Worms did not completely cut off all Jewish connections; he was one of the signatories on a presentation to Cardinal Manning made in 1890 on the occasion of the latter's Silver Jubilee in acknowledgement of his help for the cause of the Russian Jews. Over a further ten years, contact with the association became less frequent. When Edward VII became king various public groups, including the Anglo-Jewish Association, attended a court reception on 3 May 1901 to tender loyal and congratulatory addresses.

Henry, now Lord Pirbright, was not included in the group headed by Claude Montefiore, the president of the association, although he was the only living past president. He was, however, present at the declaration of Edward VII in St. James's Palace on 23 January 1901.[38] Henry de Worms' period of office in the Anglo-Jewish Association gave him access to the most important members of government, including the Marquis of Salisbury, at that time foreign secretary, and who after 1885 became leader of the Conservative Party. He had many opportunities to perfect his public-speaking technique and made appearances on the European stage. In all, this was an excellent apprenticeship for his entry into Parliament in 1880 when the Conservatives were in opposition, and by 1885 he held a minor position in the new Conservative government.

5

Banking and Marriage – the Austrian Connections

> *Who hold the balance of the world? Who reign*
> *O'er Congress, whether royalist or liberal?*
> *Who rouse the shirtless patriots of Spain?*
> *(That makes old Europe's journals squeak and gibber all.)*
> *Who keep the world, both old and new, in pain*
> *Or pleasure? Who makes politics run glibber all?*
> *The shade of Buonaparte's noble daring? –*
> *Jew Rothschild, and his fellow Christian Baring.*
>
> *Those, and the truly liberal Lafitte,*
> *Are the true lords of Europe. Every loan*
> *Is not a merely speculative hit,*
> *But seats a nation or upsets a throne.*
>
> Byron, *Don Juan*, Canto XII, Stanzas V & VI.[1]

The Bankers

The family of Worms was closely related to the Rothschilds, the Cohens, the Montefiores and the Samuels. Members of this group, known as 'the cousinhood', were immensely rich financiers and businessmen who became the masters of the universe of the nineteenth century. They were joined later by members of the Sassoon family, Ernest Cassel and Edward Lawson. Many from this set became friends of Edward Prince of Wales, a friendship often satirised because they were thought to have much influence over him. The end of this friendship is noted in a cartoon by Max Beerbohm, drawn after the death of Edward, in which the remaining members of the circle are asking 'will we be welcome now' [by the new king, George V].[2] Edward Lawson, who after 1887 became Henry Worms' brother-in-law, appears in the cartoon alongside two Rothschilds. Edward Lawson attended Lord Pirbright's funeral and Alfred Rothschild, shown in the cartoon, sent a wreath.[3]

With such an extended family it is little surprise that Solomon Worms became a banker and broker. Nathan Mayer Rothschild and his four brothers had built up a network of banks across Europe with offices in London, Frankfurt, Paris, Naples and Vienna. This group assisted with the transfer of finance from London to the Holy Alliance between Austria, Prussia and Russia (1815–1825), whose objective was the maintenance of Conservative politics. In practice Metternich (1773–1859) controlled this alliance from Vienna. Austria acknowledged financial help from the Rothschilds in 1822 by raising all five brothers to the rank of baron. The family motto is still *Concordia, Integritas, Industria* [Harmony, Integrity, Industry].[4] Solomon Worms began his working life for the Rothschild group in London and was likely involved in the transmission of funds between London and Vienna. Henrietta Worms, Solomon's sister, had in 1821 married one Salomon Mayer Schnapper, a banker of Frankfurt who soon moved to Vienna, and this gave Solomon Worms a friend in that city.[5]

As Solomon's sons grew up he founded the brokerage firm of G. & A. Worms for George and Anthony. The firm operated from offices at 1 Austin Friars in the City of London with George as head from 1856 to 1880, specialising in Austrian bonds.[6] It filled a niche in the markets opened up by the new German railway system which made Austria more accessible from England. When Anthony died in 1864, Henry joined the firm as a director. It was a substantial and well-regarded operation.

Marriages in Austria

Solomon Worms' daughter, Ellen Henrietta, was the first of the children to marry – one Adolf Landauer (1829–1885), a banker, whom she met through the Viennese connection. Adolf came over to London for the ceremony. In 1860 George, the eldest son, married his cousin Louisa Samuel, a daughter of the Denis Samuel who had make a fortune in Brazil and Portugal. The second son, Anthony, married Emma von Schey in 1860; they had also met through the Viennese connection. She was the daughter of a prominent Austrian banker and former business partner of Adolf Landauer's father. Anthony died in 1864, after which his wife returned to Vienna, taking their baby daughter, and later made a second marriage with Joseph Unger in that city.[7] The youngest son, Henry, was married in 1864 at the age of 24 to a Viennese lady, Franziska (Fanny) von Todesco, then aged 18 and the daughter of Eduard von Todesco (1814–1887), the most prominent Austrian banker and industrialist. The Todescos thought Henry an excellent catch because of his father's close relationship to the Rothschilds. Franziska was considered the most beautiful lady in Vienna and Henry declared he would kill himself if he could not marry her.[8]

Both the Schey and the Todesco families were of immensely rich Jewish banking and industrialist stock. Jews had gained equal civil rights in Austria-Hungary by 1868 and both families gained the title of Freiherr (baron) for services to the state. Frederick Baron Schey von Koromla (1815–1881), Emma's father, was the son of a well-to-do merchant, and he studied at Vienna's Polytechnic Institute before becoming an apprentice at the banking house of Wertheimstein. In 1839 he became a partner in a banking house with his brother-in-law, Joseph Landauer. After Joseph Landauer's death in 1855 Schey established his own banking house, acting as financial advisor to Archduke Albrecht and having most of the high Austrian aristocracy as his clients. He was involved in manufacturing enterprises and the promotion of the Kaiserin-Elizabeths-Bahn, linking Vienna with Munich. Schey patronised music and the arts, and the salon of his house was a meeting point in Vienna for artists.[9]

Eduard Baron von Todesco (1814–1887) was director of the private bank of Hermann Todesco und Söhne and a director of the Northern Railway (Kaiser-Ferdinands-Nordbahn) linking Vienna with Cracow, an enterprise initiated by the Rothschilds. In 1858, Eduard and his brother Moritz (1816–1873) took over the Marienthal textile factory, situated near Vienna, from their brother Maximilian and transformed this into one of the most modern integrated cotton factories in Europe. They were pioneers in looking after the housing and health needs of their workforce. Eduard and his father Hermann provided money to build schools and hospitals in Austria.[10]

Banking and Trade

The firm of G. & A. Worms had two main business lines. When a foreign government requested a large loan from one of the giant banking firms such as Rothschild or Barings, the bonds were offered to smaller firms, like G. & A. Worms, at a discount to broker on the Stock Exchange. Owners of the bonds then became clients of the brokering firm that was responsible for the distribution of interest transmitted to London by the foreign government. Coupons were attached to the bonds to be presented at the appropriate time for payment, and the transactions attracted a fee. This constituted the first line of business of G. & A. Worms.

The other main business involved facilitating trade between Britain and Austria. The Austrian Empire at that time was a large and important European power. It controlled modern Austria, Hungary, the Czech and Slovak Republics, Slovenia and Slovakia, together with a part of northern Italy. The following is an example of this type of banking operation: before construction of the Suez Canal, the cotton factory of Marienthal imported its raw material from a supplier in London; when a price had been agreed, the factory owners, in this case Eduard and Moritz von Todesco, paid money into their bank in Vienna, which was Todesco & Söhn, and a bill of exchange was sent by normal post to the supplier in London. On presenting this to the corresponding bank there, which was G. & A. Worms, the supplier was paid in sterling, minus the appropriate commission. Now, when a London merchant bought sugar from Austria, he paid the costs to the bank of G. & A. Worms and this was noted against the bill of exchange from Todesco & Söhn, who later paid the sugar merchant in Vienna. Bills of exchange could be split into smaller sums or traded with other firms – all, of course, for a fee. The system depended on trust and on contacts. The marriages arranged by Solomon Worms for his children provided the contacts, which extended further to the firm of Bleichröder in Berlin.[11]

Throughout the existence of G. & A. Worms the currency of Austria was not stable. The gulden was based on a silver standard between 1754 and 1892 and paper currency was introduced by the national bank from 1848. There was usually a discrepancy in value between metallic and paper gulden, and this became considerable around 1871 when silver fell in value relative to gold. Only in 1892, after G. & A. Worms had closed, did Austria define the gulden in gold. The sovereign had long been defined in gold, so banks had to watch currency fluctuations closely so as to avoid possible losses. The House of Worms kept sufficient cash reserves and was considered a solid firm in a business sector that was not always secure. The largest London brokerage firm of Overend and Gurney collapsed in 1866 after it had had invested much of its reserves in railway shares, which soon fell in value, so that the firm could no longer cover its debts.[12]

The firm of G. & A. Worms was dissolved in 1880 by which time the brokerage business had become overcrowded and much less profitable.[13] Solomon had long since retired and George wished to retire, while Henry wished to devote time to Parliament. George and Henry Worms continued to use the same address for purposes of business until 1887, when the lease on premises at 1 Austin Friars was sold.[14] Both brothers continued an interest in the Land Mortgage Bank of India, which had a consortium of directors and operated from the City of London until it was liquidated.

This brokerage transfer system was susceptible to forgery, as when an employee of the Hungarian Credit Bank at Pest presented forged bills in Paris and London on Messrs G. & A. Worms, as well as some on Messrs Rothschilds. The safeguard against such problems was that firms were aware of any preliminary business negotiations and knew when to expect a genuine bill. This particular employee was apprehended in London and charged with forgery to the value of £10,000.[15]

Solomon died in 1882, leaving a personal estate of around £400,000, bequeathing £80,000 to his daughter in Vienna and £50,000 to the widow and child of his late son Anthony, both now in Vienna.[16] The remainder of the estate was divided equally between his sons George and Henry. His country house, The Lodge, Egham, was left to whichever of his sons, in succession, wished to live there.

A Grand Ceremony

The Todesco family maintained a house in Vienna and the imposing Villa Todesco situated in the nearby village of Mödling. During the 1860s they grasped an opportunity to build on one of the most prestigious sites in Vienna. An imposing zigzag bastion, built under the orders of Archduke Ferdinand (1503–1584; Emperor from 1558) after Turkish armies had laid siege in 1529, defended the old city. The bastion proved a great asset, withstanding two assaults by Protestant armies during the religious wars of the seventeenth century and the Turkish siege of 1683, but by the nineteenth century it was no longer of use. Clearance during the 1850s left a circle of prime building land around the city centre and this was sold off by the government at enormous prices to help offset its debts. Henry Worms visited the city as a boy, probably in connection with the marriage of his sister Ellen Henrietta in 1857, when these clearances were in progress.[17] By the 1850s, Austria had confirmed property rights on Jewish buyers of real estate, so the Todescos and Scheys took advantage to build their imposing palaces in this prestigious area.

The Palais Todesco, completed in 1864, was the first construction on this land. It had about 500 rooms and stands opposite the Vienna Staatsoper on Kärntnerstrasse. The building was large enough to house the Todesco family, the family of Eduard's wife Sophie (née Gomperz) and later that of his son-in-law, Ludwig von Oppenheimer. Eduard's brother Moritz lived there with the two children by his long-time mistress Jetty Treffz (1818–1878), a mezzo-soprano and opera star known across Germany and in London.[18] Jetty Treffz met Johann Strauss, Söhn, 'the Waltz King', in a previous Todesco house and left Moritz to marry him in 1862, after which she acted as his muse for the writing of such operettas as *Die Fledermaus*. The Todesco, Gomperz and Oppenheimer families each kept their own salon. The

Todesco salon was sumptuously decorated, with the adjoining dining room having a painted ceiling depicting the Judgement of Paris, and these rooms were used for the reception at the marriage of Henry Worms. Sophie Todesco was a gifted hostess, entertaining all the great in Vienna. The Palais Todesco remained in the hands of the family until 1935, when it was sold to an insurance company. It was damaged during bombardment in 1945 and later restored. The grand reception rooms are used today to host meetings and as a restaurant in the Imperial style. The catering company Gerstner Beletage is directly descended from the one that catered for Henry Worms' reception and other Todesco entertainments.[19]

The smaller Palais Schey was built close by at about the same time. It was sold in 1881 on the death of Friedrich Baron Schey, when the banking business was closed; his son was not interested in banking and became Professor of Law at Vienna University. Today the Palais Schey houses various shopping outlets, offices and apartments.

The grand reception rooms of the Palais Todesco were first used to hold Henry Worms' pre-wedding reception, and the scene is described in a Vienna daily paper:[20]

> *The Salon of the Palais Todesco was opened yesterday when all celebrated the completion of this newly built house, superbly decorated by Hansen and Rahl, along with the imminent union of the daughter of Eduard Ritter von Todesco with Herr Henry Worms. All those present stared in wonder at the gleaming apartments, which number up to 500 rooms, and appreciated the unusual union of splendour with artistically perfect taste in the decoration. This skill was also mirrored during the rest of this attractive evening. First Frau Rettich and Frau Haizinger, then Herr Beckmann spoke earnest but cheerful words pertinent to the significance of the occasion, Fräulein Arnôt, then Herrn Everardi and Fioravanti performed with songs and Herr Tausig performed on the pianoforte. Among the guests we can name: Ministers Schmerling, Lasser, Hein and Plener, Count Wickenburg, the British ambassador Lord Bloomfield, the Netherlands attaché Baron Heeckeren, the attaché of Baden Baron Edelsheim, the Switz commercial attaché v. Steiger, Baron J. Kalschberg, Governor Count Chorinsky, Area-chief v. Lewinski,* [Anselm Salomon] *Baron Rothschild and many representatives of the First Viennese Bankhouse and Institute: Bauerfeld, Kuraanda, La Roche, Prof. Unger, Prof. Hanslik, the Hon. Mautner, Rahl, Hansen, Lewinsky, Dessof, Hellmesberger etc. The company was very animated and conversed among each other for one hour. Supper was served after the concert, laid out in long attractive buffets all arranged under the personal direction of Herr Franz Hauptmann.*[translated by the author]

BANKING AND MARRIAGE – THE AUSTRIAN CONNECTIONS

This illustrious guest list includes some of the most important persons in the Austrian Government. Anton Schmerling (1805–1893) was effectively the prime minister during 1860–65 (the titular prime minister was a nephew of the Emperor). In the previous year he had proposed a scheme for reform and unification of Germany under Austria. Plener was the minister of finance and Lasser (1815–1879) the minister of political administration. Count Wickenburg (1839–1911), a civil servant, was to become a well-known poet. Members of the diplomatic corps included Lord Bloomfield, a career British diplomat, and Baron Heeckeren, who had been attaché at St Petersburg in 1837 when his adopted son killed Pushkin in a duel. The banking fraternity included Baron Rothschild (1803–1874), a cousin to Henry Worms' father, along with higher employees of the banks. Both Solomon and Anthony Worms were in Vienna, but they are not recorded as present at the reception. If they did attend, the reporter may have thought them of no interest to the Viennese public.

The wedding was solemnised on 4 May 1864, according to the Jewish rite. Solomon Benedict, his son Anthony and his son-in-law Adolf Landauer, together with Eduard von Todesco, acted as witnesses and the marriage settlement provided a substantial dowry.[21] Henry Worms returned to London with his wife, she preferred the name Fanny, and their first child, Alice, was born on 2 April 1866. They lived in a residential apartment in St George's Place associated with the Alexandra Hotel, which had bought and refurbished numbers 15–21 in 1864. This complex continued in business until it was destroyed by bombardment in the Second World War. A post-modernist office block, 25–27 Knightsbridge, built in 1993–5, now occupies the site. The Alexandra Hotel looked across Knightsbridge into Hyde Park and had an excellent view of the Wellington memorial. It was a good address for the Worms family, with a splendid view and aristocratic neighbours, but the accommodation did not match up in size to that which Fanny had been used to, especially compared with the Palais Todesco in Vienna.[22]

Fanny's sister Anna, then aged 18, came to London in 1866 and stayed with Fanny, hoping to find her destiny with a rich, handsome and single man. Soon afterwards Henry had business in Vienna and then returned to London to campaign for a parliamentary seat. Anna began to complain of nervous disorders and was sent to convalesce in Egham, where Solomon Worms had acquired a house. Fanny probably accompanied her. Egham did not impress Anna, who poured out her thoughts in German poetry. *Frühling 1867 in Egham* [Spring in Egham], in which every line ends *'lang wird der Tag'* [long is the day], was followed by *Krankenzimmer* (1867) [Sick-Room], which speaks of her confinement to bed and of the use of alcohol and morphine.

After two years she returned to Vienna and in 1871 she made a happy marriage with Leopold von Lieben (1835–1915), president of the Vienna Stock Exchange. They had five children. Anna was very intelligent but suffered from a serious psychological disorder. For periods between 1887 and 1889 and again in 1891 she was referred to Sigmund Freud for treatment; her case is documented under the name of 'Cäcilie M.' in many of Freud's works.[23]

Politics in Austria

Henry Worms visited Vienna alone in 1867 and again in 1869–1870, this time with his wife and children. The second visit was prompted by one of his children requiring medical attention; this is likely to have been Dora.[24] She had been born in 1869 and was poorly throughout her life. Henry had an introduction to the political scene in Vienna through his mother-in-law, Baroness Todesco, who was well known in society and gave receptions attended by aristocrats, artists and politicians. Both visits coincided with a period from 1866 when the Austrian government had great difficulty in servicing the loans she had taken out in previous years. A confidential report of 1866 from the Austrian Creditanstalt Bank to Gerson Bleichröder (1822–1893), the important German banker and friend of Bismarck, indicated that the country was literally bankrupt. Henry was needed to look after the affairs of the firm of G. & A. Worms in Vienna during this emergency.[25]

Austria's financial problems had built up over most of the nineteenth century. Towards the end of the Napoleonic wars, the English Rothschilds were involved with the transfer of gold and silver to the more insolvent of Britain's allies, and Austria received some of this. The military engagements with revolutionaries pursued by the arch-Conservative Austrian chancellor, Prince Metternich (foreign minister from 1808; chancellor from 1821 to 1848) early in the century caused expenditure to exceed income. At first Austria preferred to use its own banking system to raise covering loans. After 1820 these sources of money proved insufficient and the house of Rothschild succeeded in obtaining administration rights for loans to the Austrian government; Solomon Worms was one of those involved in brokering the loans.[26] More loans were required in 1824 to defray the costs of suppressing a revolution in Austria's Italian provinces and of sending an army to put down a revolution in Naples. These transactions are the ones referred to in the quotation from Byron given at the start of this chapter; the French banker Jacques Lafitte (1767–1844), there mentioned, was unsuccessful in advocating intervention by his country in favour of the Italian revolutionaries. War is an expensive business, and Austria required a further loan in 1859 to cover the costs of an engagement with Sardinia and France. The result of this was defeat for Austria and loss of territory to the partly reunified Italy.[27]

Throughout this period, Austria continually attempted to defend her position as the principal state of Germany against the upcoming Prussia. In 1864 war broke out between the German Confederation and Denmark over the succession to the duchies of Schleswig and Holstein, with Austria and Prussia defending the position taken by the Confederation. The Danish crown had held the two duchies for centuries, and a crisis arose when the Danish king, Frederick VII, died childless. Denmark wanted to keep the duchies, but the laws of feudal succession differed in all three territories. Saxony's summary of the situation was: 'The big boy in this situation is Denmark and the poor little boy is Holstein. It is a question of privilege not a question of power.'[28] Austria and Prussia combined to act on behalf of the 'little boy', Holstein, part of the German Confederation, favouring the Prince of Augustenburg[29] as the lawful successor. Their combined forces defeated the Danish Army and occupied the two duchies. Lord Palmerston, then the British prime minister, famously summed up this whole problem, which was mired in a swamp of ancient feudal privilege, with this quip:

The Schleswig-Holstein question is so complicated that only three men in Europe have ever understood it. One was Prince Albert and he is dead, the second was a German professor who became mad, I am the third and I have forgotten all about it.[30]

Austria's finances were put in serious disarray as a consequence of these operations and the crisis forced a change in government. In July 1865, Richard Count Belcredi (1823–1902) replaced Schmerling, effectively Austria's first minister at the time of Henry Worms' marriage, while Count Larish replaced Plener as minister of finance.[31] Investigations showed a huge anticipated budget deficit as future income was largely pledged for interest and other payments, but the government did little to solve the problem.[32]

Austria and Prussia had won the Danish conflict but failed to solve disposition of the newly acquired territories. Prussia began to act alone. She appropriated Schleswig and expelled the Confederation's troops from Holstein. This was definitely German territory, so Austria, on behalf of the German Confederation and supported by Saxony and Hanover, went to war with Prussia in 1866 in support of the claims of the Prince of Augustenburg to the duchies. Most of Europe thought Austria was very strong, so it was a great shock when the Austrian Army was defeated at Königsgrätz in eastern Bohemia (now Hradec Kralove in the Czech Republic) on 3 July of that year. Austria was unwittingly manipulated and seriously weakened by the masterful intrigues of Bismarck (1815–1898), chief minister of Prussia from 1862 to 1890, whose ultimate aim was a united Germany with Prussia at the head.

Prussia had been able to finance this war through a clever move of the Berlin banker Gerson Bleichröder, who organised a sale of the state's holdings in a railway constructed through the Ruhr district while Austria fell deeper into financial trouble. Unease was felt in the European markets because the Austrian government issued paper money with no financial backing.[33] In an effort to bolster Austria's diplomacy, Emperor Franz Joseph (1830–1916; Emperor, 1848) appointed Friedrich von Beust as foreign minister. In a final masterpiece, Bismarck organised a peace settlement with von Beust, which kept Austria and Saxony intact while Prussia absorbed Schleswig, Holstein and Hanover. This permanently cost Austria its power in Germany. The peace treaty required Austria to pay a large indemnity to Prussia, which further increased its financial pressures.

Friedrich Ferdinand Count von Beust (1809–1886; made a count in 1868) had a long career as a statesman of the Kingdom of Saxony. That country was heavily defeated during the skirmishes of August 1866 and Beust felt obliged to resign his position in its government. Emperor Franz Joseph of Austria, looking to modernise his government and break the mould of rigid Conservative politics, called in the outsider, Beust, and this proved a highly successful move. Beust became Foreign Minister of Austria on 2 November 1866 and Prime Minister on 22 December 1867 (Imperial Chancellor from February 1868). He referred to this move of the Emperor by saying 'my God! he has given me his lingerie to wash.' Two important pieces of this lingerie were the dissolution of the German Confederation and the reconstitution of Austria as the Austro-Hungarian dual monarchy.[34]

This appointment unwittingly provided a catalyst for the rise of the House of Worms. Beust regarded the House of Worms highly and probably had a personal acquaintance with Solomon Benedict. The period when Beust was in power in Austria coincided with the time Henry Worms made long visits there. Beust was replaced as Chancellor of Austria-Hungary in 1871 to become the country's ambassador to England, where he had much social contact with Henry Worms. In 1878 Beust transferred to Paris and in 1882 he retired from public life. Over the period 1867–1878 he proved an invaluable ally for the social and political advancement of the House of Worms.

During August 1867, Henry Worms travelled to Salzburg, where a meeting between Napoleon III (Emperor of France 1852–1870) and members of the Austrian government had been organised by Count Beust. This meeting aimed to settle differences between France and Austria and patch up relations after French involvement in Mexico that culminated in the execution there of Emperor Maximillian of Mexico, the Austrian emperor's brother. It was also hoped that France would support Austria financially in some way. The House of Worms had an interest in any financial outcome from this meeting since its business was dependent on a stable Austrian currency.

Henry Worms had taken a personal interest in the 'Eastern Question', which was of great importance in Austria's politics. This question of how to deal with the decaying Empire of Turkey plagued European politicians for decades. Henry had corresponded with Hofrath (Councillor) von Hofmann, an official in the Austrian Foreign Office, and Hofmann had shown the correspondence to Count Beust. Beust was much impressed by the arguments there proposed, and on learning that Henry Worms was visiting Salzburg during August 1867, he requested that Hofmann arrange an introduction.[35] The two men had a discussion in Salzburg over several hours about politics and the state of Austria, all of which was of concern to the banking business of the House of Worms. From that time a lifelong friendship developed between the two men. A friendship between Henry Worms and Napoleon III and his wife Empress Eugénie also developed from that time.

When Henry Worms, his wife and two children were in Austria during 1869–1870, he was in daily contact with Count Beust. Henry was given an office in the government buildings and access to state papers in order to write a history of the development of the Austro-Hungarian dual monarchy. This was published in German in 1871, and an English version appeared later. Beust arranged invitations to diplomatic receptions for Henry and his wife, and their life in Vienna must have been very agreeable. Henry was being groomed for a position in the Austrian Foreign Office and at some point Beust offered him a post in that government department. The offer was wisely declined since it would have caused considerable unrest in Conservative Austria to have a Protestant Imperial Chancellor and a Jewish assistant foreign minister. Henry Worms would also have had to take Austrian nationality and this would have prevented him from taking any active part in the politics of the United Kingdom, which was his ambition.[36]

Austria's financial standing in Paris and in London had reached such a low point after the defeat at Königgrätz that Beust had to plead with the French House of Rothschild to prevent a collapse of Austrian bonds on the Paris Bourse.[37] In 1868 the Austrian government took drastic and unilateral measures with its sterling bonds, reducing interest payments to a level it could afford and then passing a law under which these bonds were converted to internal stock and an income tax of 16% was imposed on the interest payments. Payments into a sinking fund associated with this stock were suspended. These measures were to be temporary to keep some of the money in Austria until the financial situation improved. Count Beust apprised the British government of the situation in a letter transmitted through his ambassador in London,[38] but still these measures caused uproar on the London Stock Exchange. A committee of Anglo-Austrian Bondholders was formed in London, together with a Council of Foreign Bondholders, to press for some change in this decision of the Vienna government. The Paris Bourse also pressed Vienna for change.[39]

In 1870 financial markets became concerned at the rumblings of war between France and Prussia over a candidate for the vacant throne of Spain. The Spanish royal family had been exiled and Bismarck supported a German prince as King of Spain, while Napoleon III had another candidate. The Berlin banker Gerson Bleichröder was so afraid of a collapse of Austrian finances in 1870 should the country enter any Franco-Prussian war on the side of France that on 11 July he ordered his correspondent in London, the firm of G. & A. Worms, to sell holdings at any loss. France, manipulated by Bismarck, declared war on Prussia while Austria prudently stayed outside this conflict.[40]

G. & A. Worms, with George in London and Henry in Vienna during 1869–1870, attempted to mediate in the financial dispute between London and Vienna. Henry appeared to make progress in terms of the introduction of amending legislation in Vienna. Meanwhile, in London, some bondholders exchanged their old bonds for the issue on which the new rules applied. Those bondholders who refused to accept the new situation applied for certificates from the Anglo-Austrian Bondholders' Committee in lieu of the old bonds, which Austria no longer recognised. These certificates could be traded, like bonds, on the Stock Exchange, which on 24 May 1870 had suspended dealings in the new Austrian bonds, much to the annoyance of the government in Vienna. George Worms had pleaded with the Stock Exchange to prevent this move – a move which, of course, scuppered Henry's efforts at mediation in Vienna.[41]

In a letter of 13 June 1870 the Austro-Hungarian Ambassador, Count

Above: Park Crescent, London: Henry Worms was born in one of the houses to the right of this photograph. His brother George's house was near the centre of the photograph. A blue tile marks the residence of Professor Wheatstone. (Photographer J.G., 2012)

Below: Palais Todesco, Vienna, one of the Grand Mansions on the Ringstrasse. Its Grand Salon looks out onto the centre balcony. (Photographer Czihak, Vienna, about 1880)

Above: Ballroom at the Gerstner Beletage at the Palais Todesco, Vienna: formerly the Grand Salon of the Palais Todesco, refurbished as original. Henry Worms' pre-wedding reception was held in this room. (Photographed for Gerstner, 2012)

Below: Salon Paris at the Gerstner Beletage at the Palais Todesco Vienna, refurbished as original. This room to the right of the ballroom was used for the buffet. (Photographed for Gerstner, 2012)

Top: The Judgement of Paris by Carl Rahl at the Gerstner Beletage at the Palais Todesco, Vienna. This ceiling painting is in an ante-room off the ballroom. (Photographed for Gerstner, 2012)

Above left: Henry Worms aged twenty four. (Photographer L. Angerer, Vienna, 1864)

Above right: Franzisca (Fanny) von Todesco aged about seventeen. Henry judged her so beautiful he would kill himself if he could not marry her. (Photographer F. Luckhardt, Vienna, 1863).

Above: Eduard von Todesco, banker and industrialist, a millionaire of the Vienna Ringstrasse. (Photographer L. Angerer, Vienna, ca. 1860)

Left: Sophie von Todesco, Eduard's wife and a noted Viennese hostess.
(Photographer L. Angerer, Vienna, ca. 1860)

Above: Wedding photograph of Henry Worms and Franziska von Todesco. (Photographer L. Angerer, Vienna, 1864)

Left: Friedrich Ferdinand von Beust, Chancellor of Austria 1869-1871 and Austrian ambassador in London 1871-1878, who supported Henry Worms' early career in British politics. (Engraving by Weger, Leipzig in the author's collection)

Above: Schloss Trauttmansdorff, Meran. Fanny de Worms rented part of the castle. The grounds were by then developed as orchards and vineyards.
(Painting by Johanna von Isser-Grossrubatscher, 1859)

Below: Fanny de Worms' lover, Count Moritz von Léon, owner of Schloss Trauttmannsdorff. Identification of the sitter is probable but not certain.

Top: Henry's oldest daughter Alice photographed ca. 1900 when she was Mrs. McLaren Morrison. (Photographer Bourne and Shepherd, India)

Above: Henry's oldest daughter, Alice de Worms, in court presentation dress, London, 1884.

Left: Henry's youngest daughter, Constance de Worms, introduced to society in Munich ca.1894. (Photographer Bros. Lützel, Munich)

Above: Grosvenor Place, London. Henry de Worms' residence, No. 42, was destroyed and later rebuilt as part of an office block. It was the end house of a block on the far left of the photograph and a grand house similar to, but the mirror image of, the end of this block. The house faced the gardens of Buckingham Palace to the north-east and a small square to the south-east.
(Photographer J.G., 2014)

Below: Henry de Worms' country seat, Henley Park, Surrey. He constructed the wing to the right of this photograph housing the Grand Salon on the ground floor.
(Photographer J. Horne, Normandy, Surrey, ca. 1905)

Apponyi, gave thanks to George Worms for the efforts of his firm at mediation but regretted that, since the Stock Exchange had suspended the quotation of Austrian bonds, his government would desist from any further attempt to modify the law of 1868.[42] In 1871, the Austrian government, while Beust was still Chancellor, showed gratitude to the Worms family for their efforts to ameliorate Austria's financial situation by conferring a hereditary peerage on Solomon, head of the banking house of Worms, making him Baron de Worms (in German, Freiherr von Worms). The warrant notes that 'Solomon Worms has acquired particular merit in respect of his financial interests [in] the Austro-Hungarian Monarchy'. The motto chosen was VINCTUS NON VICTUS [bound not conquered], which seems appropriate given the financial state of Austria following the restructuring of its national debt. The Worms coat of arms has the shield quartered, two sections bearing a German eagle in black with a red tongue looking inwards, the other sections bearing a right-leaning gold key with an acorn-shaped ring. A small shield bearing a right hand holding three outspread silver arrows with golden shafts, denoting either Solomon's three sons or Solomon and his two brothers, is embossed on the centre.[43]

Under the terms of this Patent of Creation, all sons were entitled to the prefix of Baron but with the distinctive addition of their forename; thus the sons became Baron George de Worms and Baron Henry de Worms. Solomon Baron de Worms quickly laid plans to have these titles recognised in Britain. First he had to obtain British nationality, as so far he only had permission to reside in the country; he described himself as 'a native of the free city of Frankfurt on the Main, not in any trade, profession or occupation and a widower'.[44] As such, he could legitimately use his title in Britain but it could not be passed on to his sons who were of British nationality by birth. British nationality was granted on 21 May 1874, and he once again became plain Solomon Benedict Worms.

Solomon now had to petition for recognition of his title in Britain, and this was achieved with the help of Count Beust and the British Foreign Minister, Lord Derby (15th Earl), both of whom had been known to Solomon in the past. Count Beust, now the Austrian ambassador, wrote in June 1874 to Lord Derby at the Foreign Office requesting that Solomon Worms be give the same privilege as the Rothschild family had in 1838 and the Golschmidt family in 1841 when their Austrian titles were recognised in Britain. The Home Office proved most reluctant to grant this privilege since it would create a precedent for others to exploit. Anticipating this reply, Count Beust had simultaneously sent a more strongly worded request in a private letter to Derby, saying: 'the House of Worms is not unknown to you, having been their host during your stay in the Indies and having had the opportunity to judge their activities which I am told have given a great push for commerce between the island of Ceylon and Europe.' Lord Derby forwarded this second letter to the Home Office with a note saying: 'Mr. Worms is a useful and deserving person. I knew him many years ago in Ceylon and shall be glad that he gets what he wants.' The Home Office agreed to this request in August 1874 and issued the necessary Royal Warrant.[45] On the death of Solomon, Henry's elder brother George became Baron de Worms and the title continued. After the First World War a warrant revoking all licences allowing the use of German and Austrian titles was issued on 1 March 1920 and this extinguished the barony.[46]

Back in 1872, diplomatic intervention was required to heal the deep rift between London and Vienna over financial matters. The British Foreign Office acknowledged[47] a request to intervene on 8 January 1872 and the Council of Foreign Bondholders was able to report a completely satisfactory settlement in its annual report for the year 1872.[48] However, trust between the two financial centres was damaged, and after 1869 German rather than British capital was funnelled into Austria-Hungary through the efforts of the Berlin banking house of Bleichröder and Hansemann.[49]

Return to London

Henry returned to London with his wife and two daughters in 1870 and took the lease of a more impressive house, South Lodge, about one kilometre west of St George's Place along Knightsbridge Road. The accommodation comprised three floors and a basement with ample room for servants. He extended the house and had elaborate decorations carried out. Clearly, his financial affairs were vastly improving, as were those of his brother George, who bought Milton Park, Egham, around the same time. In an effort to placate Fanny, and with no expense spared, the house was made over so that it could function with a salon after the style of the Palais Todesco. South Lodge had a first-floor ballroom, which was given a painted and guilded ceiling by John G. Cace & Sons. Kriepenkerl of Munich painted a first-floor anteroom. The drawing room had a ceiling painted by Chaulemont of Vienna and wood and silk panels by Kieser of Vienna. One drawback to this otherwise desirable residential area of London was the presence of the cavalry barracks at Knightsbridge. These had been an eyesore for many years and a deputation of residents in the area, led by Baron Henry de Worms, as he had become by then, petitioned the War Department to have the barracks relocated as a result of being unsightly, unsanitary and being surrounded by 'objectionable associations'.[50]

Henry Worms both gave and attended entertainment in London after the lavish style of *la belle époque*. But although Fanny now had a house approaching the Palais Todesco in splendour, Henry did not have the contacts in London to equal those he had acquired in Vienna. He rented a house in Cowes during August 1871 and after a particular party, Nathaniel, later Lord Rothschild (1840–1915), remarked to his parents that the Worms 'aired as usual their relationship to the Rothschilds'.[51] Count Beust, now ambassador to London, befriended the Worms family inviting them to a dinner during May 1872 attended by other ambassadors, along with Ferdinand de Rothschild.[52]

The Worms family was also in Cowes during the season of 1872 when Henry had an unusual visitor, the Archduke Ludwig Victor of Austria, youngest brother of the Emperor. He must have carried the letters patent for Henry's Austrian title. After this visit Henry began to use the title of Baron in Britain, although this was forbidden until allowed by royal licence.[53] The deposed French emperor, Napoleon III, was staying with his family at Beaulieu House on the Cowes promenade, so Henry grasped the opportunity to speak with him; the two had been introduced previously in Salzburg.[54] Napoleon died shortly afterwards and Henry Worms was among the crowd who offered condolences to the widowed Empress Eugénie at Chislehurst, Kent.[55] When her son, the Prince Imperial, was killed serving in the British Army during the Zulu wars, Henry, at the time president of the Anglo-Jewish Association, sent a letter of condolence on behalf of the association noting that it was thanks to Napoleon I that the ghettos throughout Europe had been closed. Henry remained in contact with the Empress throughout the remainder of his life and she sent a telegram of condolence to his family at his funeral.[56]

A Mozart Institute had been organised in Salzburg by the Austrian government and during 1874 a European-wide campaign was arranged to generate funds for this institution. The institute provided tuition to budding students at a nominal rate. Henry, as Baron Henry de Worms, received donations for the fund at the Austrian embassy and a gala concert was organised at the Royal Opera House to support this initiative. The list of sixteen patrons for the event included Count Beust, Baroness Henry de Worms, Baroness Lionel de Rothschild and six dukes and duchesses. Henry was using all means to introduce his wife into the highest levels of society.[57]

Between 1872 and 1876 Henry de Worms and others started a new business venture operating as the British and Foreign Exchange and

Investment Bank. It began with an issue of 500,000 shares at £5 each and had Baron Henry de Worms as deputy chairman with Adolf Landauer, his brother-in-law, as a director in Vienna.[58] It was an investment bank, dealing in large deposits, stocks and shares, bills of exchange and foreign exchange, and it had contacts in Paris through the firm of Léon et Dreher. Unfortunately this business had been started just as the world was falling into a deep trade depression caused by rampant speculation and a flood of liquidity from the payment of reparations from France to Germany after the unification of Germany and the stabilisation of Austria-Hungary. The immediate causes of depression were a collapse of the Vienna Stock Exchange in 1873 and the boom and bust resulting from cheap-money advocates in the USA. The firm's business proceeded very slowly, and after the shareholders' general meeting of 1874 a reduction in capital was agreed, with some capital returned to shareholders. The firm was, however, sufficiently prosperous to allow a dividend of six per cent.[59] During that year, Herman Gfrörer, the chief bookkeeper of G. & A. Worms, stole some of the company's bank records and attempted to blackmail the firm, saying he knew the true state of the British and Foreign Exchange and Investment Bank. This he would reveal unless he was given sufficient money to emigrate to New Zealand. His bluff was called without injury to the bank and he was dealt with severely in the courts.[60] The innuendo, however, did have some basis in fact, as business overall was poor, and closure of the British and Foreign Exchange and Investment Bank was decided at the shareholders' general meeting in 1876. The connection with Léon and Dreher had been liquidated in April 1875. Shareholders placed no blame on the directors, who were sufficiently trusted by them to be put in charge of the liquidation.[61]

Henry de Worms made a visit to Egypt in early 1876, probably to investigate the financial situation of that country on behalf of G. & A. Worms.[62] The Khedive of Egypt and Sudan, Isma'il Pasha, had modernised his domain, employing the best European contractors, and in 1869 contributed to the building of the Suez Canal. By 1876 Egypt was spiralling into debt and could hardly pay interest on its bonds. An earlier sale of the Khedive's Suez Canal shares did little to help the situation, and by late 1876 a mission on behalf of British and French bondholders established dual control of Egyptian finances. Henry probably also wanted to see the canal for himself, as a debate years previously at King's College had concluded that its construction was impractical.

A Criminal Conversation

Fanny de Worms was not happy in London: she missed the social scene of Vienna and Henry had developed few social contacts outside the Jewish community. She became seriously ill after their youngest daughter was born at South Lodge in 1875 and the eldest daughter also developed pneumonia around this time. In June 1876 she left with her three children to recuperate at Carlsbad (now Karlovy Vary in the Czech Republic), a well-known spa town and play area for the rich, later moving to Vienna.[63] She did not find London society agreeable and was not impressed by the city's polluted atmosphere. In those days the combination of smoke from coal fires and the damp London atmosphere generated a thick yellow fog. Count Beust, at that time the Austro-Hungarian ambassador in London, complained of 'living miserably here under the fogs'.[62] After a short stay at the Palais Todesco, Fanny went on to Meran in the South Tyrol.

Meran (now Merano in Italy) is famous for its mild, healthy climate; the district was made fashionable by the Empress Elizabeth of Austria, who rented Schloss Trauttmansdorff from the owner, Count Moritz von Léon (1843–1899), for the winter of 1870/71. She travelled with her two daughters, Gisela (age 14) and Valerie (aged 2), and Emperor Franz Joseph stayed with them on two occasions. Reports that Valerie had been cured of her illness in this mild climate greatly enhanced the reputation of the resort.[64]

On a visit to Meran around 1847, Count Joseph von Trauttmansdorff (1807–1867) had discovered the ruined gothic castle left by his ancestors, which he restored and enlarged and then lived in. He enlarged the estate by buying the adjacent castles of Pienzenau and Fragsburg with their farms and orchards and formed a model farming enterprise of wine and fruit growing. He never married, and when he died Moritz von Léon, probably an illegitimate son, inherited the estate and lived in Schloss Trauttmansdorff with his wife.[65]

Fanny de Worms took up residence in Meran for the winter of 1876 at the Villa Aders. She soon made the acquaintance of Moritz von Léon, who was by now almost penniless. He had sold off Fragsburg and in the winter of 1877/8 he let a portion of Schloss Trauttmansdorff to her while residing in another wing. The two soon became very close 'friends'. Henry visited each year, urging her to return to London, but the excuse always was that her health required her to reside outside England. Suspecting his wife was unlikely to return to England and realising that South Lodge was much too large for one person, he sold the house in 1877 to John Allan Rolls, the father of C.S. Rolls, the co-founder of the firm of Rolls-Royce.[50] Henry moved to the Lodge at Egham, which his father Solomon Worms had inherited from Maurice Worms, while Solomon still kept the house in Park Crescent, London.[66]

During 1879 Henry had grave suspicions about his wife's relationship with Moritz von Léon as reported by her servants in Meran, though all of the Todesco family denied any improper behaviour. He brought his eldest daughter to London in the hope of persuading his wife to return, but with little success. Fanny returned briefly to London in February 1880 only to seek the return of her daughter, and his father and brother persuaded Henry to allow mother and daughter to return to Austria.[67] Henry then took temporary accommodation in the Albany, a building off Piccadilly that contained bachelor apartments and that was very convenient for Parliament, as he was now MP for Greenwich.[68]

Henry visited the family in Austria that autumn and then again in 1882 and 1883, on the latter occasion staying with them in Schloss Trauttmansdorff and later at the Palais Todesco in Vienna.[69] The visit in 1883 was prolonged – Henry left Dover on 17 August and was not seen again in Britain until February 1884.[70] He must have made a serious attempt to save the marriage, and with some success, for his wife and three children came back to London with him. Henry had decided to have his eldest daughter, Alice, who was now 18 years old, back with him in London so that she could be presented at court and enter society. He was now high in the circles of the Conservative Party and such a move was one of necessity for a Tory grandee. The occasion resulted in a whirl of balls and parties where they became well acquainted with Sir Benjamin Phillips and his divorced daughter Sarah, who was to become an important figure in this story. Around this time, Fanny was described as 'a handsome, stately woman, possessing a fine, voluptuous figure, and [someone who] has long been the leader of a fashionable circle and a general social favourite'.[71] This description of her figure is probably correct, but her social status has been exaggerated.

The resulting social engagements now required Henry to vacate the cramped quarters of the Albany and to rent 4 Old Burlington Street instead. A short distance away from the Albany, this street comprised a terrace of narrow five-storeyed townhouses described at the time as being 'dingy'.[72] Only number two of this terrace exists today, the remainder having been demolished and replaced by an office block. Its only advantage to the de Worms family was one of convenience for the social whirl following Alice's presentation at court. As was deemed appropriate, Baroness Henry de Worms escorted her daughter to parties and organised a ball at the New Club on 19 June 1884 to celebrate her coming out into society.[73] Miss Alice de Worms caused a good deal of interest at the evening reception given by Benjamin Phillips when a recital of one of her Austrian poems was given in English.[74] Alice was extraordinarily beautiful, her launch into society was successful and she was married in April 1886 to John Henry Warner.

The reconciliation between Henry and his wife did not last long, for Fanny returned to Trauttmansdorff and Moritz von Léon in August 1884, bringing her other two daughters with her to Austria. She never returned to England. Henry visited in September 1884 and on this occasion his wife confessed to debts of £6,000, as a result of lavish spending and which had been paid by her family. It soon appeared that the debts amounted to £25,000. Further, at some time she had changed her bank so that now the allowance sent by her husband was cashed at the bank used by Moritz von Léon. Most of this money was used to finance von Léon. The relationship between Moritz and his wife had become distant, with Fanny and Moritz occupying different floors in the same wing of the castle while his wife lived in another wing. Detailed evidence of adultery was presented at the divorce proceedings Henry opened in London in July 1886, after the wedding of his eldest daughter. Two witnesses from Meran testified to having seen Fanny and Moritz passing between one another's rooms. The two floors had been connected by the main staircase until a more private wooden staircase had been constructed from the ground floor to Fanny's boudoir.

The case was uncontested and Henry obtained a divorce, winning costs and custody of the children. Although it had been specified in the marriage settlement of 1864 that if the couple separated Henry would have to repay £6,000, the divorce court extinguished this liability.[75] Whilst coping with these domestic upheavals during 1885–6, Henry was in government serving as parliamentary secretary to the Board of Trade. In July 1885 he wrote to the Anglo-Jewish Association, of which he was president, regretting his absence from the annual general meeting due to pressure of work as a member of the government. Without mentioning his domestic problems, he stated that doctors considered a rest at the seaside to be a necessity for the good of his health.[76]

In spite of obtaining money through Fanny de Worms, Moritz von Léon found it difficult to maintain his properties. The hard winter of 1879–80 and an epidemic of grapevine downy mildew brought financial disaster to the fruit business, so Pienzenau was sold in 1884, and only the vineyards and Trauttmansdorff were retained. Production of grapes continued to suffer as ash from the volcanic eruption that occurred in 1884 at Krakatoa caused a deterioration in climate over a number of years. Moritz turned to tourism to increase his income, and Trauttmansdorff was advertised in Bädecker as a pensionat with 40 rooms. Empress Elizabeth of Austria visited Meran one more time in 1889 after the suicide of her son, the Crown Prince Rudolf, renting Schloss Trauttmansdorff from Moritz von Léon, who moved out for the occasion. She dressed only in black and remained sequestered in the castle, rarely venturing outside. Moritz von Léon's remaining assets in Meran were all sold in 1892, just three years after this last visit of Empress Elizabeth. He then moved to Vienna, where he died and was interred in the crypt of the church at Trauttmansdorff Castle.[77] Fanny was supported from a fund bequeathed by her parents who specified that, on her death, the money be transferred to the daughters.[78]

Trauttmansdorff became a luxury hotel in German hands until Italy confiscated it in 1918 when the South Tyrol became Italian territory. It was used as emergency accommodation, and then during the Second World War as a storage facility for the German military. As a result, the building fell into decay. Finally, in 1977 restoration of the castle was begun and it was adopted as a museum which opened in 2001. Schloss Fragsburg, a short distance outside Meran, has become a luxury hotel. Schloss Pienzenau, again just outside Meran, has been renovated to serve as a centre for business meetings. One other memorial of Moritz von Léon remains in the form of a unique breed of horse that he had spotted on farms near his castle of Fragsburg. These animals were brought to the notice of the Austrian Minister of Agriculture in 1875, after which bloodlines were recorded. This Haflinger breed is recognised today and these horses are bred in Europe and America.[79]

Marriages in London

The marriage of Alice de Worms, the eldest daughter of Henry, to Mr. John Henry B. Warner was solemnised at St. James's Piccadilly on 18 April 1886, the officiating clergyman being a cousin of the bridegroom, and Henry himself gave the bride away. The bride was richly dressed in silk draped with lace and wore a diamond necklace, a gift of the bridegroom, a diamond brooch from her father and diamond stars in her hair, the gift of her uncle George. The bridesmaids included the bride's two younger sisters and two young granddaughters of Benjamin Phillips – Henry de Worms had become very friendly with the Phillips family and especially Sarah, the daughter of Benjamin. Sarah presented the lace for the wedding dress together with a jewelled cross, whilst her brother Samuel Henry gave a set of silver gilt apostle spoons. There were also presents from the bride's relations in

Vienna. The actor Henry Irvine gave a necklace of blue enamel and pearl. The breakfast was held at the Burlington Hotel, where the bride and bridegroom sat together at the principal table, the bride being supported by her father and by Baroness von Todesco, her grandmother, who travelled from Vienna. Sarah Phillips was also on the principal table. It was this wedding which greatly upset the more orthodox Jewish community along with the board of the Anglo-Jewish Association, for not only had the bride married out of the Jewish faith, but the father had also condoned and supported the ceremony. He had given the bride away and celebrated with an elaborate wedding breakfast.[80]

After the wedding reception, the couple departed for Paris to begin a world trip, travelling via Marseilles, Egypt (the Nile, the Aswan cataracts and the Red Sea), the Seychelles and Mauritius to Australia – quite an adventure for a Victorian lady. The bridegroom, John Henry Warner, was private secretary to the governor of South Australia and a commissioner to the Jubilee Exhibition held in Adelaide. On completion of duties related to his job, the couple visited Melbourne, Sydney, Brisbane, New Zealand, Tasmania, and Hawaii, returning home via San Francisco, New York and Le Havre. Back in England, Mr and Mrs J.H.B. Warner, along with Henry and Sarah, were invited to the state ball on 3 July 1889 in honour of the Shah of Persia.[81]

The Warner family held estates in Leicestershire and Yorkshire. John Henry's grandfather, Edward Warner, had purchased Quorn Hall in Leicestershire in 1855, at the same time becoming master of the Quorn hunt. He also bought land at Kepwick near Thirsk in Yorkshire, erecting Kepwick Hall there in 1873. The married couple lived largely in Kepwick Hall, which was extensively renovated for them. After the death of Edward Warner in 1886, John Henry's father, Captain W.P. Warner, became master of the Quorn hunt. From 1906, the hunt was housed in more modern buildings, and after the death of W.P. Warner in 1929, his family left the district to live in Kepwick. Quorn Hall was first converted to a country club and when this failed, the buildings were transferred to Loughborough Training College for use as a students' residence. Presently it is the Leicestershire International Education Centre.[82]

John Henry Warner became ill soon after the marriage and died in April 1891. In his will he left the use of Kepwick Hall to his wife during her lifetime.[83] Alice remarried in June 1892 to a friend of his, David McLaren Morrison (1849–1924). David was 16 years older than Alice and had business interests in Calcutta, where he was manager of a cotton mill. The two were frequently in India and David became the honorary Austro-

Hungarian consul in Calcutta. When in England they lived at Kepwick Hall. Alice became a well-known breeder of show dogs, which she kept in kennels at Kepwick.[84] There were two daughters from this marriage, Ester (b. 1899) and Theodora (b. 1900).

After their wedding in 1892, David and Alice spent some time with Alice's grandmother and their Oppenheimer cousins at the Palais Todesco in Vienna. The Austrian poet, novelist and librettist Hugo von Hofmannsthal (1874–1929) was a friend of Felix Oppenheimer and frequented the house, where he became enraptured by the oriental beauty of 27-year-old Alice Morrison. She was the inspiration behind some of Hofmannsthal's work, including the 1896 poem *Lebenslied*.[85]

The two younger daughters of Henry de Worms had been placed in the care of their father by the divorce court, but although they had been born in London, they had spent most of their lives in Austria, so as soon as they could they returned to their relatives in Vienna. Constance was presented to society in Munich and became acquainted with Count Maximilian von Löwenstein-Scharffeneck, an official at the court of Bavaria. The two were married in Munich on 4 November 1895, when Constance was 20 years old. After the ceremony the pair left for England so that Constance could present Maximilan to her father. Maximilian's family was a side branch of the royal house of Bavaria, once Protestant, but his father had reverted to Catholicism. The family had a position in society but little money, so this union would have been advantageous to both parties; two daughters and three sons resulted from the marriage. Henry's middle daughter, Dora, never married and died outside England some time before 1903. She is not recorded in her father's will.[86]

The final decree of Henry and Fanny's divorce was granted on 18 January 1887, and on 25 January Henry de Worms married Sarah Phillips in a civil ceremony at Westminster register office. Her father, Benjamin Samuel Phillips, had served on the committee of the New Synagogue together with Henry. He had begun in business with a small bead shop in London, eventually becoming a prosperous merchant and head of the firm of Faudel and Phillips. Montague Williams, friend of Henry de Worms from their student days, described Benjamin Phillips as follows: 'He never claimed to be anything but what he was – a plain citizen and a self made man.'[87] Sarah had acted as host for her father after the death of her mother in 1880. She took a great interest in the thought-reading experiments of Stuart Cumberland, and her early meetings with Henry de Worms were during thought-reading sessions in 1882 and again in 1884. She moved to her own establishment at 17 Grosvenor Street in 1885, holding Wednesday-evening parties there.

Soon she started the Grosvenor habitation of the Primrose League, a Conservative fellowship in memory of Disraeli, and Henry de Worms became a member of her habitation in September 1885. This habitation must have been very fashionable, for its members included the Duchess of Marlborough, along with other titled ladies, as well as Henry Drummond Wolff, Henry's brother (by then Baron de Worms) and Theodore Martin, who played a part in Henry de Worms' later life. The thought-reader Stewart Cumberland referred to Sarah after her marriage as a lady of 'great tact and delicacy'.[88]

The circle of Jewish friends around Henry and Sarah included the Levy family. Joseph Moses Levy (1812–1888) became the principal proprietor of the *Sunday Times* in 1855 and later acquired the *Daily Telegraph*. His son Edward became editor of the latter. Edward (1833–1916) lived in Twickenham, and the Sunday parties given by him and his wife were famous. The contingent from town included Henry de Worms, the celebrated soprano Adelina Patti (1843–1919) and many others. A sister of Edward married Sarah's younger brother.[89]

By 1880 Henry had felt himself sufficiently wealthy to enter Parliament, and after 1886 he held a minor position in government. This second marriage connected him with another prominent mercantile family of London, and his new wife became one of the leaders of fashion. Thus the scene was set for a political career and for an appearance in *la belle époque*.

6

House of Commons: House of Lords

Intelligent toryism [Baron Henry de Worms]
(Caption to *Spy* cartoon of 1880)[1]

Into Parliament

When Henry Worms formed an ambition to enter British politics as a Conservative, representation in the House of Commons had already been reformed, but the electoral franchise still comprised only a small proportion of the male population. The Liberal party was determined to redress this situation after the death of Lord Palmerston in 1865. When a general election was held that year and returned an overall Liberal majority, Lord John Russell (created Lord Russell in 1861) introduced a further reform bill. However, the Liberal Party divided over this bill, so it was defeated and the Liberal government resigned; Conservative opponents of the bill included Disraeli and Cranborne (later the Marquis of Salisbury). After the Conservatives, led by Lord Derby (1799–1869, 14th Earl from 1851), had formed a government, Disraeli steered a new reform bill through the House of Commons despite the fact that he had organised the blocking of Lord Russell's bill. Huge meetings around the country were convened to demand action and the Conservative's bill passed with support from some Liberals, including Gladstone. This 1867 act, the Representation of the Peoples Act, vastly increased the size of the electorate in boroughs to include all males who paid rates in person. Rural constituency electorates, though, remained unchanged, with the same few landowners having a vote. Many constituencies still elected more than one member.[2]

Disraeli (1804–1881; created Lord Beaconsfield in 1876), who by 1866 had become Chancellor of the Exchequer, was a member of the Jewish race. He had been baptised in the Anglican faith at an early age but he remained receptive to Jewish causes. With Prime Minister Lord Derby in the House of

Lords, he was the leader of the Conservative Party in the Commons. Henry Worms saw a chance of becoming a candidate for one of the boroughs with its newly increased electorate, but to be proposed, he first had to gain patronage and an introduction to Disraeli. Such could not come from his Jewish relatives, even though some of them were MPs, because they all belonged to the Liberal Party.

Fortunately it was at this juncture that his friendship with the Austrian Chancellor, Count Beust, developed through a series of coincidences. Count Beust must have been very impressed at their first meetings in 1867 as he obliged with a letter of introduction to Disraeli, whom he had known since being minister to London for the Kingdom of Saxony. By another fortunate coincidence, Disraeli became prime minister in February 1868 when Lord Derby retired after a serious attack of gout. Soon afterwards a general election was called, and as a result of his new contacts, Henry Worms obtained the nomination in the election of 1868 as a Conservative candidate for the borough of Sandwich, Deal and Walmer in Kent.[3]

Electioneering led to considerable private expense in 1868 when political parties were only just beginning to establish local organising committees. Sandwich returned two members to the House of Commons and the allegiance of the voters had oscillated between Liberal and Conservative. At the general election of 1865 they had returned two prominent Liberal politicians, but soon after, one of these, Lord Clarence Paget, who was also a naval officer, was given command of the Mediterranean fleet and resigned his seat in Parliament. In the by-election that followed, the Conservative candidate, Charles Capper (1822–1869), who had been defeated previously, stood against the Liberal Henry Brassey and was this time elected. There was some hope that the Conservatives would win again in the general election of 1868, but Capper was not able to stand so Henry Worms was introduced to the electorate, opposed by two Liberal candidates.

Henry Worms set forth his election manifesto on 11 July 1868 in a circular posted around the town.[4] It praised the Conservative government for carrying through the Reform Bill of 1867 and commended in glowing terms the youthful Conservative cabinet headed by Disraeli. Worms' candidature soon attracted vile anti-Jewish propaganda, with the comment 'who will "worm" itself to the surface and have its pound of flesh' directed specifically at him. The two Liberal opponents emphatically repudiated these remarks, made in an unsigned circular letter, and the author was never identified.[5]

Two important questions of the time concerned the Irish Church and the Permissive Bill. The Anglican Church of Ireland was established by law, was supported by the government and collected tithes even though the majority of the population adhered to the Roman Catholic hierarchy that had been allowed to return earlier in the century. The injustice of this situation caused agitation in Ireland and Gladstone (1827–1902), leader of the Liberal Party, had spoken in Parliament on 23 March 1868 in favour of disestablishment of the Church of Ireland. The Conservatives, including Henry, opposed this move and it might appear that in his manifesto, Henry, a Jew, was merely following the Party line. His overall political career, however, indicates his firm conviction that a country should have a state religion.

The second important topic of the time was the Permissive Bill. This was first introduced in 1864 by Sir Wilfrid Lawson (1829–1906, Liberal MP for Carlisle), a lifelong campaigner against alcohol. It proposed a veto on the basis of a two-thirds majority in any district against the granting of a licence for the sale of intoxicating liquor. The Conservatives, including Henry, were against this veto, and it was never embodied in any act, although Wilfrid Lawson tried often to introduce his bill. Pamphlets were distributed and meetings held all over the country to debate this subject that F. W. Newman (younger brother of Cardinal Newman) deemed 'more urgent than any franchise'.[6]

Many candidates during and before the 1860s resorted to bribing voters and causing riots to scare the opposition's supporters. The small franchise which existed before the 1867 act made bribery easier, and since voting was by open declaration the briber could see his wishes being carried through. A number of acts had attempted to curtail bribery, beginning with the Treating Act of 1696 which banned candidates from offering meat, drink, money, entertainment or provisions to the voters. An act of 1863 ordered that election committees be obliged to report to the House the names of people found guilty of bribery and corruption. In spite of this, bribery had been rampant during the 1865 election, so the Election Petitions and Corrupt Practices at Elections Act was passed in July 1868, setting up a formal route for complaints.

Bribery and treating were rife during the 1868 elections, as were riots aimed at intimidation, and one incident of riotous behaviour involving Henry Worms was reported in the reminiscences which followed his elevation to the peerage. His journey from Sandwich by coach had been blocked by a group of Deal boatmen, Liberal supporters who refused to give way. During the arguments it had been decided that Henry would fight one of the boatmen for the right to travel on. Henry had become proficient at boxing during his studies at King's College and defeated his opponent with little difficulty. Later during the election he was surprised to see these boatmen sporting his Conservative colours. 'His antagonist of Deal Road fame declared that, having been deservedly licked, both he and his friends considered that Baron de Worms was the best of the three candidates, and, politics or no politics, they intended to vote for him.' Writing in retrospect, the reporter had elevated Henry Worms to the title of baron long before the letters patent were granted.[7]

In spite of this declaration of support, Henry Worms was defeated and two Liberal MPs were elected. Knatchbull-Hugessen (1829–1893; created Baron Braebourne in 1880) was a Kent landowner, while Brassey (1840–1891) was the son of an immensely rich railway engineer and contractor. The votes cast were as follows:

SANDWICH (1868)
E. Knatchbull-Hugessen (L)   932
H. Brassey (L)   923
Henry Worms (C)   712

This trend was followed nationally, and the Conservatives under Disraeli lost the general election, having only 271 seats to the 387 of the Liberals. When the new Parliament assembled in 1868 with Gladstone as prime minister, the Irish Church Bill was indeed drawn up and the Anglican Church of Ireland disestablished.[8]

After this defeat in 1868, Disraeli asked John Gorst (1835–1916) to reorganise the party machinery and make it more democratic, a move which paved the way for Henry Worms to achieve his ambition to have a role in government. In the general election of 1874 a substantial Conservative majority was returned, due in large part to the reforms Gorst had initiated in the party management. However, Sandwich again elected the same two Liberals in 1874, with two opposing Conservatives being defeated, and both Liberals stood again unopposed in 1880.

In 1880, Knatchbull-Hugessen was elevated to a peerage, causing a by-election in May, when a Conservative candidate with Edwin Hughes (1832–1904) as his electoral agent stood in opposition to a wealthy Liberal and won with a large majority. Complaints of widespread bribery became so numerous after this by-election that a thorough investigation into the affairs of the borough was demanded. It was clear that the Conservative candidate won the by-election because Edwin Hughes had surpassed the efforts of his opponent in bribery, and not through legitimate persuasion. The Parliamentary Commission set up in 1881 declared that 'we cannot doubt that electoral corruption had long and extensively prevailed in the borough of

Sandwich'.⁹ As a result, the May 1880 by-election was declared invalid, the seat was abolished and the electorate incorporated into adjacent areas.¹⁰ Perhaps during his election campaign of 1868, Henry Worms had not understood the importance of bribery to the electors of Sandwich, but later a whiff of bribery from that time came back to haunt him during the 1885 election when he employed Edwin Hughes as electoral agent.

When the general election of 1874 was imminent, Count Beust, now the Austro-Hungarian ambassador in London, gave a helping hand to Henry de Worms' political ambitions by inviting Benjamin Disraeli, along with Baron and Baroness Henry de Worms, to a political dinner.¹¹ This election returned a Conservative government with Disraeli as Prime Minister, but Henry de Worms did not try for a seat. It is likely that even then he had domestic problems, and two years later his wife left for Austria with the three children. He devoted himself to making money, improving his skills at oratory through his chairmanship of the Anglo-Jewish Association and moving up the ranks of the Conservative Association.

It was common knowledge that Henry wanted to stand for the City of London or some adjacent borough. Thus, as the election of 1880 approached, a deputation from the City asked him to consider nomination, along with another, should two of the sitting Conservatives retire from politics. The City of London returned four members of Parliament, and in 1874 those elected were three Conservatives and one Liberal. In the event only one of the Conservatives retired, so the provisional agreement with Henry fell through.¹² An article in the *Jewish World* spoke strongly against Baron de Worms as a representative for the City, maintaining that the Liberal party was the party to which Jews owed their allegiance. Three Conservative and three Liberal candidates stood for the City of London in 1880, and of these, the three Conservatives and one of the Liberals were elected. Even though Henry never stood for this electoral district, the affair was later raked over during heated libel suits between him and Edwin Hughes, who had been one of the Conservative Party agents in London.

In Opposition

A deputation of Conservative electors asked Henry de Worms to stand as MP for the borough of Greenwich at the 1880 election alongside the sitting member Thomas Boord (1838–1912). The party agent for both candidates was the same Edwin Hughes who had tried to broker an arrangement in London and who had acted as agent at the invalidated Sandwich by-election of 1880. Greenwich returned two MPs, and two Liberal candidates stood for election along with these two Conservatives. The other sitting member for this borough before 1880 had been the Liberal Party leader, William Gladstone, who retired to the backbenches after his government's defeat in 1874 and did not intend to stand again in Greenwich, where his policies had resulted in much unemployment. Henry's electoral address supported the policies of Disraeli and indicated that he was firmly opposed to any measures that could lead to the disintegration of the Empire. He remained opposed to the Permissive Bill, echoes of which still rumbled through Parliament, and was opposed to the efforts of the Secularists to exclude religious teaching from schools. He also declared that he would resist any attempts to interfere with the position of the Established Church, a move mooted by Liberals after passage of the Irish Church Bill. Henry's opposition was again based on his conviction that a country must have a religion.[13]

Both Henry de Worms and Thomas Boord were returned as members for the borough of Greenwich, the full poll for this borough being as follows:[14]

GREENWICH (1880)
Boord, T.W. (C)	9,243
Worms, Baron de (C)	9,240
Saunders, J.E. (L)	8,152
Stone, W.H. (L)	8,141

The authorities had thought that there might be public unrest during the Greenwich election, so the troops in garrison at Woolwich were ordered to keep in barracks. Men employed in the Royal Arsenal at Woolwich were given a half-day holiday so that they could vote. In fact the election passed off peacefully.[15]

It was at this election that Gladstone had a change of heart and determined to return somehow to the front line political scene and to regenerate the Liberal Party. He stood for a seat in Midlothian, the district around Edinburgh, where he campaigned from a private train giving whistle-stop speeches in which there was fire and passion. One of his points was that 'the foreign policy of England should always be inspired by love of freedom'.[16]

The important question related to freedom at that time was the Irish Home Rule Bill. Gladstone's campaign led to a substantial Liberal victory with a majority of 137 over the Conservatives, but with the Irish Nationalists constituting a substantial third party with 65 seats. He returned as prime minister and leader of the Liberal Party and soon debates on Irish home rule came to dominate Parliament. Disraeli retired after the election and

Conservatives were led under the dual control of Sir Stafford Northcote (1818–1887; created Earl of Iddesleigh in 1885) in the Commons and the Marquis of Salisbury (1830–1903; 3rd Marquis from 1868) in the Lords, a system which soon led to serious friction within the party.

Parliament had continued with attempts to curb bribery and corruption during elections. The Ballot Act of 1872 had made provisions for voting in secret, whereas previously voting had been by open declaration. Legislation passed on 24 March 1880, just before the general election, defined the maximum sum which candidates' agents could spend on conveyances, on employment of clerks and messengers and on committee rooms. The new act also removed some restrictions on the conveyance of voters, for there had been an anomaly between borough and county election practice. The long distances between polling stations made conveyancing necessary in the country but the extension of this practice to boroughs led to complaints of influencing voters. Both sides in the borough of Greenwich resorted to the practice of carrying voters to the poll in style when this became lawful.[17]

The new government continued these attempts, passing draconian measures against corruption; an act in 1883 curbed expenses such as payment for conveyances, employment of voters and wearing of party favours or marks of distinction.[18] This matter of conveyancing was a sore point for Henry de Worms, who referred to the problem during a House of Commons debate. He was in the position of being able to afford a carriage. 'He represented a large constituency of working men, and was able to say that in that district there were more Liberals who polled in wagons and carts than there were Conservatives who polled in carriages. If the hon. Member [for Wolverhampton] could see corruption in Conservatives going to the poll in carriages which cost 200 guineas, he would like to know whether he would say there was corruption in driving Liberals to the poll in coal wagons.'[19]

The Parliament of 1880 had five members of the Jewish faith: Sir Nathaniel de Rothschild, Serjeant Simon, Sidney Woolf and Arthur Cohen, all Liberal; and Baron Henry de Worms, Conservative. Serjeant Simon and Arthur Cohen were associated with Henry de Worms in the Anglo-Jewish Association. The first Jewish Conservative MP had been Saul Isaac (1823–1903), a coal owner who from 1874 to 1880 represented Nottingham before losing an election. The 1880 election also returned a declared atheist, Charles Bradlaugh (1833–1891), as MP for Northampton. Bradlaugh refused to take any oath in the name of God, stating that such an oath would not be binding on his conscience, and he had much popular support. Several times he presented himself at parliamentary sessions only to be ejected, on occasion with the aid of the police, because he had not been sworn in.[20]

This Bradlaugh affair occupied parliamentary time for over eight years. At first, Gladstone proposed to refer the business to a committee, and Stafford Northcote, Conservative leader in the House of Commons, was inclined to agree. It was to this proposal of Gladstone's that Henry de Worms made his maiden speech on 24 May 1880. The question was, should Mr. Bradlaugh be allowed to affirm allegiance to the Crown in place of the oath? Henry de Worms remarked that the Affirmation had been provided to accommodate Quakers whose members refused to swear oaths. 'He should like to know in what capacity Mr. Bradlaugh could possibly have taken the Affirmation? Certainly not in the capacity of a member of the Society of Friends.' He protested in the name of both Jews and Christians against 'confounding that which was religious with that which was not religious'.[21] Henry Drummond Wolff (1830–1908) and Lord Randolph Churchill (1849–1895, MP for Woodstock) were two Conservative members who spoke to oppose Galdstone's proposal. They and Henry de Worms were to mount fierce opposition to many of the government's actions, but Henry was later to isolate himself from their strategy of combining opposition with attempts to oust Northcote from his leadership of the Conservative Party. Effective speeches from the opposition benches bring the speaker to the notice of party whips; Henry de Worms won a future under-secretaryship and Randolf Churchill a cabinet post when the Conservatives gained power.

Eventually, Gladstone introduced an Affirmation Bill, allowing a person to affirm allegiance as an alternative to swearing an oath, and this received support from the Liberal Jewish members, but he could not command a majority in Parliament for this measure, so the Bill was dropped. Henry de Worms was among those who voted against this bill on the grounds that an affirmation had no meaning since it was not made in the name of a higher power. Many of those who considered the bill an extension of the measures allowing Jews and other non-Anglicans into Parliament censured him. Osborne Morgan, the judge advocate general directed the phrase 'it only shows how easy it is for the victims of persecution to become persecutors themselves' specifically at Henry.[22] Within the country as a whole there was much support for Gladstone's measure. The nonconformist Congregational Union of England and Wales came out strongly in favour of freedom of conscience and of the Affirmation Bill, adding that 'Christianity was insulted when it was offered such support as that which had been given by Baron Henry de Worms, Mr. O'Brien and Mr. Ashmead-Bartlett'. These three gentlemen who voted against the bill were particularly pointed out because they were respectively a Jew, a Papist and a High Churchman.[23] Henry later gave his reasons for voting against the measure at a public meeting in

Greenwich: 'Many conscientious men opposed Catholic emancipation and the removal of Jewish disabilities because they thought these measures would destroy the Protestant character of the House of Commons. But what would be said if at the first moment a real struggle came on in which the very principle of religion was involved, the Catholics and the Jews who had seats in Parliament sat by and allowed religion to be successfully assailed. It was because he [Henry] and others thought that a country should have a religion that they voted against the Affirmation Bill.' He pointed out 'how intimately connected atheism was with those communist and revolutionary principles which would destroy society'. Other speakers in the Commons debate on this bill had also noted the connection between atheism and three of the past revolutionary movements in France. Within living memory a commune had briefly been set up in Paris during the anarchy which followed the fall of Napoleon III.[24]

Serjeant Simon was a supporter of the defeated Affirmation Bill and during 1886 he succeeded in organising a compromise in which the words of the official oath were followed by 'omitting any words of imprecation or calling to witness'. After reading this modified oath, Charles Bradlaugh took his seat. Finally the Oaths Act of 1888 clarified the situation by allowing allegiance to be solemnly affirmed rather than sworn. From the start, this affair became one of the sources of discontent between Henry de Worms and Serjeant Simon, respectively president and vice-president of the Anglo-Jewish Association.[25]

The Liberal government found it difficult to push measures through this Parliament and the press commented vigorously on the time wasted by the constant questioning of ministers and by extensive debate on Irish legislation. Statistics compiled from January to Whitsuntide in 1881 showed 1,531 questions put down by 311 members; Henry de Worms came sixth in the list with 20 questions, while higher up the list were Henry Drummond Wolff and some Irish MPs. Henry was intent on embarrassing the government as well as making a mark.[26] He was so much in the public view that a scurrilous newspaper, *Christian and Jew*, whose avowed object was 'to counsel a crusade against the Jews', specifically denounced him. The paper maintained that '[they Jews] have entered into a combination to make Baron Henry de Worms Prime Minister of Great Britain.' Parliament discussed this matter and William Harcourt for the government thought the best course would be 'to recommend this gentleman's health [the paper's editor] to the attention of his friends.'[27]

Henry sported a large moustache, which was seized upon by the political cartoonists of the day. Very soon, his usual seat was behind the front opposition bench, where he was described as 'a cool and sententious speaker, who orates with a smiling brow and gleaming teeth, and contrives thus and thus to wet the lips of the hon. gentlemen opposite with vinegar and myrrh'. Later, when he attained government office, one observer remarked: 'Baron de Worms would be styled a good looking foreigner whose features have only just escaped being English.'[28]

In a conversation with Conservative friends after his first parliamentary session, Henry remarked that the ABC of Liberalism was A for anarchy, B for Bradlaughism (the continuing row over the oaths bill), and C for *clôture*. Anarchy was the result of their policies in both the Transvaal and Ireland, whilst filibusters by the Irish MPs caused wastage of parliamentary time, hence the need for *clôture* (i.e. enforced closure of debate). Ireland was an integral part of the United Kingdom and returned both nationalist and unionist MPs. Large sections of the agricultural population were opposed to the landlords and the previous Conservative government passed a statute of coercion to assist in control of the country. Gladstone had campaigned against this and the statute was allowed to lapse when he came to power. His government, however, soon found it had to introduce its own coercion bill and later, on 7 April 1881, it introduced the Irish land reform bill aimed at improving the lot of tenants. Debates on Irish affairs became such marathon sessions that Gladstone introduced a discussion paper on new rules of *clôture* on 3 February 1882; these were debated fiercely for the remainder of that year, with Henry in the opposition's camp. In all, though, he took little interest in the substance of Irish affairs.

Henry's contributions to the question of *clôture* were made both inside and outside Parliament. At a Conservative meeting in north Wiltshire he strongly condemned such procedures and censured Gladstone for refusing to give a firm statement on what the government would do for Ireland before the coming Easter recess. During speeches in the House of Commons he argued that *clôture* was against the principle of freedom of speech, which alone should govern the business of the House, and he contrasted the procedures at Westminster with those in the German and Austrian Parliaments. Both of these countries adopted *clôture* to control debate, and while the Austrian Parliament had successfully governed for three years by an absolute minority, Prince Bismarck, now Chancellor of Germany, had defied the chamber openly, saying he was not to be governed by their will. In spite of many objections, Gladstone in December 1882 pushed through new Rules of Procedure to control the debates. Henry's final words on the subject in a speech to Gravesend Working Men's Association expressed the opinion that this move was made in order to prove to Liberals that their government was worth saving.[29]

Intelligent Toryism

The new breed of intelligent Tory recognised that an increasing number of voters were working men. This was the case in Greenwich, so its new MP took care to address the grievances of this borough, which housed both Army and Navy establishments. The Navy administered Greenwich Hospital, which was housed in an elegant building facing the Thames and founded by William and Mary in 1694 as the naval equivalent of the Army's Chelsea Pensioners' building. During a debate on Admiralty supplies, there was a scandal over the administration of Greenwich Hospital and Henry de Worms took up this cause on behalf of the retired seamen who should have been housed there. The charity housed pensioners in the building until 1869, when the operation was deemed too expensive and the old seamen were boarded in the town. Its resources were then devoted to paying pensions and educating orphaned children. Serious maladministration was demonstrated, for not all the pensions were paid and the buildings themselves were let for the paltry sum of £100 per year. Henry argued on behalf of the retired seamen that 'a contract was made with them by which they were morally and legally entitled to live in Greenwich Hospital or, failing that, they were entitled to a pension in compensation for not living there'.[30] Others entered the argument and gradually the charity was put on a firmer foundation. As the years passed the available funds did not meet all of the hospital's obligations. Even when Henry reached the House of Lords, Parliament had to approve additional sums by vote. Successive acts of Parliament have limited the objectives on which the funds of the Greenwich Hospital may be expended and it continues today as a Crown charity.

The Army barracks at Woolwich were within the borough of Greenwich and concern had been raised over administration of charities associated with the Army. The Patriotic Fund was set up in 1862 after the Crimean War to support the widows and orphaned children of dead sailors and soldiers. It paid some army pensions and ran a school for boys in Wandsworth together with a convalescent home for girls in Margate. It was the constant badgering by Henry de Worms that forced the secretary of state for war to make enquiries into the state of this fund. Serious mismanagement was discovered, the school and the convalescent home were closed and a new set of commissioners was appointed to oversee expenditure. Formally gazetted in October 1881 were the Duke of Cambridge as president and Baron Henry de Worms as a commissioner, along with others. Subsequent acts of Parliament have modified the administration of this fund and it continues today to provide assistance for the widows, orphans and other dependants of deceased members of the armed forces.³¹ Henry's appointment as administrator to a charity soon led to his involvement with other London-based charities, along with hospitals, school boards and the London Orphan Asylum. A third Greenwich-based charity was the Dreadnought Seamen's Hospital, founded in 1821 to provide treatment for distressed and sick seamen of all nations. From 1882 this became the Seamen's Hospital Society and after 1881 Henry became one of the subscribers, supporting the management committee and speaking at their annual meetings. Such committee work gave one advantage to Henry at the period in his life when his wife had left for Austria with the children. He lived a bachelor existence, so this work provided opportunities to attend boardroom and charity dinners, and after a few years he gained a reputation for good living. Curiously, later cartoon representations of Henry de Worms show him as a more and more rotund figure.³²

Henry was a strong constituency MP, introducing several measures directly to alleviate conditions in Greenwich. A serious concern was the lack of communication except by ferries between the two banks of the Thames east of London Bridge while Henry de Worms was MP for Greenwich. A non-elected body, the Metropolitan Board of Works, was responsible for management of transport in the London area and during 1882 Henry headed a deputation of his constituents to ask that steps be taken immediately to improve matters. It had little effect because the board had become notoriously corrupt. The board was abolished in 1888 and replaced by an elected body, which started to plan a tunnel under the river. This was successfully completed and the Blackwall Tunnel opened to traffic in 1897.³³

The Borough of Greenwich also faced a serious problem during the 1880s from the number of human bodies found floating in the river Thames with its incoming and outgoing tides. Most were the results of crimes of robbery and murder in the capital, from where they were washed downstream, and those not recovered became more and more objectionable with time. Any parish recovering a body had to bear the costs of burial while the waterman who recovered the body received only a pittance for his loss of time, so there was no incentive for this work. All parishes were aware of the debt of some £1,200 which had fallen on the parish of Woolwich as a consequence of the disaster in the Thames when an excursion paddle steamer, the *Princess Alice*, foundered on 3 September 1878 with the loss of over 650 lives. In an act of charity, Woolwich had recovered the bodies. Previously, there had been a five-shilling grant for each such burial, which the County of Kent had just withdrawn and did not wish to reinstate, so the parish fell into debt and others did not wish to follow this route. A letter from the local coroner to Henry de Worms pointed out this lack of an incentive to recover the bodies and the problem was discussed in Parliament. Henry proposed to introduce a bill to rectify the situation by setting up a treasury fund to cover costs. The home secretary, Sir William Harcourt, did not see that this was 'a charge which should come upon the general funds of the Exchequer', but Henry disagreed and pressed on to introduce his Tidal Rivers (Interments) Bill. This was intended to be retrospective so that the parish of Woolwich could recover its expenses. The government announced no intentions to oppose the legislation but neither did it make any effort to assist its passage. The measure was never discussed, partly through lack of interest but also because of pressures on the House's time due to crises in foreign affairs and the tortuous debates on the Irish bills.[34]

Debates on a private bill for the Sunday closure of public houses in Durham offered Henry another opportunity to lecture the Liberal government on its treatment of the working man. He was the representative 'of a large working-class constituency' and asked whether it was right that government members 'who had the means at their command of gratifying their desire for drink at any time ... should deprive the great mass of the people of what hon. Members themselves enjoyed.' Did the honourable members know 'that a working man with his family frequently occupied only two rooms and he was only too glad to be able to leave them on Sundays'?[35]

Women were also included in Henry's view of Tory democracy. His concern over the treatment of women led him to ask of the home secretary in 1881 'whether in view of the prevalence of aggravated and felonious assaults upon women and children, he will introduce a Bill this Session ... so as to extend the punishment of flogging to persons convicted of such assaults'.[36] Henry's interest in women's causes received comment because this was not a usual Tory position. A pamphlet entitled 'The Wife Beaters' Manual: A Guide to Husbands' Connubial Corrections' was published in support of his position 'dedicated to that eminent political guide and philosopher the Baron Henry de Worms, in whom women, good and bad, find a ready champion.' The author, Henry Romeike, had collected a list of the relatively trivial fines imposed by the courts on men convicted of wife beating. He was pleased that Baron Henry de Worms was 'one gentleman bold enough to advocate flogging as a remedy for wife-beating'.[37]

Women at that time had no vote so the question of female suffrage received an airing in 1883 during debates on enlarging the franchise. At a public meeting in Greenwich Mr E. Hughes, Henry's electoral agent, moved and Henry seconded a motion 'that in the opinion of this meeting any Reform bill to be satisfactory should include provision for extending the franchise to duly-qualified women householders.'[38] It was carried by an overwhelming majority. In parliament a motion in favour of female franchise was proposed by Mr Mason (MP for Ashton-under-Lyne) and seconded by Baron Henry de Worms, who made a long and impassioned speech advocating votes for women. The idea of votes for women was however rejected by parliament at that time, not to be realised for many years.[39]

Colleagues on the Conservative front bench gave Henry de Worms so favourable a reception during his first parliamentary term that he invited a number of them to a fish dinner on 3 August 1881 at the Ship Inn in Greenwich, to mark the end of the session. At the time he was living in cramped bachelor apartments in the Albany which were unsuitable for entertaining, so this was his response to the receptions he had attended given by Tory grandees. The party travelled by private steamer from Westminster to Greenwich and partook of an excellent dinner at which the finest wines were served and the dessert was a notable feature. After dinner, fine cigars were distributed and speeches were made. Sir Stafford Northcote, leader of the Party in the Commons, proposed Henry's health in very flattering terms. The guests left around midnight in good humour and when later the Conservatives came to power, his investment reaped the reward of a junior ministry. The Ship Inn itself was destroyed during World War II; it was the Conservatives' favourite inn in Greenwich.[40]

This first parliamentary year for Henry saw an increased number of Conservative Clubs catering for both professional and working-class men. As a prominent Conservative, he spoke at the opening of the West Kent and Greenwich Carlton Club and the Dover Carlton Club. A Conservative Workingmen's Club was also inaugurated in Greenwich, using a room formally belonging to the Crown and Sceptre public house. The opening ceremony included a smoking concert during which Mr Boord and Baron Henry de Worms gave speeches on Conservative policies. Such concerts were a common entertainment at that time and much favoured by the Conservative Party. Professional entertainers could be employed and communal singing from distributed song sheets was usually included. They were a means of connecting with all classes of voter. Such entertainment can still be experienced today in a few of the London clubs, though smoking is no longer permitted. The Liberals disdained such concerts in favour of more genteel tea parties.[41]

A family card game, *The Game of Parliament*, was marketed in the mid-1880s with cards depicting 23 Liberal and 23 Conservative politicians, each illustrated with a caricature drawing. Each politician was given a comic name. Baron Henry de Worms appears as Baron de Caterpillar, caricatured with a moustache and bearing a strong resemblance to Disraeli. He had arrived on the lower rung of the parliamentary ladder and his advocacy of the aims and opinions of Disraeli had been noted. On the cards Gladstone appears as W.E. Grindstone and Salisbury as Lord Salisbury-Plain. At that time a pack of these cards cost 1 shilling (5p.).[42]

The Primrose League

Disraeli, now Lord Beaconsfield, resigned as leader of the Conservative Party in 1880 and died in 1881. His status as a great politician was universally recognised and a commemorative statue paid for by public subscription was ready to be unveiled in 1883 by Stafford Northcote. Lord Randolph Churchill used the form proposed for this ceremony to stir up controversy among Conservatives over the future leadership of the Party. He wrote three letters to *The Times* criticising the Tory establishment. The first, dated 29 March, was signed 'A Tory' and complained that Northcote and not Salisbury had been invited to unveil the new statue, suggesting there was a plot to obtain the overall Party leadership for Northcote. The second letter appeared on 2 April under Churchill's name and blamed all the Tory leadership for the poor showing of the Party at by-elections. Henry de Worms wrote in reply giving examples showing how Churchill's tactics in the House, without previous consultation with Northcote, severely hampered the latter's room for manoeuvre. He wrote 'it would seem that Lord Randolph Churchill's idea of Conservative leadership is that the Conservative members should follow him'. In the third letter of 5 April, signed 'M.P.', Churchill questioned the voting procedure at the Conservative National Union Council which nominated Salisbury as leader. To this, Worms, who had been present at the meeting, stated that delegates had in fact negated the proposed resolution in favour of Salisbury 'in the sense that it was absurd of a body like the National Union arrogating to itself the right of nominating a leader to succeed Lord Beaconsfield'. This view was supported in separate letters from Northcote and an anonymous MP. They agreed that the National Union was never more than a discussion group without powers.[43]

Northcote unveiled the statue of Lord Beaconsfield as planned on 19 April. Churchill then became even more strident against him and contributed an article to the *Fortnightly Review* arguing that Conservatives needed a leader who could move the hearts of households. Churchill engineered his nomination to the Council of the National Union of Conservative Associations in July. The Council members had voted equally in favour of and against this move and Churchill was elected by the then chairman's casting vote. Henry George Earl Percy (MP for Northumberland North), who had been chairman of the council from 1879, afterwards resigned, to be replaced by Churchill on 1 February 1884. Both Northcote and Worms resigned from the council over an election carried through in this manner. Such infighting indicated that joint leadership was not a satisfactory arrangement, and the matter had to be rectified before a general election took place.

Randolph Churchill's agenda was to have himself elected leader of the Party. The majority of the Party considered Northcote too weak, and furthermore, doubts over Salisbury's leadership began to grow among the highest tory grandees as feelings were growing on the necessity of having the prime minister in the Commons. The liberal statesman Lord Rosebery was later to give an unfavourable commentary on Northcote's character: 'Where he failed was in manner. His voice, his diction, his delivery, were all inadequate. With real ability, great knowledge, genial kindness and a sympathetic nature – all qualities indeed which evoke regard and esteem – he had not the spice of the devil which is necessary to arouse zeal and elation.' The leadership problem was discussed at a private council of Conservative grandees summoned by the Marquis of Abervagenny in late October when Salisbury was retained as leader but clearly on probation. Henry de Worms was abroad in Austria at the time from 17 August until November, investigating the conduct of his wife.[44]

The Primrose League had been formed shortly after Disraeli's death to perpetuate his memory and was so called because members wore a primrose, his favourite flower, on the anniversary of his death (19 April). Because Henry was so fond of quoting from the opinions of Disraeli, he was rumoured to be the originator of the league and on the first anniversary he was one of the few Conservative MPs who did wear this flower. On the second anniversary, when the memorial statue was unveiled, the whole of the Conservative Party in the House of Commons wore the flower. The Primrose League opened officially in November 1883, at which point it became plain that Lord Randolph Churchill, Sir Henry Drummond Wolff and John Gorst had founded it to support their own views on Conservatism. They were in favour of vigorous opposition to the government and Churchill alluded to the importance of competing with the Liberals for working-class votes. Within the House of Commons they formed the so-called 'Fourth Party' to embrace intelligent Conservatism and hoped to draw others to their way of thinking. (Conservative, Liberal and Irish Nationalist were the other three parties.) Henry de Worms was in favour of the aims of this Fourth Party but not at the expense of breaking with the

Conservative Party leadership. The Fourth Party had only a brief existence and soon collapsed for lack of supporters, Randolph Churchill then returned to the orthodox party fold. The Primrose League became closely associated with the Conservative Party, having Sir Stafford Northcote as Grand Master (1885–1887), followed by Lord Salisbury (1887–1903).

Henry was a member of the league from its early days, belonging to the Grosvenor 'habitation' formed by his future wife, Sarah Phillips, in 1885. He occupied the chair at the general meeting of the Marylebone district habitations in March 1887 and in later years can be found as principal speaker at meetings of the league around the country. The league was popular because it was inclusive of all classes. Anyone could be a member on payment of a very modest subscription and its meetings allowed the humblest member to mix with the party aristocrats. The wide range of members proved useful to the Party for the organisation of unpaid canvassing.[45]

Imperial Interests

During the latter part of the nineteenth century, successive British governments had found it necessary to undertake military intervention in Asia and Africa. Henry de Worms was interested in foreign affairs and in 1877 had published a book on 'England's policy in the East' so he relished being able to attack the government over its actions in Afghanistan, Egypt and also the Transvaal. Government policy in Afghanistan and Egypt was aimed at curbing any Russian moves which threatened British interests in India. This strategic rivalry between the British and Russian empires became known after around 1840 as 'The Great Game'.[46]

After the Balkan crisis and the Russo-Turkish war, the 1878 Treaty of Berlin was signed; it was designed to curb Russian expansion in Europe. During the treaty discussions, Henry de Worms, as president of the Anglo-Jewish Association, lobbied for the inclusion of clauses to regulate the treatment of Jews in Romania. In spite of this treaty, concern over Russian expansion southwards, this time in Asia, soon flared up again when the Russian government established a mission in Kabul. Britain under Disraeli countered by demanding its own mission in that city. When that demand was rejected in 1879 a large British invasion force was sent into Afghanistan. The Liberal government entering power in 1880 had to deal with the situation and was faced with a backlash from the Afghans. British forces became besieged in Kandahar, so here was fertile ground for parliamentary questions directed at the foreign secretary.[47]

After the successful relief of Kandahar by General Roberts (1832–1914; created Lord Roberts of Kandahar in 1892), a British agent was placed in Kabul, but Russia's forces continued to push her frontier south at the expense of Afghanistan. Henry de Worms read all the major European newspapers, including those from Russia, and repeatedly questioned the British government on current events in Central Asia, taking the House through lessons in history and geography. War over Russian territorial expansion was averted by the British government's acceptance of the newly established border between Russia and Afghanistan, but the affair added to Conservative scorn over the appeasement policy of the Liberal government.

Henry Romeike (1855–1916), who ran a complete newspaper-cutting business, had Henry as one of his many clients, and it would have been Romeike who compiled the newspaper articles used after 1881. He was born in East Prussia and educated in Munich. He emigrated to London in 1881 to set up a business providing newspaper cuttings on specified subjects for a fee. Romeike was very successful and in 1887 moved the service to the United States. His pamphlet of quotations on the mistreatment of women was dedicated to Henry de Worms in the most flattering terms.[48]

The main crises of imperial interests in the nineteenth century concerned African affairs. These built up over the years when Henry de Worms was in opposition and came to a head under the government of Lord Salisbury in which Henry had a junior post in the colonial office. Britain had acquired the Cape from the Dutch at the end of the Napoleonic Wars, and the original Dutch settlers, the Boers, soon became hostile to British rule, wishing to preserve their backward-looking patriarchal society from any restrictions imposed from outside. They made the Great Trek north in 1836, setting up two republics, the Orange Free State and the Transvaal, outside British South African jurisdiction. Hostile tribes surrounded the remote Transvaal, with its most dangerous enemies being the Zulus, some of whose land the Boers had taken to form the republic. The inhabitants of the Transvaal were also divided on doctrinal principles, so that a government serving only a small white population, with limited agriculture and no industry, could barely maintain itself. Disraeli's Conservative government had devised a scheme for a confederation of British South African States. It annexed the Transvaal, sent the Army in 1879 to crush Zulu King Cetshwayo (1826–1884), and finally succeeded despite a catastrophic defeat in the Battle of Isandhlwana. Cetshwayo was exiled. In the words of Henry de Worms, 'they [the Transvaal Boers] proved totally unable to protect themselves – to collect taxes or indeed to perform any of the functions of government.'[49]

When Gladstone came to power in 1880, he sought a solution to the Zulu problem by dividing their lands between the tribal chiefs. Cetshwayo was brought back from exile in 1883 and restored to some power. Faced with a British liberal government, Paul Kruger (1825–1904) organised passive Boer resistance to the annexation of the Transvaal and hoped that Gladstone would restore self-government. Gladstone, immersed in the Irish problem, did nothing for the Boers, so by December 1880 Kruger had led his people into active opposition, declaring independence and starting the First Boer War. During this uprising, British forces were defeated at Majuba Hill (27 February 1881), a consequence as much of the superior skills and tactics of the Boers as of poor leadership of the British forces. Gladstone's Liberal government then entered negotiations and in 1881 agreed to the Boer Convention, which restored complete self-government to the Transvaal under the status of a protectorate. This new state took as its name the South African Republic, with Paul Kruger as elected president from 1882. The Orange Free State remained independent and gradually aligned to the South African Republic. The neighbouring states of Zululand and Swaziland became independent British protectorates.

When the Conservative opposition gained debating time over the terms of the Boer Convention a condemnatory resolution was introduced by Michael Hicks Beach and seconded by Henry de Worms. Henry poured scorn on Gladstone's references during the Midlothian campaign to the annexation by the previous Conservative government of a 'Model Republic', pointing out that it 'was so enlightened and religious that it tolerated and practised slavery in its worst forms'. He and other members complained that the House had not been given an opportunity to debate the agreement before it had been effected. This was the subject of Henry's first important speech in the House of Commons, delivered in a pugnacious style.[50]

All was not well either in the north of Africa. The affairs of Egypt had proved a serious problem to the Disraeli government, and continued to do so through the Gladstone administration. Khedive Isma'il Pasha of Egypt and the Sudan (reigned 1863–1879) had borrowed money to finance modernisation of his country but was unable to pay the interest. After many twists and turns he was obliged to sell the country's only major financial asset, shares in the Suez Canal. Disraeli, then prime minister, purchased shares on 25 November 1875 giving Britain command of the canal, controlling the shortest route to India. Henry de Worms had visited Egypt in early 1876 after this move and was well aware of the value of the Suez Canal to British trade. He approved of the move but even this drastic step did not remove Egypt's financial crisis. Finally a joint Franco-British mission intervened to establish dual control of Egyptian finances and virtually controlled its government after 1879. Isma'il Pasha was replaced in 1879 as khedive by his son Twefik Pasha (reigned 1879–1892).

The British Liberal government of 1880 was faced with an Egyptian backlash. A charismatic Army officer, Ahmed Urabi (1841–1911), began to agitate against the influence of foreigners in his country. He was made a member of the Khedive's cabinet and soon rebelled, taking over the government. Alarmed at this situation which threatened their investments, the British and French governments sent a fleet to Alexandria in 1882 and so the stage was set for military intervention. British troops were dispatched to Malta and Cyprus, but a crisis in relations between France and Germany caused France to withdraw from any operations. The French fleet returned to base, leaving Britain with a free hand in Egypt.[51]

Henry followed events closely through the newspapers and the debates in the French Chamber of Deputies, probably also with the help of Romeike's service. He first began to question ministers over the naval demonstration at Alexandria in May 1882. During June and July he repeatedly expressed concern over the possibility of destruction of the canal from its banks, citing General Wolseley's opinion that such an operation was easily possible. Henry Drummond Wolff in particular supported Henry in the Commons. In June a riot occurred in Alexandria, killing about 50 Europeans; it was quelled by Urabi's troops but as the situation in the country deteriorated, British warships began a bombardment of Alexandria on 11 July, in part to destroy the seaward-facing gun emplacements. During a debate on the request for funds to defray expenses in Egypt, Henry de Worms criticised the government for letting affairs deteriorate so far without intervention.[52]

A large British force under the command of Wolseley (1833–1913; created Lord Wolseley in 1882) landed in Alexandria but was prevented from approaching Cairo by strong resistance. Fears for the safety of the canal persuaded Wolseley to transfer his forces to the Canal Zone, which they occupied and secured by 6 September. Wolseley then advanced towards Cairo and defeated the Egyptian Army at Tel-el-Kebir some 20 miles west of the canal on 10 September. He proceeded to Cairo and reinstated Khedive Twefik Pasha to power. The Egyptian general Urabi was captured and exiled, while Suliman Sami, Urabi's lieutenant, was condemned to death for carrying out the burning of Alexandria. The speedy trial and execution of Sami caused uproar in the House of Commons, led by Randolph Churchill and assisted by Drummond Wolff, and to which Henry de Worms contributed a speech in agreement with the protests, asking why the whole affair had been carried out in such haste.[53]

Egyptian affairs continued to dominate Parliament during 1884. In January the government sent General Gordon (1833–1885) to Khartoum to organise the evacuation of the Egyptian forces from the Sudan, which was now in revolt, under its charismatic leader, the Mahdi, against its Egyptian control. Robert Bourke, MP for King's Lynn and Conservative under-secretary for foreign affairs in the previous government, led an attack on the government's foreign policy in Egypt and elsewhere, as set out in the Queen's speech. Henry de Worms joined this attack, condemning, in strong terms, the vacillating policies of the Liberal government. 'A government without cohesion – a policy which led to disasters in Egypt. The defeat at Majuba Hill resulting in the Boer Convention; at Alexandria when no action was taken until the disaster had happened; and in Ireland they did not understand the position of affairs until after the murders in Phoenix Park.' The reference to Phoenix Park, Dublin concerns the murder there in 1882 of Lord Frederick Cavendish, chief secretary for Ireland and MP for Yorkshire (West Riding) Northern.[54]

As affairs in Egypt progressed, a rebel army in the Sudan laid siege to General Gordon at Khartoum and a poorly organised relief operation failed. During the debate on the government's actions Henry accused them of vacillating between attack and withdrawal. Gordon's situation worsened and Henry castigated the government during the debate of May 1884: 'The House had waited with breathless expectation to hear that the Government were prepared to do something towards the relief of General Gordon, towards preserving the safety of that man, whose responsibility the right hon. Gentleman had adopted, whose success he would have taken, and whose defeat he was now to share or prevent. But all the right hon. Gentleman [Gladstone] told them was, that when time and circumstances and weather should be sufficiently propitious, Her Majesty's Government might, perhaps, conceive some plan, which might ultimately lead to the relief of General Gordon.' More strong words were exchanged when, during a discussion on the appropriation of money to support the Army in Egypt, Gladstone accused Henry of introducing a 'dishonouring imputation which the Hon. Member thinks himself entitled to cast on Her Majesties Government'. Khartoum fell to the rebels and General Gordon was killed in January 1885. Stafford Northcote proposed a vote of censure on the government and a long reply from Gladstone followed. Henry de Worms then rose to oppose the prime minister, condemning the government and raising again the whole Eastern Question using a quotation from Napoleon I. 'The possession of Egypt is decisive for India. That European power who is the mistress of Egypt is, in the long run, the mistress of India.' In the Lords, Salisbury vigorously condemned the government's actions in Egypt: 'Egypt stands in a peculiar position. It is the gateway to India.'[55]

After this Egyptian crisis, tension arose again between Britain and Russia over further Russian expansion southwards at the expense of Afghanistan. In March 1885 Afghan forces were heavily defeated at Penjdeh and for a time it looked as if Russia would expand its frontier to the Indian Ocean. Henry de Worms was among those who badgered the government, asking for confirmation of reports he had read in foreign newspapers about this Penjdeh incident. After a while anxiety lessened and an international body charged with defining the disputed frontier was established. The Russia-Afghan frontier was placed well away from the Indian Ocean.[56]

Reform and Litigation

The election of 1880 had involved far from universal male suffrage, for the act of 1867 had given the vote to all rate-paying householders in the towns and householders rated at £12 per annum in the counties, women had no vote at all. Lord Cranborne (from 1868 Marquis of Salisbury) resigned from the Conservative cabinet of 1867 in protest.[57] Gladstone and the Liberals in 1884 wanted to extend voting rights in rural areas, but Salisbury, still not in favour of any extension of the franchise, opposed this in the Lords, where the Conservatives had a majority. Salisbury chaired a meeting in the St James Street Club at which Henry de Worms proposed 'that this meeting is of the opinion that the House of Lords is justified in refusing to accept the Franchise Bill unaccompanied by a measure for the redistribution of seats'. The Conservative proposal coupled the increased franchise with a radical redrawing of constituency boundaries.[58]

This compromise was accepted in Parliament: Gladstone had his way over the increase in male suffrage (but still around 40% of males had no vote) and the Lords were allowed to introduce a Redistribution of Seats Bill. Previously many constituencies had elected two or even more representatives, but under the new proposals, towns with a population of between 15,000 and 50,000 lost one of their MPs to become single-member constituencies. Larger towns and the county constituencies were subdivided into single-member constituencies and the northern industrial towns received better representation. The measures affected Greenwich, which had its representation reduced to one seat, with further seats established in the neighbouring towns of Deptford and Woolwich. Liverpool, which previously formed one constituency with three members, was split into eight constituencies of which Liverpool East Toxteth would become Henry de Worms' future constituency.[59]

As the Redistribution of Seats Act was passing its final stages in the House of Commons, the government also proceeded with a Customs and Inland Revenue Bill, and a minor Conservative amendment over tax on liquor received support from the Irish Nationalists. Surprisingly, 76 Liberals did not vote and the amendment was carried by 264 votes to 252. The announcement of this result was received by long opposition cheers, many members rising to their feet and throwing their hats in the air.[60] Gladstone resigned as prime minister on 9 June 1885, but since administrative work on the redistribution of seats had not been completed, it was impossible to hold a general election. This defeat was arranged by the Liberal chief whip, Robert Duff (1835–1895) because the government could not find a way out of their difficulties over Ireland. He hinted that a number of the party supporters need not come back to the House after dinner, so a defeat was secured.[61]

The Queen asked Lord Salisbury to form a minority government and he accepted. 'Umpire called Over! And field changed sides' was how this situation was portrayed by *Punch* magazine.[62] Salisbury retained for himself the position of foreign secretary, while Stafford Northcote was sidestepped as party leader, promoted to the Lords as Lord Iddesleigh and made First Lord of the Treasury, a post usually held by the prime minister himself. Henry de Worms had followed foreign affairs closely during his time in opposition, particularly concerning the Eastern Question, so there was much speculation that he would be offered the post of under-secretary of state for foreign affairs, which he was clearly hoping for. Newspapers in Paris, Cologne and Vienna tipped him for the post but this ambition was not realised. His connections with Jewish causes and with Austria were too obvious for the government's liking, so instead he was offered the post of parliamentary secretary to the Board of Trade.[63]

When in the Commons as Robert Cecil, Salisbury had spoken out against and voted against the Jewish Oaths Bill on 22 March 1858. His view softened over time, and Henry de Worms' stance over the Bradlaugh affair counted in his favour for a post in government. Henry de Worms, of Jewish persuasion, had achieved a seat on the government front bench, for his chief, the president of the Board of Trade, was an old Tory, the Duke of Richmond (1818–1903; 6th Duke from 1860), who sat in the Lords. Henry had to do all the government work in the Commons, but a seat in the Cabinet was denied him. The Liberals, now in opposition, took great pleasure in questioning their former tormentor and he was required to respond to many questions in the House. His work in government took up so much time that he was obliged to resign as president of the Anglo-Jewish Association. The Duke of Richmond was relieved of his post in the Board of Trade after less than two months, to be replaced by Edward Stanhope (1840–1893), who sat in the Commons. The consequences of the redistribution of seats were becoming clear during 1884, and in this year, while the Liberals were still in power, Henry de Worms acted swiftly to have himself nominated to stand in any subsequent election for the new single seat at Greenwich. The Greenwich Conservative Club adopted the following resolution in early December 1884: 'That this association accepts the candidature of Baron Henry de Worms for the borough of Greenwich about to be constituted under the Redistribution Bill.' The old Tory machine, however, disputed this resolution and there was a scramble between Henry de Worms, Mr Boord and Mr Hughes for the two safe Conservative seats of Greenwich and Woolwich, leaving Deptford for the unlucky runner-up. Boord was the senior of the two MPs for the old constituency of Greenwich, while Hughes had been election agent in 1880 for both Conservative candidates. The fight became hotter when a deputation from the Greenwich New Conservative Association met in January 1885 to invite Boord to become their candidate for Greenwich and Edwin Hughes received an invitation from Woolwich. None of the three candidates wanted Deptford, which was considered an unsafe Conservative seat, though in fact it remained Conservative after the election. Edwin Hughes had been the Conservative election agent during the notorious Sandwich by-election of May 1880 and Henry de Worms was determined to oppose both him and Mr Boord.[64]

The argument over who should represent the new constituency of Greenwich rumbled on for many months, with Henry de Worms and Boord sending increasingly acidic letters to the newspapers. A suggestion of arbitration by delegates from the central Conservative Office was followed up but the delegates were unable to obtain any resolution to the problem. For a time it looked as if a test ballot would have to be run in the constituency, until the problem was finally solved on 21 October 1885, when delegates from the new constituency of Liverpool East Toxteth invited Henry de Worms to be their Conservative candidate. He accepted and proceeded to campaign vigorously in Liverpool. The electors expressed delight at having such a well-known politician stand, for Henry had made his mark at Conservative rallies and in Parliament. His Greenwich supporters made a last attempt on 22 October to induce Mr Boord to retire from candidature by presenting a letter of request. A churlish Mr Boord did not appear at his London residence, so the letter could only be left for his earnest attention; he ignored it, stood as the Conservative candidate, opposed by a Liberal, and was subsequently elected for Greenwich. When the dust had settled, Conservatives from the old parliamentary borough of Greenwich presented

Baron Henry de Worms with a testimonial and a piece of silver plate 'as a mark of respect and admiration'.[65]

During April 1885, at the height of these arguments over the nomination for Greenwich, Henry de Worms organised the wedding of his eldest daughter and also sued Edwin Hughes for libel. A counterclaim for slander came from Hughes. The libel was contained in letters from Edwin Hughes, dated January 1885, claiming that when Henry de Worms was a candidate for Greenwich in 1880 he had admitted to Hughes that certain people in Sandwich had unpaid claims against him in respect of the election in 1868. The slander against Mr Hughes was contained in a speech made at Greenwich Conservative Club in December 1884 when Henry de Worms had accused Hughes of using his position as a servant of the City of London Conservative Association in about 1880 to ensure that Worms would contest one of the City of London seats and Hughes would contest Greenwich. Hughes was also named as being involved in bribery whilst the Conservative agent for the Sandwich by-election of May 1880.[66]

The libellous claims against Henry de Worms were soon discovered to be unfounded, with judgement in his favour and £500 damages awarded to him. Only one small outstanding claim for expenses had been found, incurred by the former Conservative member for Sandwich, Mr Capper, who had died soon after his election. Henry paid the debt out of courtesy. The claim of slander against Edwin Hughes appeared more substantial, but as his character was probed, Hughes was found to have an unsatisfactory reputation as a Conservative agent. He had indeed been charged with bribery after the 1880 election, but he had turned Queen's evidence and so escaped prosecution. In consequence, the jury considered that since Hughes already had an unsavoury reputation the remarks of Henry de Worms were not slander; but this was not the end of the matter. Edwin Hughes brought a libel action in March 1886 claiming £10,000 from the editors of the newspaper who had reported the speech given by Henry de Worms. This article had attacked Hughes' loyalty to the Party over the London seats affair and his standing because of the Sandwich election affair. Now even more dirty linen was washed in public and finally the jury upheld the charge of libel, but awarded damages of one farthing. Clearly they thought Edwin Hughes' character so black that no speech against him could make it worse.[67] Later that month Edwin Hughes sought a retrial of the 1885 libel case on the grounds of misdirection of the jury and excessive damages. After discussion between both sides it was agreed that the verdict in this case should stand but that the damages should be reduced to £300.[68]

In Government

The minority Conservative administration continued for six months until elections were called in November 1885. Henry de Worms was returned as member for Toxteth East, the full result of the poll being:[69]

LIVERPOOL (East Toxteth) (1885)
Baron Henry de Worms (C) 3,598
John Charles Bingham (L)   2,608

He now had another Conservative Jewish colleague, Lionel Louis Cohen (1832–1887), MP for Paddington North 1885–1887, a grandson of Levi Barent Cohen. In the new Parliament, the Liberals had a majority of 86 over the Conservatives and the campaigns of Charles Stuart Parnell (1846–1891) in Ireland led to 86 seats for Irish home rulers. For a time Parnell was able to support Salisbury, who continued as prime minister until his minority government was defeated on 27 January 1886 over a minor agricultural measure. Gladstone then formed a cabinet from the Liberal Party and introduced an Irish Home Rule Bill on 8 April. The political waters soon became muddied as rumours surfaced of an affair between Parnell and Mrs O'Shea (1846–1921), a prominent Nationalist. These rumours were correct and in 1891 Mrs O'Shea divorced her husband to marry Parnell. It was she who channelled communications between Gladstone and Parnell, and Gladstone's hold over the Liberal vote was weakened in part because of this Parnell affair.

One Cabinet member, the Marquis of Hartington (1833–1909; MP for Rossendale and from 1891, 8th Duke of Devonshire), belonged to the Cavendish family and was a brother of Lord Frederick Cavendish, the Liberal-minded Viceroy of Ireland, murdered in Dublin during 1882. Infuriated by his brother's early death and unhappy about the Irish policy, Hartington split with Gladstone on the Irish question and led a breakaway group of Liberal Unionists.[70] On 8 June 1886 the second reading of the Irish Home Rule Bill was defeated in a full house by 343 votes to 313, some 93 Liberals voting against, and Henry de Worms counted among the opposition Conservatives. There was uproar in the House at the declaration of the result, with loud cheers from the opposition and cries of 'the grand old man' from Gladstone's supporters.[71]

Parliament was dissolved and in the subsequent election of 1886 Henry de Worms was returned unopposed for Liverpool Toxteth East. The country proved much more anti-home rule than were the members of the old

Parliament and the new House now had 394 anti-home rulers (the Conservatives plus 78 Liberal Unionists), with only 276 supporters of Gladstone (the Liberals plus 85 Irish Nationalists). Gladstone resigned at once and Lord Salisbury returned to office with help from the Liberal Unionists. Henry de Worms was expected to return with the higher rank of president of the Board of Trade and a seat in the Cabinet, but this eluded him and he continued in the same position as parliamentary secretary. The president of the Board of Trade was now Frederick Stanley. Lord Iddesleigh became foreign secretary and Randolph Churchill chancellor of the exchequer.

Henry's situation over a Cabinet post was analogous to the situation which applied in 1870 when the Austrian Chancellor, Count Beust, offered him a post in the Austrian Foreign Office. Then Beust was a Protestant while Henry was Jewish and the Austrian Cabinet would not have accepted two dissenters from the state religion. Now Salisbury, the High Church Anglican, had appointed Henry Mathews, a Roman Catholic, as home secretary and the Cabinet would be unlikely to stand for Worms, another dissenter. Mathews was the first Roman Catholic Cabinet minister since the time of James II.

Randolph Churchill continued to plough a furrow in opposition to the rest of the Cabinet. When the other members refused to accept his proposals for reduction of defence expenditure, he resigned on 23 December 1886 in the hope of forcing Salisbury and the rest of the Cabinet to change their minds. Salisbury accepted the resignation with mock reluctance while the rest of the Party, tired of Churchill's quixotic behaviour, did nothing. Later, Randolph's old friend and Liberal politician, Lord Rosebery, remarked about him that 'he was often petulant, had something of the spoilt child about him'.[72]

George Goschen (1831–1907; created Viscount Goschen in 1900) was invited to take the post of chancellor of the exchequer. He had followed Hartington as a Liberal Unionist and the offer helped Salisbury cement a coalition between the Conservatives and that branch of the Liberal Party. During 1892 Goschen formally joined the Conservative Party. Goschen was a well-respected economist who had been largely responsible for solving the Egyptian debt crisis, but he was no longer a member of Parliament. He stood as a Liberal Unionist and had been defeated in his East Edinburgh seat during the 1886 general election. Goschen stipulated that he would accept the post if Iddesleigh was removed as foreign secretary. This was agreed and Salisbury took the position of foreign secretary as well as that of prime minister, leaving Iddesleigh to take voluntary retirement. Goschen was then proposed as a candidate in a by-election for Liverpool Exchange caused by the death of the sitting member. Henry de Worms campaigned on his behalf but Goschen lost the election to a Gladstonian Liberal by a margin of seven votes. The government's budget had to be postponed until Goschen was returned on 9 February 1887 with a 4,157 majority for the safe Conservative seat of St George's Hanover Square, obligingly vacated by the incumbent, Lord Algenon Percy, younger brother of Henry George Percy.[73]

Frederick Stanley, appointed president of the Board of Trade in August 1886, was soon moved to the House of Lords as Lord Stanley (from 1893, 16th Earl of Derby). Henry was again left as front bench spokesman in the Commons and had to fend off the Liberal opposition, who took great delight in badgering him with some 40 questions during four weeks of intense pressure in August and September. To his credit, questioners received calm and clear answers from him on subjects ranging from railway safety, false trademarks, civil service salaries and fishery regulations to communication between lighthouses and the shore. He became responsible for guiding much useful legislation through the Commons.

One long enduring piece of legislation drafted by Henry concerned the marking of goods with their country of origin. For a number of years there had been complaints from, amongst others, the cutlery trade and the watch trade over the presentation of imported goods as of English manufacture. The Board of Trade had to deal with these matters, and while Henry contributed much to the drafting of legislation designed to prevent these frauds, Lord Stanley introduced this in the House of Lords. One watchmaker stated to the select committee that watchcases stamped with the English hallmark were frequently filled abroad with foreign watches and then sold on as English-made watches. Henry as chairman produced his own gold watch worth £45 for examination during that session to be told, much to the amusement of the other committee members, that the movement was not an English one as he supposed; he had been duped by a dishonest trader. A bill to suppress such behaviour was presented in the Lords by the president of the Board of Trade and came into force on 31 December 1887 as the Merchandise Marks Act. This required for the first time that the country of origin should be marked on imported goods and that goods manufactured in the United Kingdom should bear the name or trademark of the manufacturer. It remained in force until supplanted by the Trade Descriptions Act of 1968.[74]

Another important piece of legslation supporting British trade was drafted at this time. Manufacturers frequently complained about the charges that railway companies applied to the transport of goods. Especially where one line had a monopoly of transport, it could and often did favour one industry over another. Companies often charged less to transport foreign goods from a port of entry than for corresponding English goods, though Thomas Farrer, permanent secretary to the Board of Trade, justified this procedure. He pointed out that, for example, goods imported via Liverpool for London may be diverted directly to London by sea if the cost of rail travel was too high.[75] The Board of Trade devised a Railway and Canal Traffic Bill in 1887 to regulate this situation but this did not reach the statue book. The bill was resuscitated in February 1888 for the next session of Parliament, but soon afterwards Henry de Worms moved from the Board of Trade to the Colonial Office. Though this railways bill contained much that was down to his efforts, he took no further part in the final polishing. The second reading was in May 1888, presented by Michael Hicks Beach, now president of the Board of Trade, and the bill finally appeared as the Railway and Canal Traffic Act of 1888. It required all companies to submit their rates for review at a public hearing and all rates had to be listed in a rate book, which was available to the public. A panel was also set up to resolve disputes.[76]

Sugar and Spice

The major task Henry undertook during his period in government was to act as chairman of the International Sugar Convention, which attempted to regulate the international sugar trade. Prior to the Napoleonic wars, world sugar production depended on sugar cane grown in the tropics, and production in Jamaica and other British West India possessions during the eighteenth century created families with great wealth. Some of their relatives came to live in England and formed a sugar lobby to achieve preference for their trade, and indeed one of these sugar barons, William Beckford (1702–1770), was twice Lord Mayor of London. Following the slave revolt in the French colony of St Dominique (from 1804, Haiti) and the collapse of it as a major sugar-producing region, Jamaica experienced a huge increase in demand for its sugar. The West India Dock in London was completed in 1802 partly to service the import of crude brown sugar, and the refineries in East London producing white sugar prospered greatly. Refineries in London, Glasgow and Bristol became large employers of labour.

During the Napoleonic wars France had found it impossible to import cane sugar. It had also lost its major producing area, so French chemical engineers were instructed to find an industrial process for the extraction of sugar from beet. By 1813, mills were producing sugar by this process in France and in countries in central Europe. France especially began to subsidise exported sugar while recouping some of the costs by imposing an internal duty. The biggest importer of sugar was Great Britain, and part of Napoleon's economic strategy had been to ruin British West Indian sugar trade. Subsequent French governments continued the subsidies in an effort to ruin cane sugar production and hand a monopoly to the beet sugar producers.[77]

An attempt to create a level playing field in this trade was made at the 1864 convention in Paris. Signed by Prime Minister Palmerston, Foreign Secretary Earl Russell and Chancellor of the Exchequer Gladstone, it proposed that importers be allowed to impose a contravening duty which would equal the value of the subsidy applied. Nothing, however, was done and complaints against the practice of applying the subsidies, known as sugar bounties, grew in Britain during 1877. The then Conservative government did little beyond setting up a committee of enquiry and the Liberal administration that followed did nothing. When Lord Salisbury came to power he determined to seek a remedy to improve the lot of both the colonial producers and the British sugar refiners, both of whom found it impossible to compete against subsidised beet sugar. Startling trade figures appeared; in 1886 the export of sugar from France suddenly rose by 100% due to the bounty system and the payment of the London trades council to unemployed sugar workers rose by some 150% in the same period. There was also an upside, for between 1877 and 1887, because of the bounty system, the price of refined sugar to the British consumer fell by half. However, something had to be done to prevent the total collapse of both sugar growing in the colonies and the British refining industry. In a letter to the National Association of Agricultural Labourers Henry de Worms wrote: 'it is for Great Britain a question whether one of its industries, giving employment to thousands of persons, shall be sacrificed to a principle indefensible alike in theory and in practice'.[78]

During 1887, successive European governments agreed to attend a Sugar Bounties Conference in London, and the first meeting of this body was held on the afternoon of 24 November. Lord Salisbury was absent in Oxford, so Baron Henry de Worms as parliamentary secretary of the Board of Trade received the delegates at the Foreign Office. He was elected president, with Count Küfstein (1841–1918), the Austrian delegate, as vice-president. After a general conversation on the scope of the conference the delegates adjourned and later attended a banquet given by Henry in the Foreign Office. The conference held seven sittings and the ensuing protocol, written in French, was signed by all the representatives on 19 December. In his ensuing remarks Henry said that 'we have contributed towards an important act of justice regarding international commerce'; he was very pleased with the results. Count Küfstein, offering to Henry on behalf of the delegates 'our warmest thanks for the courteous manner in which you have directed our labours', described Henry's efforts as a work from the heart. Henry spoke excellent French and German and these skills were required during the conference. Salisbury hardly made an appearance, for at the Congress of Berlin in 1878 the Russian plenipotentiary Count Schouvaloff was heard to remark in a derogatory manner that Lord Salisbury spoke 'foreign office' French.[79]

The principal recommendation in this protocol was that governments should remove any bounty system operating in their country. Lord Salisbury was absent also from this final session, opening a new Conservative club in Derby. In a speech there, he praised the careful management of the conference by Baron Henry de Worms, pointing out that the recommendations, contrary to the views of others, were not false to the doctrine of free trade.

Issuing the protocol was, however, only the end of the beginning of the work of the president of the conference. The conference had recommended that extraction and refining of sugar should be carried out in factories under the strictest government control (in bond), from where it could be taxed and sold on to the export market or for home consumption. Manufacturers could manipulate the profit on refined sugar by underestimating the quantity of sugar in the intermediate molasses they had bought. This protocol supported the ideas both of free trade, not distorted by a tax regime, and of fair trade. Unfortunately, Belgium objected to manufacture in this way and proposed to continue with its old system. The convention was due for ratification in April 1889, so Henry immediately began conferring with European governments to remove any difficulties and his new wife accompanied him on a journey around Europe. A visit to Paris gained the support of the French government for the visit to Brussels, where the Belgian methods of manufacture were examined. The Belgian factories used the new saccharimeter, described as an ingenious machine, to estimate yields of sugar from crude material. This gave a firm basis for pricing molasses. While in Belgium, Henry had an audience with the King and then continued to Berlin to obtain the approval of Prince Bismarck, Chancellor of Germany. The journey had to be terminated without visits to Russia and Austria as Henry had to return to London for the opening of a new session of Parliament in February 1888 and a government reshuffle.[80]

The audience with King Leopold II of Belgium (1835–1909) was an interesting encounter; the two men became friends and on several occasions the King was entertained in London by Henry. The connection between them went back to the time when Henry's father was a young apprentice at the Rothschild office in London. Leopold II's father (the future King Leopold I of Belgium) was then only Prince Leopold of Coburg (1790–1865). He arrived in a shabby hackney carriage with letters of introduction and credit, having come to England to pay his addresses to Princess Charlotte, daughter of the Prince Regent. Nathan Rothschild severely berated him on the impropriety of driving about London in a hackney and sent him back to the Prince Regent at Carleton House in a glass coach. Solomon Worms, who was present, often told this story. Leopold and Charlotte married in 1816, but sadly Charlotte died in 1817 after the birth of a stillborn child. Leopold was chosen as king of the Belgians in 1831.[81]

This journey of Henry de Worms across Europe during the first two months of 1888 seems to have had a hidden agenda, for at the time there was fear of war over the governance of Bulgaria. That country had elected a ruling prince who was not in favour with Russia. If Russia invaded Bulgaria in order to impose its own candidate, then Austria was likely to declare war and Germany would be involved under the terms of the Austro-German Alliance. This situation was certainly under discussion, as well as the sugar convention, during the meeting in Berlin, and Bismarck told Henry de Worms in conversation that Germany would not fight for Bulgaria but 'as soon as Austria and Russia were at war, I fight France'. The information was duly relayed to Salisbury.[82]

The Cabinet reshuffle of 1888 was caused by the placement of Lord Stanley as Governor General of Canada and by accommodation of the veteran politician Michael Hicks Beach (1837–1916; created Viscount St Aldwyn in 1915), who was looking for a Cabinet position. He had suffered an eye problem which had prevented him from taking any post for two years, but he was now in recovery. Hicks Beach agreed to return as president of the Board of Trade on the condition that Henry de Worms was not his deputy. This condition was accepted and Henry was moved to become under-secretary of state for the colonies, from where he continued as president of the sugar convention, the outcome of which was also of importance to the colonial sugar trade. The colonial secretary was Lord Knutsford, who remained in office for the rest of the parliamentary term, so Henry was still a principal spokesman in the Commons. The government was criticised over this chopping and changing of ministerial duties and clearly Henry had difficulty in fulfilling all the demands on his time. He had to deal with problems over the convention, which involved further visits to Paris, so he was absent for periods during 1888 when there was important colonial business concerning Zululand. John Gorst, now under-secretary of state for India, had to reply in debate on behalf of the Colonial Office.[83]

Parliamentary expenses are always under scrutiny and Mr Biggar (MP for Cavan) asked under what heading the charge for expenses in connection with the banquet and the visits to Paris, Brussels, Berlin and The Hague would appear. The First Lord of the Treasury replied that there was no public charge in connection with the dinner and that the mission abroad was not intended to involve any public charge whatever: 'The honourable member [Henry de Worms] undertook this journey solely out of zeal for public service, and the public are greatly indebted to him for what he has done.' The French continued to make fresh demands to protect their sugar industry so Henry, now in the Department of Colonial Affairs, had to travel to Paris for two weeks of negotiations during July/August, missing an important debate on Zululand. The convention resumed its session in London to work out final details of the agreement and Henry again smoothed its passage by hosting a dinner for the delegates on 16 August 1888 at his residence, 42 Grosvenor Place. A final text of the convention was agreed on 30 August. Some months later Salisbury gave great praise to Henry's efforts at a Conservative conference in Bristol: 'with regard to the Sugar Bounties Convention, Baron Henry de Worms has been to a very large extent instrumental in carrying that through and I have every hope it may be ultimately successful'.[84]

Signatories to the convention agreed not to take sugar from countries paying a bounty although France still dithered over committing itself to taking part at all. The document was immediately criticised by Thomas Farrer (1819–1899), the retired permanent secretary to the Board of Trade who was hostile towards Toryism; he was also the brother-in-law of Stafford Northcote, Lord Iddesleigh. The system, he said, would not put an end to bounty-fed sugar but would divert the stream from countries that boycott it to countries that would receive it, tending to make sugar cheaper to Britain's neighbours and rivals. Gladstone also stepped up to criticise the convention by writing to Robert Peel, the Liberal candidate at a Brighton by-election, and charging him to follow his illustrious father 'who set free the importation of food [in 1846] by opposing a law that would [in 1889] make sugar scarcer and increase its price'. The Liberal posters at that by-election proclaimed 'Peel and Cheap Bread' as opposed to 'Ritchie and Dear Sugar'. Charles Ritchie (1838–1906; created Baron Ritchie of Dundee in 1905) was the Conservative president of the Board of Local Government who had reduced the grants given to local authorities. He was MP for Tower Hamlets, a district of London where many sugar refineries were situated.[85]

In order to enact the provisions of the convention, the signatories had to pass appropriate ratifying legislation by 1 August 1890, after which the convention would come into force by 1 September 1891. Manufacturers and workers in the sugar trade across the country were in favour of the provisions in the convention but Gladstone and the Liberals still grumbled over dearer sugar and interference with free trade. Henry moved around Britain promoting the aims of the convention and pointing out the costs to France, Germany and Austria of the bounties system and the distortion of trade which this system produced. A speech on this subject given at Greenock was published for distribution. City corporations as well as manufacturers showed their appreciation for his efforts with presents of silver bowls and caskets. For the sustained diplomatic effort which had resulted in this sugar convention, Henry de Worms was created a privy councillor in the New Year's honours list for 1889.[86]

Sugar refining in France, Germany and Austria was controlled by cartels that had made large profits from the bounties system, and these foreign manufacturers lobbied their governments against the convention. Britain was the most important market for imported sugar and these cartels also aimed to break British resolve to implement the results of the conference. If through the bounties system they could push cane sugar out of the market, then beet sugar would be king and they could dictate the price. The production of beet sugar in the 1888–9 season was very much reduced, probably by design, so the reserves of refined sugar became low and prices rose. British opponents of the convention blamed it for the price rise in spite of the fact that its provisions were not yet in force.[87]

Henry de Worms introduced the Sugar Convention Bill in the House of Commons in April 1889. In the course of his speech he managed a swipe at Gladstone through an allusion to the Liberal Party's attempts to prevent sugar bounties in 1864 'when the member for Midlothian [W.E. Gladstone] was Chancellor of the Exchequer'. An international conference made proposals at that time which were totally ineffective. Henry's bill would have enabled Britain to act against importation of sugar carrying a bounty and it received a very hostile reception from the Liberal opposition, which was in favour of free trade, even subsidised 'free' trade. The delegates to an international commission set up under the chairmanship of Baron Henry de Worms continued to meet in London to review progress towards implementation of the terms of the convention and Henry again smoothed the process by entertaining the delegates to dinner at his home. France still dithered and its sugar industry lobbied for retaliatory measures on imports from Britain if it was excluded from the British market.[88]

Agitation against the bill was vigorous from both sides of the House. Many Conservatives who identified with 'free trade' became opponents of the scheme, as did Lord Hartington and many of the Liberal Unionists. In later years, as Lord Pirbright, Henry justified the sugar convention thus: 'We have to deal with adversaries who are bent upon promoting their commercial interests at the expense of ours, and we are told by disciples of the Cobden Club that the principles of Free Trade prohibit our using the only effective weapons at our disposal. Every principle of Free Trade is undoubtedly violated by the bounty system but so long as the result is cheapness to the consumer the bigoted Free Trader is ready to condone the situation.'[89] He singled out Thomas Farrer, a member of the Cobden Club, for particular scorn.

The core Liberal Party was against the bill on the grounds that it interfered with free trade, so the bill was likely to be defeated and also to cause a split between the two parties of the governmental coalition. The Sugar Convention Bill quietly disappeared after its first reading in Parliament and the sugar conference of 1887–8 collapsed, having achieved nothing.[90] Many years later, in the House of Lords, Henry remarked: 'I had the honour of introducing the enabling bill in the House of Commons in February 1889 which was read for the first time, but for some occult reason, which, perhaps, will never be disclosed, the Second Reading never took place.'[91]

Trade and Industry

Henry de Worms, in the Colonial Office from 1888, found himself with a double burden of work. Hicks Beach, in spite of his original objections to working with Henry in the Board of Trade, used him to assist the passage of its business through the Commons. Hicks Beach's new under-secretary, Lord Onslow, was unavailable since he sat in the other House. Members noted that of the seventeen principal ministers of the government at that time, eleven sat in the House of Lords, and the House of Commons raised a debate on this unfair ratio. The prime minister, Lord Salisbury, sitting in the Lords, heard little of this debate, and did nothing.[92]

Hicks Beach and Worms, working together in the Commons, introduced a Weights and Measures Bill which provided for the inspection of weighing instruments, for the delivery of coal in specified amounts and for the sale of bread in loaves of specified weight. The measures were discussed at some length, but because of difficulties in specifying quality of goods as well as quantity, this particular bill never became law.[93]

This same pair introduced the Regulation of Railways Bill in July 1889 following the Armagh railway disaster of 12 June when many lives were lost because of a failure in the simple manual braking system then used. Part of a packed excursion train had run away backwards downhill and into a following train. At the time this was the world's worst rail disaster. The bill introduced compulsory use of continuous automatic brakes (vacuum brakes) on all trains. It passed swiftly through Parliament to be enacted on 30 August, and with amendments this bill remains in force. Accidents caused by failure of the coupling and the braking systems used on railway wagons had been brought to the notice of Henry de Worms when he was in the Board of Trade but little was done to improve the situation before the Armagh disaster. Hicks Beach some two years later still complained of the difficulties in enforcing this act on the remote small railways in Scotland and Ireland.[94]

The two politicians continued to co-operate and Henry de Worms was nominated to the select committee for the consideration of all bills related to trade and industry. Hicks Beach began to recognise Henry's expertise in the area of trade and probably regretted having forced him out into the Colonial Office. Henry sat on the committee convened to look into the operation of the Merchandise Marks Act and usually acted as chairman. This committee dealt in particular with the marking of cutlery and cotton goods with the name of the manufacturer and its work was embodied in an amending Merchandise Marks Act 1891, brought in by Henry de Worms.[95]

Strikes for better pay and conditions of work became more frequent after 1888, by which time, fortunately for him, Henry de Worms had left the Board of Trade. The match girls' strike on 2 July 1888 was over working conditions in a factory using the toxic yellow phosphorus. These terrible conditions were only slowly ameliorated by the introduction of red phosphorus as a replacement. The London dockers' strike, which began on 14 August 1889, was over poor pay and it resulted in victory for the strikers and the establishment of a strong trade union. The London Trades Council had decided to demand a nine-hour day for building workers, which they had previously pushed for through a strike in 1859. The strike was defeated at that time but demands for a shorter working day continued and by 1889 the unions were in favour of an overall eight-hour limit to the working day.

In 1890 the new German emperor, William II, anxious to make a mark in the international field, organised a labour conference in Berlin to begin on 15 March, to regulate hours of work in coal mines, Sunday working and the employment of women and children. The enforcement of the eight-hour day, standard practice in most countries today, was prominent in these proposals.[96] It was at this point that Bismarck, the unifier and leader of Prussia and Germany for nearly 30 years, was dismissed on 18 March by William II, who wished to take a more prominent role in government. William had absorbed the sermons of court preacher Adolf Stöcker and had strong anti-Jewish feelings.[97] The proposal that Henry de Worms would be the British delegate to the Berlin Conference was consistent with his previous work at the Board of Trade, but he was Jewish. Henry diplomatically refused this appointment on the grounds that he would have had to juggle his time between the conference and the Colonial Office. Instead, John Gorst, Randolph Churchill's old ally, was named as chief British delegate to Berlin. He had an interest in social welfare but was now under-secretary of state for India. Probably Henry also sensed another doomed international conference like the sugar conference had been because, from the outset, the organisers had decided that its conclusions would not be binding on the delegations.[98]

This Berlin conference was discussed in Parliament when Cunninghame Graham (1852–1936; Liberal MP for Lanarkshire NW) proposed the gradual introduction of an eight-hour day. Graham had been prominent in both the match girls' and the dockers' strikes He introduced a bill in 1890 to regulate the working day but this never received a second reading since too many in the government party were not in favour. Henry de Worms was never in favour of a compulsory eight-hour day though he strongly advocated the fair treatment of workers. In speeches to his Liverpool constituents he consistently opposed the cheap labour sweating system used by some manufacturers to make their prices more competitive.[99]

Together with Hicks Beach, Henry de Worms was on the select committee looking into the hours worked by railwaymen, and was often in the chair. The committee heard evidence of incredibly long working hours and trade union witnesses took the opportunity to advocate the eight-hour day. They were subjected to harsh cross-examination and Henry was clearly not in favour of legislation to fix hours of work. He maintained that such a measure would require extensive policing and would probably lead to absurd situations. Arguments over railwaymen's hours continued but no legislation was introduced until the next session of Parliament.[100]

Imperial Obsessions

Alongside this work assisting the Board of Trade, Henry de Worms also processed routine business as spokesman for the Colonial Office in the Commons. In February 1888 there was a debate in the House on liquor traffic in the British dependencies. In a long speech, Henry showed himself to have been well briefed by the Colonial Office, citing the measures which the government was taking to suppress liquor trade in areas as far apart as the Pacific islands and South and West Africa. He declared, 'It was the duty of the Government, and a duty which they would certainly not neglect, to spread the benign influence of religion and civilisation wherever British power or influence extended.' The indefatigable Wilfrid Lawson, by then MP for Cockermouth, was again against any sale of alcohol and managed to introduce an ineffective plea for its prohibition in Britain. He also managed a favourable comment on Henry's very excellent and satisfactory speech.[101]

The granting of responsible government to Western Australia was a piece of business left unfinished by the previous secretary of state for the colonies. A deputation from the colony was sent to London, where Henry de Worms had become chairman of the select committee in charge of negotiations over the constitutional proposals. Discussions lasted until July 1890, when the colony became self-governing and Henry was invited to stand for the post of governor, though he preferred to remain in London. A subsequent major step, involving the federation of the Australian states, was achieved in 1901.[102]

Africa also kept Henry busy in this period. Zululand had not remained peaceful for long after Gladstone had reinstated Cetshwayo in 1883. Intertribal warfare broke out and Usibepu killed Cetshwayo, who was his rival. The Boer people, who had self-government from 1881, sent mercenaries in support of Cetshwayo's son Dinuzulu (1868–1913) in the hope of gaining territory and an outlet to the sea. They demanded so much land from Dinuzulu, including a sea outlet, that the Conservative government of Salisbury became alarmed and in 1887 formally annexed Zululand to Natal. Transvaal did gain more territory from this expedition but was denied sea access. When Henry de Worms arrived at the Colonial Office he had to deal with the consequences of annexation. A number of the Zulu chiefs were tried and imprisoned, while Dinuzulu was exiled to St Helena from 1890 to 1897. Chief Usibepu (1841–1904), who had used no Boer mercenaries and was defeated in the tribal fighting, was considered to have been loyal to the government and had his lands restored to him.[103]

The discovery of gold deposits in the Transvaal during 1886 made that country prosperous and profoundly affected the stability of the region. The city of Johannesburg developed through an influx of miners and soon rivalled the capital of Pretoria in size. Railway construction and extension of the Natal railway to join the Transvaal system by 1891 caused great rejoicing. President Kruger and the governor of Natal opened the border station, while in London a banquet was held, presided over by Henry de Worms. He read the telegram of good wishes he had sent to the governor and to President Kruger, which ended, on behalf of the government, with 'an expression of our cordial good wishes for the continued welfare of the South African Republic and Natal'. The Natal section was financed by British capital, while Transvaal in 1884 had awarded construction of railways to the Netherlands South Africa Railway Company. It completed the Natal line northwards to Johannesburg and also built a line from Pretoria to the Portugese port of Lourenço Marques (now Maputo) in Delagoa Bay.[104]

In spite of this expression of cordial good wishes, all was not well between Britain and the Transvaal. Kruger's government was now awash with money and used the route from Delagoa Bay to import modern armaments without passing through British territory. This government feared that the influx of miners, mostly British and German, to Johannesburg would swamp the Boer population. The behaviour of President Kruger's government occupied most of Henry's later political life and his last philanthropic act attempted to alleviate the suffering of discharged soldiers wounded in the consequent colonial wars.

A group headed by Cecil Rhodes in 1889 formed the British South Africa Company, which the British government agreed would administer territory to the north of the Transvaal. As under-secretary of state, Henry de Worms outlined the aims of this company as being to open up its territory by constructing telegraph and railway connections with the Cape Colony. It was obliged to eradicate slavery, govern according to native customs and also regulate the sale of liquor and arms to the Matabele under their chief Lobengula (1845–1894): 'I [Henry de Worms] think it will be seen that these provisions afford satisfactory evidence of the enormous civilising influence which this Charter must exercise over the vast territory to be administered by the Company.'[105] In 1890 Cecil Rhodes sent a pioneer column of settlers, protected by his British South Africa police, through Matabele territory into Shono territory to establish Fort Salisbury (now Harare). The Matabele, like the Zulu, were a warrior tribe, but Lobengula managed to avoid confrontation with the British South Africa Company's forces until 1893, when the Matabele wars began, and fortunately for Henry, he was then out of office. Lobengula was defeated in 1894 and his capital of Bulawayo captured.

A desire to develop the area of Africa around modern-day Kenya led Salisbury to negotiate a treaty with Germany to exchange some small 'spheres of influence'. As a bargaining tool, Britain offered Germany the Island of Heligoland, which was under the control of the Colonial Office. In private, Henry de Worms was not in favour of relinquishing this island which in Napoleonic times had been used as a base for smuggling goods into the Continent. His Rothschild relatives had profited from this business, transporting cotton cloth from Manchester to Germany. Henry expressed his opinion diplomatically when replying to a parliamentary questioner who contended that Great Britain had no interest in retaining the island. 'If the fact that the island was very near to the German coast were sufficient argument for its relinquishment, the Channel Islands would have to be surrendered to France and Gibraltar to Spain.' Salisbury, however, took a different view and proceeded with the negotiations for a treaty, which was signed on 1 July 1890. This provided for the exchange of Zanzibar for Heligoland and recognised British control over what are now Kenya and Uganda. Parliament ratified the arrangements during the month of August. An anonymous critic pointed out that Salisbury had in 1886 surrendered the British protectorate of Zanzibar to Germany so as to gain Bismarck's support for British policy in Egypt, and so was only repurchasing what he had given away.[106]

Swaziland is adjacent to Zululand and has a long border with the Transvaal. It had been recognised as independent under British protection and the King of Swaziland proceeded to sell mining concessions that were sometimes in conflict with each other. The trivial amounts of money involved were spent on debauchery and his country rapidly fell into disorder. During 1890 the Colonial Office negotiated a convention with the Transvaal government over the governance of Swaziland and Henry de Worms had the task of explaining all the arrangements to the Commons during heated exchanges in August and September. Discussions ranged over all the problems of central Africa and the final convention allowed for Swazi independence with an independent administration presiding over white settlers by means of a joint Transvaal-British court. There was provision for this joint administration to be terminated after three years if previous notice was given by either party.[107]

Boer settlers from the Transvaal Republic, concerned at interference with their way of life, began to talk of a large northern trek to a country outside British rule and into areas where the British South Africa Company already had an interest. A scramble for good agricultural land was developing and a group of Boers, as many as 5,000 men, proposed to assemble and cross the Limpopo River on 1 June 1891. They intended to found a Republic of the North in what is now the eastern section of Zimbabwe. It would have bordered British South African Company on the west and Portuguese territory on the east, extending north as far as the Zambezi River. Such a move was against the provisions of the agreement between Britain and President Kruger, which bound the Transvaal to use its best efforts to support the British South Africa Company. Henry de Worms announced firmly in 1891 that such a move 'will not be tolerated [and] will be deemed an act of hostility against the Queen', and the trek was abandoned.[108]

The mastery of facts required for answering questions relating to colonial affairs was achieved at considerable government expense. Simple questions could be answered easily, but often the members asked for more specific and detailed statistics. To answer in detail, the Colonial Office had to seek a response by telegraph and this was expensive. Expenditure on telegrams caused a row in the Commons, but if the information was needed quickly then the costs had to be borne. A telegram to Western Australia at that time cost eight shillings [40p] a word.[109]

When Henry Raikes (1838–1891), the Postmaster General, died, another government reshuffle was triggered. Henry de Worms had made a very creditable performance in the Commons on colonial affairs, so there was speculation that he would be advanced further. James Fergusson (1832–1907), previously under-secretary for foreign affairs, filled Raikes' old position, so now there was more speculation that Henry might be moved from the colonies to the Foreign Office, a move he would have very much liked. His long introduction to the memoirs of Count Beust, published in English in 1887, notes Henry's youthful escapades into Viennese diplomatic circles and forms a creditable curriculum vitae for a post in the British Foreign Office. However, in the end a new member of the government, James Lowther (1855–1949), filled the post of under-secretary for foreign affairs and Henry remained at the colonial office and was denied fulfilment of his ambition. Salisbury was determined to remain fully in charge as foreign secretary.[110]

Opposition Again

The Parliament elected in 1886 ran its full course and was dissolved on 28 June 1892. A general election then returned 268 Conservative, 45 Liberal Unionist, 272 Gladstonian Liberal, 81 Irish Independent and 2 Independent Labour members. Baron Henry de Worms, opposed by a Gladstonian Liberal, was re-elected for East Toxteth and he took the parliamentary oath in the Jewish fashion, wearing his hat. Nearby Liverpool Exchange, as in 1886, returned a Gladstonian Liberal, defeating the Liberal Unionist by a small majority. One of the new Labour members of this Parliament was J. Keir-Hardy (1856–1915), elected for the first time in West Ham (South).[111] The votes cast in East Toxteth were as follows:

LIVERPOOL (East Toxteth) (1892)
Baron Henry de Worms (C)   3,707
Edward Paul (G)   2,200

The previous government had remained in power through a coalition between the Conservatives and the Liberal Unionists. There were now fewer MPs in this combination than there were Gladstonian Liberal and Irish Independents, so a Conservative government could only continue in office by winning support from Gladstonian Liberals, and Lord Salisbury was not willing to do this. In the Queen's Speech, Queen Victoria wished only that her government would continue 'the path of useful and beneficial legislation', without listing any particular course. The Liberal member Herbert Asquith proposed 'that it is essential that Your Majesty's Government should possess the confidence of this House and of the Country, and respectfully to represent to Your Majesty that such confidence is not reposed in the present Advisers of Your Majesty'.

A motion of no confidence was agreed by 350 votes to 310, which represented the split between Liberals and Irish Nationalists on the one hand against Conservatives and Liberal Unionists on the other, and the government resigned on 12 August. In this division, Henry de Worms voted with the Conservative minority. Gladstone then formed a Liberal administration with the support of Irish Nationalists and Henry de Worms now sat on the opposition benches. In his electoral address Gladstone had promised a raft of social legislation, home rule for Ireland and the disestablishment of the Scottish and Welsh Churches, but debates on home rule took up so much parliamentary time that other matters were pushed into the background.[112]

This Liberal government now had to deal with the tribal problems in central Africa left by the previous government, and Henry maintained a vigorous barrage of questions over its way of conducting colonial affairs. He took little part in the debates over Matabeleland but kept a stern eye on the government's negotiations with President Kruger of the South African Republic over the future of Swaziland. The crisis in Matabeleland erupted into war by 1893 and the chief, Lobengula, was soon defeated. Henry's experience as under-secretary for the colonies led him to conclude that whenever a tribe meets with a reverse in the field at the hands of white troops and its chief becomes a fugitive, it has very little rallying power left. 'We look upon the repulse of the Matabele impis as an absolute solution to the problem,' he explained. The British South Africa Corporation took over administration of Matabeleland after the final defeat of Lobengula in 1894, and the territory it administered became known as Rhodesia (now Zimbabwe).[113]

The government of Kruger continued a policy of seeking *lebensraum* (land on which to live and farm) for the younger sons of Boer farmers and looked towards the tribal area of Swaziland. The convention of 1890, signed when

Henry was under-secretary, was due for re-negotiation after three years and could be repudiated by either party up to three months before expiry. Henry, together with George Baden-Powell (1847–1898; MP for Liverpool, Kirkdale and elder brother to Robert Baden-Powell), badgered the liberal under-secretary from February 1893 in attempts to clarify the situation, always to be put off because negotiations were ongoing. In May of that year, Kruger's government gave notice of termination of the old agreement, which was replaced by another one in November. The new arrangements transferred control of Swaziland to the Transvaal subject to the agreement of the Queen-Regent of Swaziland, and this was obtained, after some troubles, by the summer of 1894. The British government's position, set out by the Liberal under-secretary, was that 'while they acquiesced in the control of Swaziland by the Transvaal, they had stipulated for the native independence of the Swazis themselves'.[114] An agreement was reached defining borders but it did not address the further problem of friction between the Boers and other settlers in the Transvaal. Several MPs criticised the Boer government for neglecting the rights of the Uitlanders, mostly British and German, who outnumbered the Boers and who ran the country's industries, generating a huge surplus of revenue for the Transvaal government. Animosity between the Boer people and the Uitlanders ultimately led to the second Boer War.[115]

The new government began a raft of domestic legislation on which Henry made little contribution in Parliament, though his public speeches indicate a willingness to vote at the call of the Conservative Party. Concerns expressed in the previous Parliament over the long hours of work of railwaymen led to the Hours of Railway Servants Act, passed in 1893. A bill stipulating an eight-hour working day for miners was introduced by private members in 1893 but never reached the statute book, for much of the debating time was taken up by the question of Irish home rule. In speeches to his constituents Henry was against general legislation to control hours of work, although he was against the sweated labour systems used by some manufacturers.

Gladstone introduced his second Home Rule Bill in February 1893; it passed the second reading in the Commons by 43 votes, and the third reading on 1 September by 34 votes. On 8 September it was overwhelmingly defeated in the Lords, whose members still had a veto on legislation. Henry de Worms did not speak to this bill in Parliament, but in addressing Conservative gatherings on the subject of home rule he became more and more stridently opposed to it. He suggested that the men of Ulster 'might very well be compared to the unfortunate Jews in Russia if Home Rule was granted'. One of his Conservative colleagues, Lord Arthur Hill (1846–1931; MP for Down West), a confirmed Ulster Orangeman, appears to have had a strong influence on Henry's opinions. These two became friends and dining colleagues, and much later Lord Arthur Hill attended Henry's funeral.[116]

After the defeat of the Irish Home Rule Bill, Gladstone continued as leader of the Liberal Party, hoping that this measure could eventually be passed, but the friction between him and his Cabinet increased. A final separation from his colleagues came during the winter of 1893–4 when a proposal was made, which he could not accept, to increase naval expenditure. The Cabinet staggered on until 1 March 1894, when Gladstone announced his intention to resign. At this meeting the Cabinet accepted the Lords' amendments to the Local Government Bill, and after making announcement of this in the Commons, Gladstone resigned as prime minister. The Queen asked Lord Rosebery, a Liberal peer, to form a government and the party continued, but with declining vigour, to press for social legislation.

The Local Government Act received the royal assent in March 1894. It changed the character of the governing bodies in villages, replacing the old select vestries, which had been connected with the Church, with elected and secular parish councils. Henry de Worms had opposed this bill when it was first mooted. In a speech given to the Worplesdon Agricultural Association he confessed he 'did not see the utility of the proposal'. (Worplesdon in Surrey is near his country seat of Henley Park.) Later addressing his Liverpool constituents he maintained that the Liberals 'were unable to resist the attempt to deprive the Church of its undoubted property'. However, when the provisions of the act came into operation he determined to ensure that the arrangements would be successful; he was elected chairman of the Pirbright Parish Council at its first meeting in January 1895 and worked hard to ensure that this council functioned properly.[117]

One of Gladstone's promised pieces of legislation was a Welsh Suspensory Bill, intended to separate and then disestablish the Anglican Church in Wales. The first Welsh Bill was introduced in February 1893 and was strongly opposed by the Conservatives. H. Asquith (1852–1928; MP for East Fife and then home secretary) remarked that 'the policy of Welsh Disestablishment is a policy to which the Liberal party as a whole is distinctly pledged', but consideration of the Home Rule Bill overtook any debate on the matter.[118] Henry followed the party line in his constituency speeches, indicating that in his opinion the bill was 'simply the preliminary to a gigantic scheme of statesmanlike burglary' because it proposed an assault on the tithe system.[119] He was not alone in this criticism. The justification given by the Liberal Party for this measure in Wales was similar to that for disestablishment of the Church in Ireland, which a Liberal government had achieved by 1869 (this act became effective in 1871). In both cases, the majority of citizens in the countries concerned belonged to a dissenting Church. Henry was not a Christian but he continued to support the established Church and followed the views of the Tory Party. A further attempt to bring in a Welsh Bill under Rosebery was overtaken by the dissolution of Parliament in 1895 and it was not finally enacted until 1920.

Two other items raised, which did not reach the statute book, were a Plural Voting Bill, whereby Liberals voiced the principle of 'one man one vote', and the proposition that members of the House of Commons should be paid. These issues had been introduced during the electioneering period, but discussions in Parliament were deferred in favour of debate on home rule. Later they were not pushed with sufficient vigour and Parliament was dissolved before they could be implemented. Henry de Worms was strongly against payment of members: 'once allow the principle of paying a man £300 a year, and they would have a collection of political adventurers and carpet baggers, who made politics their profession and who would sell their principles in the same way they would sell anything else'. He also felt that 'if a man prospered in business and had an office, say in Liverpool and a residence in Southport, he could not understand why that man should be deprived of his right to exercise the franchise in those two different places'.[120]

An item of business that had Henry's interest came up at this time. Liverpool Corporation had inherited obligations to maintain some ten churches in the inner city which now served very small congregations. The corporation introduced a private bill allowing it to pay a large sum to cancel these obligations, in order to build churches in the suburbs instead. Henry was against this bill, which he felt was a measure of local disestablishment since it removed the regular income of ten parishes. The bill was first introduced in 1893 and was rejected by a majority of nine votes. It was reintroduced in 1897 under a Conservative government, with Henry in the House of Lords, and the second reading passed by 205 votes to 95.[121]

Rosebery soon grew tired of the constant quibbling in Parliament. When his government was narrowly defeated on a minor motion to censure the minister of war over an alleged shortage of ammunition for the Army, he took this as a vote of censure on his government and resigned on 21 June 1895. A general election was postponed to later that year so as to avoid a clash with the planned wedding festivities in Twickenham of Hélène of Orléans, which were attended by most of the British royal family.[122] Salisbury agreed to form a stopgap coalition government with the Liberal Unionists and gave that party a number of places in his government, dropping some of his former Conservative ministers. Henry de Worms and David Robert Plunket (1838–1919) were relegated to the backbenches, with the promise of peerages if a Conservative government was in place after the forthcoming general election. Plunket was an Irish lawyer and MP for Dublin University who had held several posts in government.

House of Lords

At the general election held at the end of July 1895 Henry de Worms was returned for Liverpool (East Toxteth) with an increased majority. The election was a landslide victory for the Conservatives, who took 340 seats, so with 71 Liberal Unionists they had a huge majority over the 177 Liberals and 82 Irish Nationalists. This new Parliament had eight members of the Hebrew faith. Of these, Ferdinand de Rothschild, Sir Julian Goldsmid and Arthur Strauss, all of whom in the past had been staunch Liberals and opposed to Henry de Worms, now classed themselves as Liberal Unionists and were in the same camp as the Conservatives; only Samuel Montague, MP for Whitechapel, remained a Liberal Radical.[123] The voting for East Toxteth went as follows:

LIVERPOOL (East Toxteth) (1895)
Baron Henry de Worms (C)   3,628
Mr. C.Y. Dawbarn (R)   1,706

Salisbury continued his policy of introducing Liberal Unionists into the government, making Joseph Chamberlain (1836–1914) colonial secretary with Lord Selborne (1859–1942) as under-secretary. Salisbury himself retained the position of foreign secretary, with the Conservative George Curzon (1859–1925) as under-secretary.

Two displaced Conservatives were made peers: Henry de Worms became Lord Pirbright for services rendered in government, while David Plunket became Lord Rathmore. Lord Knutsford was another forced retiree; he became Viscount Knutsford. At the same time, Algernon Borthwick (1830–1908), MP for Kensington South and proprietor of the *Morning Post*, became Lord Glencorse. Borthwick had pleased Salisbury by supporting the Conservative line through the columns of his newspaper. Salisbury did not pursue a policy of giving peerages for contributions to party funds.

The newly created Lord Pirbright was the fourth person of purely Jewish descent to be raised to the peerage. The first two were born into Jewish families and later baptised into the Anglican faith: Samson Gideon (1774–1824, created Lord Eardley, an Irish peerage, in 1789 by William Pitt) and Benjamin Disraeli (created Lord Beaconsfield in 1876). Gladstone had proposed to ennoble one of the Rothschilds in 1869 but Queen Victoria vetoed his suggestion and it was not until that candidate had died that his son, Nathaniel Mayer Rothschild (created Lord Rothschild in 1885) was ennobled.[124]

Following his ennoblement, Lord Pirbright took a holiday in Spain, where he was the guest of the Spanish royal family and then had a break on the Riviera before the earls of Limerick and Kintore introduced him to the House of Lords on 11 February 1896.[125] Kintore (1852–1930) was Conservative and a government whip, and Limerick (1840–1896) was the government chief whip. Pirbright took little interest in the political questions of the day, probably seeing that there would be no opening for him in government, and the press reported his retirement from public speaking. He still attended Parliament and, remembering his connections with Liverpool, he introduced two private bills from that city. The Liverpool Court of Passage Bill was introduced to assist with speeding the application of law in simple cases, and the Mersey Channels Bill regulated the shipping lanes in the approaches to Liverpool docks. Both were practical measures and they passed unopposed. Pirbright served on several committees of the House of Lords dealing with railway bills and with Scottish bills.[126]

The sugar bounty system intensified after the fall of the sugar conference, of which Baron Henry de Worms had been chairman. Russia now entered the market and set up an efficient beet sugar industry in its western provinces, laying long tracks of light railway for the transportation of beetroot to the factories. Politically powerful sugar cartels developed in France and in Germany, all totally devoted to making money from the export subsidy system regardless of any expense to their taxpayers. As competition intensified, the British government received numerous pleas for help from the cane sugar producers in the British Empire, while sugar refineries in London, Bristol and Glasgow, which could not match the artificially low prices for sugar, closed down, swelling the ranks of the unemployed. Britain was the only European country to import sugar and the competition for the British market became ruinously expensive for foreign governments. In late 1897 Henry wrote an article, 'The Ruin of the West Indies', on these problems for the *National Review*. He advocated the imposition of an import duty, called a surtax, exactly equal to the bounty which a foreign government had granted so that beet sugar could compete on a level playing field with cane sugar.[127]

Britain's Conservative government of 1900 called for regulation of the market, but this attempt failed due to Russian intransigence. By 1902 Britain insisted that an agreement be reached against the bounty system or British borders would be closed to sugar from sources outside the British Empire. Great improvements had been made in the production of sugar in the colonies and refineries in Britain had been completely modernised so that the cane sugar industry was now more efficient and able to compete with beet sugar at the true price of manufacture. The international response to this ruinous bounty system was the Brussels Sugar Convention of 1901–02, which abolished all export subsidies from signatories, limiting them to a modest import duty, and which allocated international market shares. The British delegates to Brussels were Salisbury and Onslow; the latter had also attended the London conference. Pirbright was strongly recommended as a British representative because of his experience and because he was by far the best linguist on the government side, but he was not accepted.[128]

This agreement was the first international attempt to regulate an aspect of world trade, and a commission, which met regularly in Brussels, policed it. Henry, now Lord Pirbright, took no part in the negotiations but after the convention had been signed he made a critical appraisal in the House of Lords. This was his last major speech in Parliament and it pointed out some of the failures in the proposals.[129] Countries not exporting sugar were allowed to apply a subsidy to home-grown beet sugar, which allowed them to undercut the price of cane sugar imported from Britain. The agreement prohibited bounties on both the production and the exportation of sugar only for those countries having an export trade. It also allowed a modest surtax on imported sugar, which pleased Germany since it meant it was able to raise the price of imported sugar above that of its home-grown beet sugar. In fact it was not a 'free trade' agreement. A contemporary reporter said his audience of peers was a most depressing one consisting of 'three Liberal, a dozen Conservative peers and one real live Bishop'. On the positive side it was remarked that Lord Pirbright spoke more distinctly than lords usually do. At the height of his public career he had been much in demand as a speaker at Conservative meetings.[130]

The Brussels Sugar Convention was signed on 5 March 1902 and the Bill of Authorisation, brought in on 28 May 1903, culminated in the Sugar Convention Act of 1903. The government was bound to the terms of the convention for five years from 1 September 1903. Pirbright had described the convention as a sickly child and there were numerous objections to its operation, but the terms were renewed for a further five years until 1

September 1913. Britain then withdrew as it considered that the convention in Brussels interfered too much with free trade.

Pirbright continued to serve on House of Lords committees for this session of Parliament and took part in the coronation of Edward VII on 9 August 1902. He died on 9 January 1903, aged 62, after a short illness.

7

La Belle Époque

> *The chief enjoyment of riches consists of the parade of riches*
> Adam Smith, *Wealth of Nations* (1776)

Prélude

Henry Worms, his first wife and their family spent some time in Vienna, arriving there in 1869 shortly after the birth of their second child. Henry's father-in-law's palace there was very large and must have been rather more comfortable than their small apartment in London. Viennese society was also much more attractive to his wife Franziska, and Henry had many friends in government and in diplomatic circles. He was now on intimate terms with the Austrian Chancellor and received regular invitations to government receptions. Invitations flowed also from the British ambassador, Lord Bloomfield, who had been a guest at his wedding reception. Henry soon became a friend of the French ambassador, M. le duc de Grammont (1819–1880), and yet more invitations flowed from this source. His friends in government gave parties and there also were the public balls to attend. By comparison, life in London must have seemed somewhat lacking in amusement to Franziska.

There was even diplomatic intrigue in Vienna revolving around the possibility of war between France and Prussia, which, when it finally began in 1870, saw the defeat of France and the abdication of Napoleon III. At one reception Grammont asked Henry if he thought Bavaria would ally with France in any future conflict. Henry sought Count Beust's opinion, who maintained that such an alliance was impossible because Bavaria was a German state and would never ally against another part of Germany. This opinion was relayed to the French ambassador, who preferred rather to rely on the vague assurances of alliance given him by the Bavarian ambassador. Beust's opinion proved to be the correct one. Henry had the opportunity to discuss this matter with Napoleon III in exile at Cowes during 1872, when the former emperor remarked that Grammont had given him the impression that he could count on the alliance with Bavaria. When the war began, Bavaria allied with Prussia.[1]

On his return to London in 1870, Henry bought a splendidly large house for Franziska and had it decorated in the best continental style in order to begin a social life there. At the same time, his brother George bought the Milton Park estate in Egham, Surrey. From where did the brothers find the money for these operations?

Bismarck's banker sold Austrian bonds through his London agents, G. & A. Worms, when much of Europe, including France, believed that Catholic Bavaria and Austria would unite with France against Protestant Prussia. Austria's finances, already in a perilous position, would have been destabilised if the value of its bonds collapsed. Trusting in their inside knowledge, the brothers were able to buy Austrian stock at low prices, wait for a short period, then resell when the market improved. The war began on 19 July, eight days after the sale of the bonds had been ordered, and Napoleon's Army collapsed on 2 September. Soon after this incident, the Austrian government recognised the financial help from the House of Worms by granting it a peerage. The Austrian stock market rose after German unification, only to crash a few years later because of overspeculation.

Count Beust later became the Austrian ambassador to England. His delight with English society was sincere: 'whether it be the magnificent hospitality that one finds in England, or the loyal attachment one meets with, there is a homely feeling about the country which attracts the visitor in spite of the dreary monotony of English life and the lack of amusement'.[2] Franziska, however, found life in London dreary and monotonous with none of the positive aspects seen by the count. Even though parties were organised in London and there were the two excursions to Cowes in the season, the attractions of Vienna proved too great, and shortly after the birth of their third child in 1875, she left for Austria with the children. The temperaments of husband and wife proved incompatible: Henry was serious and ambitious, while Franziska preferred the excitement of the frivolous Viennese salon society. She returned to London only briefly for the season of 1884 when their eldest daughter was presented at court, and appears to have enjoyed the associated whirl of parties.

During the years when his wife preferred to live in Austria, Henry de Worms could regularly be seen at charity dinners. He was often chairman for the proceedings and was expected to deliver a topical speech. Even before his election to Parliament he was invited to political receptions given by Lord

Above: Henry Joseph Tenison Halsey, ca. 1920, last holder of the mediaeval title of Lord of the Manor of Pirbright.

Below: Henry Lord Pirbright outside the entrance to the Houses of Parliament. (Photographer Benjamin Stone, 1897: © Victoria and Albert Museum)

Above: The Gardens, a group of semi-detached houses in Pirbright constructed by Henry de Worms in 1895-1896. (Photographer J.G., 2009)

Below: Henry de Worms, Lord Pirbright, marked his property with monogrammed wall plaques. W 1895 and P 1896 are found in The Gardens, P 1897 is from Pirbright Terrace. (Photographer J.G., 2012)

Above: Reverend Arthur Krauss, vicar of Pirbright 1898-1924, who was never friendly with Lord Pirbright.

Left: Reverend John Dunn, vicar of Pirbright 1889-1898, and a good friend of Lord Pirbright.

Left: A village photograph to commemorate the unveiling of the Little Girl Statue. Lord and Lady Pirbright in the centre, with Lady Pirbright dressed 'like a peacock'. H. M. Briant, second chairman of Pirbright Parish Council, is the man to the right.

Below: Lord Pirbright's Hall being prepared for the opening ceremony in 1899.
(Photographer, Miss A. Long, Pirbright)

Left: Bronze medal presented to villagers of Pirbright to commemorate the coronation of Edward VII. Due to the king's illness the ceremony had to be postponed to 9 August 1902.

Below: Door lintel of Lord Pirbright's Hall. The coronets and motto were inserted in 1899. The inscription above in Latin and in English was inserted in 1901. (Photographer J.G., 2012)

Left: This cloth badge with Sarah Pirbright's initials was given to villagers in her sewing circle.

Below: A group of the Princess Christian Homes, Bisley, constructed on the initiative of Lord Pirbright in 1900 (© The Francis Frith Collection, photographed 1911)

Above: Portrait of Henry Lord Pirbright, ca. 1900, presented to the village hall. This is a copy, prepared under the artist's supervision, of an oil painting by Luke Fildes. (Photographer E.G., 2013)

Left: Oil portrait labelled Sarah Lady Pirbright presented to the village hall. From the dress fashion this must have been painted ca. 1885 and possibly before she was married to Henry de Worms. (Photographer E.G., 2013)

Left: Freifrau Fanny von Worms-Todesco, the first wife of Henry de Worms, a portrait taken probably in mourning for her mother. (Photographer J. Lorvy, Vienna, 1895)

Below: A chest tombstone marks the grave of Lord and Lady Pirbright in St. Mark's churchyard, Wyke, Surrey. Plaques round the sides of this chest mark the burial of children and relations of Lord Pirbright by his first wife. (Photographer J.G., 2011)

Salisbury and others. As a Conservative member of Parliament, he continued to receive invitations to parliamentary receptions and was invited both to address local party meetings and to attend their local dinners. Franziska missed all of this entertainment, but she would probably have thought it all very boring. Henry's essentially bachelor-like existence, however, was not suitable for reciprocal home entertainment, but his second wife, Sarah Phillips, who had considerable experience in entertaining, soon changed the situation completely and proved a great asset for Henry in developing a social life.

The Phillipses were a prominent London Jewish merchant family related to the Samuels. Sarah's grandfather was a cousin of the Alfred Phillips who set up the firm of Samuel Phillips & Co., operating in Brazil.[3] Sarah's father, Benjamin Samuel Phillips (1811–1889), 'never claimed to be anything but what he was – a plain citizen and a self made man'. He started in business with his brother-in-law as Faudel-Phillips and Sons, becoming very wealthy as wool, yarn, needlework, fancy drapery, hardware and fancy goods importers, dealers and manufacturers. He was elected Lord Mayor of London in 1865.[4]

Sarah Phillips had been married, on 10 May 1853, at the age of 18, to William Barnet according to the Jewish rite. This first husband was an East India merchant late of Canton and they set up house at 155 Westbourne Terrace, Hyde Park. There was one child, a girl, stillborn on 11 June 1854, and after this William began to show his displeasure by refusing to allow Sarah the food and wine prescribed for her by the doctor. On several occasions during 1861–3 he showed violence towards her. The level of violence escalated during 1866–7 and soon he was threatening to kill her with a knife. On diverse occasions during the marriage he committed adultery. In August 1873 he was living, cohabiting and frequently committing adultery with a female at No. 40 rue Chaeaudun in Paris. Sarah then took the matter to the court and filed for divorce on 31 July 1874. The court heard oral evidence from witnesses and had Madame Virbine Capitane, William Barnet's mistress, examined in Paris. Barnet presented a puny defence and after the hearing on 30 January 1875 Sarah was granted a divorce, which became absolute on 3 August 1875.[5]

Divorce was a great social stigma at that time, and on 4 March 1875 Sarah reverted to her maiden name by deed poll, and after this she is referred to as Mrs Sarah Phillips. She slowly re-entered society, hosting parties for her father, and from 1885 she had her own establishment at 17 Grosvenor Street. Henry and Sarah must have been acquainted for a number of years, meeting in her father's house and later as members of the same Primrose

League habitation, and two of her nieces were bridesmaids at the wedding of Henry's eldest daughter. Henry de Worms was granted a permanent divorce from his first wife on 18 January 1887 and on 25 January he married Sarah Phillips in a quiet civil ceremony.[6]

Fin de Siècle

The harsh rules which forbade the innocent female party in a divorce suit from being presented at Court were relaxed in time for the Queen's Golden Jubilee of 1887. Now the newly married Baroness Henry de Worms could be fully reinstated in society and presented to the Queen at a drawing-room party by her sister-in-law, Mrs G. Faudel-Phillips. This second marriage proved highly successful because both husband and wife had similar ideas on how a rich gentleman should behave in order to become both a swell (spending lavishly on clothes and entertainment) and a serious politician.[7]

A new bride requires a suitable house, and the pair bought the lease on 42 Grosvenor Place, which faces the gardens of Buckingham Palace. It was one of a group of town houses with party walls and little or no garden. The property was described as follows:

Built by Cubitt, and containing 10 cheerful and airy bed and dressing rooms on the upper floors, double drawing room and boudoir on the first floor, entrance and inner halls, dining room, library and excellent third room on the ground floor, and unusually good domestic offices in the basement. At the rear is the capital stabling, 42 Dorset Mews, comprising four stalls, double coach house, large harness room, men's rooms, loft etc.[8]

The *New York Times* reported that 'Baron Henry de Worms is furnishing a handsome house in Grosvenor Place at great cost and where hospitality is to be shown on a grand scale'. The stage was thus set for festivities during *la belle époque*.[9] The Worms family remained at Grosvenor Place until Henry's death, and Sarah continued to live there for some years afterwards. During 1917 the house became a club for American nurses, when it was described as having substantial comforts with ornate frescoed ceilings in the drawing room, lounge and dining room.[10] The area suffered war damage during the 1940s, and later the whole block of 36–42 Grosvenor Place was rebuilt, first to become Hobart House, the offices of British Coal, and presently to be a group of offices numbered 40 Grosvenor Place. Dorset Mews, which was the entrance to the stables, is now a gated residential area.

In the last decades of the nineteenth century, many men with money were intent on becoming a swell. The compulsion was so great for some that they bankrupted themselves in the process. Besides the swells there were 'great swells' with enormous amounts of money, who could put on fabulous entertainment, and the world of politics had some of these. Lord Hartington, a prominent member of the Liberal Party in the 1880s, was known for his somewhat Bohemian life style; he became Duke of Devonshire in 1891 and moved to the House of Lords, where he developed into a great swell. He followed the practice of the previous duke, hosting a reception at the beginning of a parliamentary session at Devonshire House in Piccadilly to which large numbers of guests, including Baron and Baroness Henry de Worms, were invited. To celebrate the Diamond Jubilee of Queen Victoria in 1897, the Devonshires gave a fancy dress ball for 3,000 guests. Clearly, for the great swell it was vital to have a fashionable house in London. Alfred de Rothschild and Ferdinand de Rothschild each had a large residence adjacent to Devonshire house on Piccadilly where they outdid each other in fantastic excess. The two Rothschilds, along with other immensely rich friends of the Prince of Wales, became known as the Marlborough House Set, entertaining the Prince as well as being frequent guests in his house.[11]

The entertainment that Salisbury offered the Shah of Persia during a state visit in 1889 illustrates the vital accoutrement of a great swell: a substantial country house. The Shah was given a reception at Buckingham Palace and later entertained by the Marquis of Salisbury at Hatfield House. His secretary, Prince Malcom Kahn (1832–1908), who had also been on the previous visit when the Shah had dealings with the Anglo-Jewish Association, accompanied him. A dinner party which included the Shah and the Prince of Wales travelled from London to Hatfield House by special train on the Sunday afternoon and stayed overnight. Lunch with members of the diplomatic corps, ferried by special train, was held on the Monday and during the same afternoon the Marquis held a reception for over 2,000 guests, who had travelled to Hatfield station in a convoy of special trains, to continue by horse-drawn carriage. Later the guests returned to London by special trains. The Shah continued his visit by train to Earl Brownlow for dinner and an evening reception. On Tuesday he had lunch with Alfred de Rothschild at Halton and dinner with Ferdinand de Rothschild at Waddleston, where he stayed overnight. At this time Henry's father-in-law was seriously ill (he died in October), so Sarah did not attend the festivities. Henry stayed in London and was present only at the reception in Buckingham Palace. There was the possibility of an important division in the House of Commons and the special train, always kept in readiness at Hatfield for the use of Salisbury, was to be used if the MPs were recalled to Parliament by telegram to take part in a division.[12]

Henry de Worms began to acquire a reputation among the satirical press for giving lavish entertainment and Dr Clark (MP for Caithness), together with Mr Conybeare (MP for Cornwall, Camborne), took an opportunity to ask in Parliament for an explanation of excessive expenditure by the Northern Lights Commission in Edinburgh. On the 15 January 1887 this body had spent £70.50 on 47 dinners and desserts plus 100 guineas on wines and spirits and an explanation was demanded from the secretary to the Board of Trade. These exchanges sparked a *Punch* cartoon showing a very rotund figure identifiable by his moustache as Henry de Worms. A reporter from that magazine remarked that the secretary to the Board of Trade (Henry de Worms) was heard to exclaim in languid terms 'that's the diet for Worms'. The official report of proceedings indicates only that Henry referred this matter to a committee for consideration.[13]

Soon after their marriage, Baron and Baroness Henry de Worms had the opportunity to enter the ranks of the swells by hosting a dinner for the delegates to the sugar bounties conference. Their new house at 42 Grosvenor Place was used for the occasion and the rooms were decorated with red and white camellias – this in December – while the band of the Grenadier Guards played for the occasion. Later Henry and his wife toured European capitals, Henry seeking support for the ideas of the convention. Some ten years after the conference and its lavish entertainment, General Wolseley remarked that he had just had lunch with Henry and his wife – 'a banquet prepared by a cook who ought to have the Garter'[14]

Lord Onslow, then parliamentary under-secretary for the colonies, was one of the guests at Grosvenor Place for the sugar conference dinner. He must have been very impressed by the cuisine, for three years later, when Governor General of New Zealand, he sent a supply of frozen sheep over to six gentlemen in London who were known to have first-class cooks, for their opinion of the meat. Head of this list was Baron Henry de Worms, followed by the Earl of Rosebery, later the Liberal prime minister, and at the bottom of the list, the French ambassador. Henry was rapidly being recognised as a swell. After the meat had been consumed, Henry, now under-secretary for the colonies, replied that 'we found it quite excellent. The freezing did not hurt it in the least in fact the greatest epicure would fail to discern that it was not home grown'.[15]

The negotiations over the sugar convention projected Henry de Worms into public view and he was elected to Fellowship of the Royal Society on 4 April 1889 as a 'member of the privileged class' – he possessed no scientific qualifications for this honour. The proposal form was signed from personal knowledge by four eminent members of the Society: G.C. Stokes (1819–1903), Professor of Mathematics at Cambridge and then president of the Royal Society; John Evans (1823–1908), an archaeologist and the treasurer of the Royal Society; J.D. Hooker, director of the Royal Botanical Gardens, Kew, and a former president of the Royal Society; and Michael Foster (1836–1907), Professor of Physiology at Cambridge and then one of the secretaries of the Royal Society.[16]

The newly married couple needed a place to retire to from London during the parliamentary recess, and so they leased a house, The Lodge, Augusta Gardens, in Folkestone. Augusta Gardens exists today largely unchanged from the Victorian period, when it was a terrace of four-storeyed houses each with a basement, The Lodge is now numbered 37; it faces the sea across a stretch of communal lawn.[17] Such an address was, however, not suitable for a Tory grandee and minister of the Crown who wished to be a great swell. He needed both a residence in town and a country seat. Henry's brother George, neither a grandee nor aiming to be a swell, had acquired Milton Park, Egham, and also kept a house on Park Crescent in London.

The Rothschilds boasted two great swells. Nathan of the English branch kept a house on Piccadilly and acquired an estate near Tring, Hertfordshire. Ferdinand of the Austrian branch, who had married a sister of Nathan and became a British subject, also lived on Piccadilly and constructed a house at Waddleston, Buckinghamshire. So when the lease on Henley Park in Surrey was advertised in December 1889, Henry de Worms acquired it from the owner, Henry Halsey. This house fulfilled all his requirements, with rooms for guests, land for formal gardens, flower and vegetable production, an area for shooting, and being close to Brookwood station for trains to London.

Henley Park began in the Middle Ages as a hunting lodge and it had gradually been converted over the years to a gentleman's residence. Henry de Worms fitted out the building in a grand manner. His business interests, together with the inheritance from his father, paid for the conversion. The work occupied seven months, during which time a new wing was constructed to accommodate a ballroom and the building was fitted with electric lighting, the current being supplied by 54 lead-acid accumulators placed in series and recharged from a 15hp steam engine and dynamo. The Palais Todesco was also fitted with electric lighting at about the same time. The expert on this type of installation in London was David Lionel Salomons (1851–1925), Henry's step-cousin.[18] The expert in Vienna was Henry's nephew, Robert von Lieben. Henley Park was also fitted with a furnace and boiler for hot water and central heating. On the second floor was a suite for the principal guest, as well as seven further bedrooms and three other bathrooms. The whole complex had fifteen servants' bedrooms.

The house was lavishly decorated and soon used to display the artwork and china that Henry inherited on the death of his uncle, George Samuel (1804–1893). Paintings, some expensive originals and some copies, hung on the walls. Guests encountered a Frans Hals portrait in the entrance hall, probably a copy of the *Laughing Cavalier*, from where they would continue across oak floors past cupboards of priceless Sèvres china and into the ballroom, also serving as a drawing room, and containing a bust of George Samuel. From there, guests were ushered into the dining room, which could seat fifty. Henry was known to boast that the kitchens could cope with a total of 140 guests and servants. The gardens could supply loads of flowers for decoration, along with fruit and vegetables, including asparagus, strawberries and exotic fruits in season. In keeping with Victorian custom, there was an orchid house.[19]

Baron and Baroness Henry de Worms took up residence in August 1890, returning to their London residence while Parliament was in session. Their first task in the county was to gain the acquaintance of local landowners, and what better place for this than to attend a meeting of the local Chiddingfold hunt in November? A future meeting of the hunt was scheduled for April 1891 at Henley Park, where Henry and his wife greeted all their guests on arrival and provided them with an excellent breakfast, after which the hunting party set off around the local countryside. Over that weekend there was also a small house party of gentry from London.[20]

The large areas of heath and woodland attached to the Henley Park estate were devoted to pheasant rearing for the shooting season. Rifle shooting had been an old hobby of Henry, and Sarah also was a good shot, so each season saw shooting parties assembled at Henley Park. Selected guests stayed at Henley Park for some days while others were invited to join them for dinner in the evenings. Shooting rights were leased on a yearly basis from Lord Onslow over a large area of agricultural as well as heath land to the east. The inhabitants of the nearby town of Guildford showed their respect for Henry by electing him president of the District Rifle and Pistol Club when it was formed in 1900. He opened the club's new range and Sarah had the honour of firing the first shot.[21]

A swell gave lavish entertainment, but if he wished to become a great swell he had to attract royalty, preferably British royalty. Members of royalty were entertained at Grosvenor Place, beginning with the King and Queen of the Belgians, whom Henry knew from the sugar bounties excursions. Lord Knutsford, secretary of state for the colonies, was also included in this luncheon party.²² The Duke of Cambridge (1819–1904), whom Henry had known since 1881 from being a member of the Patriotic Fund, became a frequent visitor; he was the Queen's uncle. Two persons of distinction had a residence in the neighbourhood of Henley Park: the Duke of Connaught (1850–1942), third son of Queen Victoria, lived at Bagshot Park, while the Empress Eugénie (1826–1920), widow of Napoleon III, resided at Farnborough Hall. These also became frequent visitors and there were reciprocal visits. Friendship with the empress led to an acquaintance with her nephew, Prince Victor Napoleon (1862–1926), titular Emperor Napoleon V, and he was entertained both at Henley Park and in London.

The Infanta Eulalia (1864–1958), aunt of the King Alfonso XIII of Spain, formed a friendship with the Duke of Connaught and became a yearly visitor to Bagshot Park. She had moved with her mother to Paris after the Spanish revolution of 1868, returning to Madrid in 1886 when her newly born nephew was declared king. Eulalia regarded the Spanish court as reactionary and whenever possible left Madrid. She stayed at Windsor Castle for the Golden Jubilee of Queen Victoria and became friendly with the Queen's youngest daughter the Marchioness of Lorne, later Duchess of Argyll. Yearly invitations then followed from the marchioness, the Duke of Connaught and the Empress Eugénie. Through these connections the Infanta became great friends of Henry and Sarah de Worms. Eulalia paid a long visit when Henry's elevation to the House of Lords was announced, staying both in Grosvenor Place and at Henley Park. Henry was now president of the Guildford Agricultural Association and the house party from Henley Park visited the Guildford Agricultural Show in style. Sarah, Eulalia, the Marchioness of Lorne and the Empress Eugénie, all of whom thought women should be allowed to have a voice of their own, remained friends for life.²³

Sarah gave regular Wednesday afternoon parties at Grosvenor Place in the season. This was the type of party where eligible daughters could meet prospective suitors. Elegant food was served while musicians and singers entertained. Henry's connection with the Colonial Office made it possible to invite members of the diplomatic corps as well as aristocratic friends and celebrities, such as Sir Arthur Sullivan and Henry Morton Stanley, for more elaborate dinners. For these special meals it was customary to invite a celebrity and one person who could give musical entertainment after dinner; there should also be equal numbers of men and women. After 1890 Eschoffier, the head chef at the newly constructed Savoy Hotel in London, set the standard for elegant meals. The meals in private houses would have many courses and the menu was written in French. It was acceptable for a guest to pass on certain courses according to his or her taste.²⁴

Evening dinners, especially in the season, were followed by a reception for more guests. Grosvenor Place, with its dining room and large first-floor sitting room, was well suited for such entertainment and it was lavishly decorated with flowers from Henley Park gardens. There must have been lively conversation, probably in French, when Henry invited two who had been his opponents during his period with the Anglo-Jewish Association: Prince Malcom Kahn, previously secretary to the Shah of Persia, was now Persian ambassador in London, while Prince Ion Ghica, the defender of the position of the Romanian government over the Jewish question, was now the Romanian ambassador.

Lord Wolseley, Commander in Chief, stayed at Henley Park on several occasions when army manoeuvres were in progress over the heathland between Pirbright and Aldershot. The frequent letters he wrote to his wife are full of praise for the kindness of his hosts. He described a visit to Guildford when Lady Pirbright was dressed in bright colours: 'no bird of paradise, no cockatoo or parrot with a tail like a carrot, ever equalled her in brilliancy and variety of colouring' – an opinion whose accuracy is fully confirmed by the dress she wore at the unveiling of the Little Girl Statue. She was well known in the town, where everyone greeted her. Elaborate dinners were served each night, accompanied by the finest wines, and with as many as twenty guests. Lord Wolseley remarked on the pictures, the china and the other works of art with which the house was filled, as well as on the standard of the cookery and the exquisite wines that were not to be surpassed. Other Army personnel entertained at Henley Park included Sir Evelyn Wood (1838–1919) and General H. Trotter (1844–1905) of the Grenadier Guards, the general officer commanding the home district. Trotter later became an adversary of Lord Pirbright over the Bisley homes affair, when Army officers disagreed with Pirbright on how to accommodate disabled soldiers from the Boer War. Evelyn Wood had been given the Victoria Cross for his action during the Indian Mutiny and was commander of the Aldershot garrison. He was promoted to field marshal in 1903.[25]

Sarah, Baroness Henry de Worms, became famous for the amount and value of the jewellery she wore. In the early years of this marriage she was the most conspicuous figure in the London drawing rooms, blazing with diamonds and with a priceless necklace, earrings, bracelets and hair adornment. The Parisian paper *Le Matin* described her as 'one of the most distinguished ladies of the United Kingdom, without doubt one of the best dressed'. In later years, as Lady Pirbright, she was known for her necklace of evenly matched pearls which, if hung at full length, stretched from her neck almost to the ground, and which she wore at the state opening of Parliament by Edward VII on 14 February 1901. She had a second, smaller necklace made from pearls the size of hazelnuts. These were natural pearls, for cultured pearls were not marketed before 1917.[26]

The dresses and jewels Lady Pirbright wore for the coronation of Edward VII reached the heights of extravagance. The coronation was first arranged for 26 June 1902, and at a prior reception in Buckingham Palace she wore a white satin dress with a train of white satin lined with mauve satin and another train of black Chantilly lace. Plumes of mauve and white feathers each with a diamond ornament in the centre were placed down each side. Her jewels consisted of a large girdle of diamonds and sapphires with a stomacher and tiara to correspond and the famous necklace of pearls. Edward later contracted appendicitis and the coronation had to be postponed to 9 August. Lord Pirbright attended the coronation itself in robes, and Lady Pirbright wore an undergarment of cloth of gold overlaid by a dress of old English point lace. The same girdle, stomacher and tiara were worn and the chain of pearls was converted to a necklace of sixteen rows.[27]

All of this show was extremely expensive, and an idea of the costs to Lord Pirbright can be gleaned looking at two well-known examples from the *fin de siècle*. Ernest Cassel (1852–1921) was the financial advisor of Edward, Prince of Wales. On one occasion the Prince's mistress, Alice Keppel, ran up a dress bill of £5,000, which Cassel paid.[28] The second example is the string of matching pearls, as long as the one worn by Lady Pirbright, which the French jeweller Pierre Cartier used in 1917 to buy premises for his firm on New York's Fifth Avenue.[29] Henry Lord Pirbrght must have found the large bequest from his uncle George Samuel very useful when buying dresses and ornaments for his wife.

Visitors to Henley Park from the neighbourhood could travel by coach or car – either their own or one sent by the host. Important visitors from London arrived by special train at Brookwood station, where Lord Pirbright met them and conducted them through the village in his carriage. Crowds assembled to cheer the visitors, and for royalty the Vicar, the Reverend Dunn, gave permission for the church bells to be rung. Soon the down platform at the station was considered not to be suitable for the use of royalty because to reach the station yard and the transport laid on to Henley Park, visitors had to cross the railway tracks by a footbridge. Hence the railway company changed its method of working for these occasions and the special train was shunted onto the up line and stopped at the eastern end of the up platform. The railway had only two tracks, so normal scheduled trains were halted for a short time while this manoeuvre was executed. A special ramp, which is still visible, was constructed for the visitor to descend to the station yard avoiding the flight of steps which ordinary passengers used. On very grand occasions this ramp was covered in red carpet. The old down platform was demolished and moved in 1903 when the railway was extended to four tracks.[30]

The visit of Helena, Princess Christian of Schleswig-Holstein (1846–1923), a daughter of Queen Victoria, to Henley Park in May 1899 caused great excitement. The special station ramp was constructed for this visit. Lord Pirbright accompanied her by special train from London Waterloo station. Flagpoles lined the whole route from Brookwood station through Pirbright village to Henley Park, where the house was filled with exotic flowers and the party was greeted by a string band of the Royal Lancashire Fusiliers playing the national anthem. The dining room had been enlarged and heightened for the occasion and was set for fifty guests, each of whom was given a buttonhole of carnations and gardenias. Guests included local dignitaries, villagers and the Reverend R.C.E. Heyle, chaplain to the Bishop of Winchester. The bishop could not attend and sent his apologies. The menu for this occasion has been preserved, and was as follows:

DÉJEUNER
Escallopes de Truite au Vin du Rhin
Cendrillons de Soles à la Princesse
Poulets Printemps à la Chevalier
Cotelettes d'Agneau aux petits Pois
Cailles aux Cressons
Boeuf rôti froid à l'Anglaise
Salade
Asperges
Suédoise de Fraises Celestine
Bombe glacée Andalouse

Unfortunately the wine list was not preserved. All the vegetables and fruit came from Henley Park gardens. The band of the Royal Lancashire Fusiliers played during the meal. Later, Princess Christian planted a Wellingtonia and left to open the village hall in Pirbright.[31]

In order to join the ranks of the great swells, Henry had to secure a visit from the Prince of Wales, and this he achieved on Tuesday, 4 December 1900. The Prince arrived at Brookwood station by special train and used the new ramp to descend from the platform, before entering Lord Pirbright's carriage. The carriage had been fitted with electric light powered by accumulators and was brilliantly lit so that all could see. They drove through the village, which was decorated with Chinese lanterns and on to Henley Park, where a party of nineteen sat down to dinner. The entire house was filled with flowers and foliage and a fresh table decoration was prepared for each day of the three-day visit. One object of the visit was to form a shooting party over the grounds, but the following day saw a rainstorm, which lasted all day. Another Wellingtonia was planted in the grounds and the party had expanded to twenty-two for dinner that evening. On the Thursday Prince Edward and his host set out to shoot and bagged nearly 500 brace of pheasant. The Prince then left for Brookwood station at about 1.30 p.m. in an open carriage, accompanied by Lord and Lady Pirbright

Visits on this scale were expensive, but Lord Pirbright was well able to bear the costs. At his death, his estate was proved at around £350,000, which has to be multiplied by a factor of around one hundred to compensate for the rise in the price index since that time.[32]

8

Baron Pirbright of Pirbright

Der Mensch fangt erst beim Baron an.
[A man only begins to be a man when he is a Baron]

Prince zu Windisch-Grätz (translated by H. de Worms)

Count Beust remembered this remark made by Prince zu Windisch-Grätz during a conversation with Henry Worms. Substitute the word Baron with its equivalent in traditional German, *Freiherr* (translated as Freeman), and the phrase becomes a pun. Windisch-Grätz (1787–1862) was the arch-Conservative Field Marshal of Austria who violently suppressed the revolutions of 1848 in Vienna, Prague and Budapest. In his view, freemen had to maintain the Conservative system. Henry Worms was an Intelligent Tory and a freeman who wished to bridge the gap between classes in society and to promote education so that all could participate in the prosperity of the country.[1]

Two Village Lords

Henry, after his second marriage, began to look for a country estate to complement his newly acquired London town house, and in 1890 he leased Henley Park near the village of Pirbright from the owner, Henry Joseph Tenison Halsey. The Halsey family had bought the title of Lord of the Manor of Pirbright in 1784, along with what remained of the medieval lands of the manor and the right to present a priest to the living of St Michael and All Angels Church in the village. Their estate included Henley Park and most of the village of Pirbright. The first Henry Halsey (1745–1807) entailed the estate to the eldest son in succession and arranged to construct a mortuary chapel on the north side of the church for family use. He clearly intended his family to live in the district for ever. When in 1877 the chapel became full his son, Henry William R.W. Halsey (1801–1885), had remains buried within the walls, the floor cemented over, and a section of the churchyard reserved for other members of the Halsey family. The mortuary chapel area is now the church vestry.[2]

Henry Halsey's arrangements proved defective, for Henry William's son Henry Halsey (1825–1869) was a wastrel who lived for most of his life in New York. His son, Henry Joseph Tenison Halsey (1857–1937), was brought up in that city by strangers, hardly knowing his immediate family, until, as the heir, he was brought to England in 1880 and assigned power over the family estates. He stayed long enough to raise a mortgage and left for New York, where he married and had one child, a daughter. Edward Joseph Halsey (1836–1905), a younger son of Henry William Halsey, lived in the village between 1872 and 1886, carrying out duties on behalf of his father, who was now very infirm. The Halsey family built some cottages in the village and organised a fête for the Golden Jubilee of Queen Victoria in 1887, giving a medal to each child and to all the ladies of the village. Edward Halsey and his wife were active in local society. On his departure from the village, the residents presented him with a silver tankard. Edward Halsey continued a link with the district and served as chairman of the Surrey County Council from 1893 until his death twelve years later.[3]

Henry J.T. Halsey returned to Britain in 1886 and took over the estate. His only interest in it was as a source of money, which he spent on living in Edinburgh and later in London. A manager was employed to collect the rents. When Henry de Worms moved into Henley Park he quietly filled the vacuum created in Pirbright society by the absence of the Lord of the Manor.

It seems probable that Henry de Worms began to covet the title of Lord Pirbright from some point in 1894, and to obtain it he needed to own land in the village. He bought various properties in the vicinity of Henley Park and in early 1895 had acquired land in and about the village of Pirbright with a view to building model cottages. He had money from his business interests and this sum had been immensely increased by the huge bequest from his uncle, George Samuel.[4]

The Liberal Party had made the introduction of district and parish councils part of its election programme for 1892, and a Local Government Act was passed in 1894 which established secular parish councils, replacing the select vestries that had been associated with the Church. When these councils were set up, Baron Henry de Worms refused the offer of a post on Normandy Parish Council, the district in which Henley Park lies, citing pressure of work in Parliament.[5] Shortly afterwards, however, he showed no hesitation in becoming a member of Pirbright Parish Council, regardless of his duties in London. This council held its first meeting on 9 January 1895, when Henry de Worms was elected chairman, a post he filled until his death.[6]

After the fall of Lord Rosebery's Liberal government on 21 June 1895, events towards the fulfilment of Henry's ambition for a title moved fast. Rumours began that Henry would be offered a peerage if a Conservative government was elected, and when Salisbury became prime minister he duly made the offer. Henry's preference for the title of Lord Pirbright was mentioned in the press and Henry Halsey woke up to a serious situation. As Lord of the Manor of Pirbright and patron of the living of Pirbright, he had strong grounds for objection. He maintained that he was by far the largest landowner in the village with which the Halsey family had been identified for nearly two hundred years. The Attorney General countered that lordship of a manor gave the owner no right to reservation of the name of the manor for prospective use in the event of his being raised to the peerage. Since Henry de Worms held freehold land amounting to about one hundred and fifty acres in the village, he was allowed to take the title. The objection from Halsey that this was only a small acreage was overruled by the Attorney General, who noted that the greater part of the manor of Pirbright was the property of the Crown. This government land had the most impoverished soils; it had been purchased from the Halseys by the War Department in 1875 and converted to an army training area with barracks. It had a railway connection at Bisley Camp and began immediately north of the village green.[7]

Henry de Worms was created Baron Pirbright of Pirbright in December 1895, and on 14 December the village welcomed him at a meeting in the school. The Reverend Dunn, the vicar, presented an illuminated congratulatory address to Lord and Lady Pirbright which remembered their many acts of kindness since residing at Henley Park, 'alleviating the sufferings and wants of the less fortunate of the inhabitants'. In his reply Lord Pirbright noted that 'where the privileges of property existed there the responsibilities and obligations ought to be'. He did not see why old traditions should prevent the development of that village into what might be in some years' time a prosperous town. He promised to do all he could to bring the benefits of modern science, modern education and modern improvements to bear upon the property he had recently acquired. Finally he announced that he would donate an organ to the church, the funds so far collected of around £101 for this purpose to be applied to refurbishing the church bells. That Christmas, Lady Pirbright provided ferns, poinsettias and chrysanthemums for decorating the church and it was generally agreed that the church had never looked so beautiful. The Bishop of Winchester dedicated this organ on 9 June 1896 and afterwards Lord and Lady Pirbright gave a luncheon at Henley Park for the Bishop, the officiating clergy, the High Sheriff and members of Pirbright Parish Council.[8]

Henry de Worms, now Lord Pirbright, adopted the same crest and motto that his father had when he was made an Austrian baron. The shield is quartered with a German eagle and a golden key (for finance) and bears a central motif of a hand grasping three arrows. It is surmounted by a British baron's coronet and above that the coronet of an Austrian noble with either five silver points or five ostrich feathers, all of this supported by two beasts.[9]

One section of Henry de Worms' land in Pirbright was that given to the select vestry in much earlier times to be held as a charity for the benefit of parishioners, and subsequently put up for sale, freehold, in 1865. Pirbright Parish Council records disposal of the money from this sale in a minute of 1895. The local builder James Faggetter (1839–1918) had acquired much of this land but by 1895 was thinking to retire. He had built a cottage for himself with an adjacent builder's yard, other cottages around Pirbright Green and in a street known as The Gardens, together with cottages on other building land now known as Fox Corner. Henry de Worms acquired most of James Faggetter's property and free land in 1895. There were further acquisitions in 1896 and 1897, all from Pirbright residents.[10]

Not all the village inhabitants approved of Henry Lord Pirbright, and Ross Lowis Mangles (1833–1905), who was a member of the District Council, caused an argument in the autumn of 1896. Mangles was born in Calcutta and spent his life as a magistrate in India, where actions during the Indian Mutiny had gained him the Victoria Cross. The family of his wife, Henrietta Anne (neé Molyneux), lived at Loseley Park near Guildford, so he retired to nearby Pirbright. He disputed Henry's behaviour in blocking a supposed right of way, probably on Stamford Common, which Henry had recently bought. The various arguments over this were presented at a public meeting of the village attended by Mangles, Henry and his wife. Here Henry spoke in brilliant adversarial style to establish that Mangles was puffing up the objection from only one person over the loss of a vague track across the heath. There was now a good road to walk along and the old track only saved a few yards on the walk from south of the village to the station at Brookwood. Henry summed up his feelings as follows: 'If the District Council considered that he [Henry] was going to allow himself to be bullied into taking a position he knew was not right, and allow questions of personal spite to be put forward as matters of public interest, then all he could say was that they were very much mistaken, and he knew enough of the fairness of the people of Pirbright to know that he should have their fullest approval to any action he might take.' The meeting completely rejected Ross Mangles' arguments. It seems that Henry thought Mangles was fighting a battle on behalf of local 'old' landlords against the new proprietors.[11]

Intelligent Toryism, as practised by Henry de Worms, questioned the immutable ordering of estate, and took the view that, through work and intelligence, man could improve his position. When Henry rejected the offer from Normandy Parish Council he gave them one piece of advice: 'There is, in my judgement, one especial object to which the Councils may with advantage address themselves, and that is the promotion of healthier dwellings for the poor, and generally in an earnest endeavour to remove the appalling ignorance which too commonly prevails in regard to sanitation.' Now, as Lord Pirbright, he put money into this view and set about improving Pirbright village. He was probably very much influenced by the actions of his father-in-law, Eduard von Todesco, who in 1858, together with Moritz von Todesco, had taken over the cotton factory of Marienthal in the commune of Gramatneusiedl near Vienna. Over the years to 1893 they established houses for the workers, a factory restaurant, a hospital with a pharmacy, baths, showers and a Turkish bath.[12]

A few industrialists in later-nineteenth-century Britain with similar views also sought to improve accommodation for workers. Across the river Mersey from Henry de Worms' Liverpool constituency of East Toxteth, the Lever brothers began to build the model village of Port Sunlight for workers at their soap factory, while south of Birmingham the Cadbury family constructed the village of Bournville for workers in the chocolate factory. These had good housing for workers to rent, along with schools, shops, a cottage hospital and other amenities. Other Tory landowners sought to improve the living conditions of their estate workers, and Lord Salisbury was one of these; he improved the town of Hatfield and the estate around. Some twenty years previously, Henry de Worms had been on the council of the Metropolitan Artisans and Labourers Dwellings Association Ltd., which built four-storeyed blocks of tenement buildings (demolished in 1983) on Battersea Park Road for occupation by families. He could see that the future for agriculture in Pirbright was not bright because of the poor soil, and sought to build a mixture of accommodation in the village, some for workers and some for middle management. These buildings were for rent and not tied to a particular occupation.[13]

The first phase of Lord Pirbright's plan was the construction of solid two-storeyed workers' houses, each with a bathroom. His views are further expressed in a letter, written in 1900, to Pirbright Parish Council:

Now we are confronted with the indisputable fact that the exodus from the country to the town has at length overwhelmed the latter and, paralysing its resources, has produced the gravest evils. It will be apparent to all thoughtful persons that it is in a great measure to our own villages we must look to secure the relief and readjustment that are urgently required. I am convinced this is especially the case in regard to the provision of wholesome dwellings, for although it may not be immediately practicable to provide work in rural parishes for the multitude which it is desirable to withdraw from the towns, at any rate it would assist to mitigate the prevalent evils if easier facilities existed for those who are occupied in the towns to have their habitation in the country. Holding to these views I am highly gratified to feel that Pirbright is being developed in this direction. I believe it has a prosperous future before it, both on account of its proximity to London and as a military centre.[14]

The first to be built were several houses in The Gardens, finished in 1895–6, and all built on the freehold land that had been sold by the select vestry in 1865. The houses at Fox Corner, including a post office, soon followed, and during 1896 to 1898 more houses were constructed around the village, including those now forming Pirbright Terrace, the additional land being bought in stages. A post office and shops also appeared on the village green. Billboards advertising houses to let appeared on some of the building sites. Lord Pirbright, proud of his work, had commemorative earthenware plaques placed on these houses, so the sequence of building can easily be seen. Plaques begin with W 1895, then, after Henry's elevation to the British peerage, P with a date, and finally, after 1897, an undated letter P. A number of outlying houses were also constructed. The village houses are mostly according to the same plan – two-storey red brick with a dormer window, tiled in dark brown and facing the road. When the whole freehold estate was put up for sale in 1916, after the death of Lady Pirbright, it produced a gross income of about £1,190 per year from around 50 houses to let.[15]

Unfortunately the W plaques display an unpardonable error. The Austrian coronet is that of a full baron – a circlet surmounted by seven silver balls or feathers, and this is what these plaques display. As the younger son, Henry was only a nobleman and thus entitled to a coronet with only five silver balls or feathers. Plaques erected around the village after 1896 do, however, display the correct coronet. The same error had first been made when Henry de Worms designed his headed notepaper, bearing an HW cipher surmounted by a coronet with seven silver balls, after he acquired the Austrian title. Probably the College of Heralds pointed out this error during the design of his British armorial bearings.

Henry J.T. Halsey proved to be very obstructive regarding Lord Pirbright's plan for improving village amenities. The antagonism, which had begun over the question of the title, was further fuelled by frequent reports in the society columns of London newspapers of Lord Pirbright's intention 'to stay for some time at his estate in Pirbright'. An important part of the plan was to construct a recreation facility on the green, which for a long time had been set aside for ball games and village fairs. Green House and its orchard, which abutted the green, were on freehold land and had been willed to Elizabeth Collyer (née Faggetter) by her husband, with James Faggetter as trustee. This property was sold to James Faggetter's son on 25 March 1897 and then conveyed by endorsement to Lord Pirbright on 24 April 1897. This roundabout transfer was probably constructed to avoid irrelevant objections being raised by Henry Halsey. Green House and its orchard were eventually developed into the village hall and children's playground.[16]

A small section of garden at Green House was developed in 1897 as a public drinking fountain to commemorate the Diamond Jubilee of Queen Victoria. The fountain had a tap providing drinking water and is surmounted by a little girl statue where the girl is some one and a half metres high and depicted as standing while reading a book. Lord Pirbright, after much thought, had bought this statue in Paris. At the base of the statue is a small drinking bowl for dogs. It was unveiled on 30 June 1897 on the occasion of a fête given by Lord and Lady Pirbright to the villagers in commemoration of the Jubilee. The village was gaily decorated for this occasion and two army bands provided music. A large marquee had been erected on land belonging to Lord Pirbright in the Green House grounds; some 900 sat down to dinner in it, including 100 guests from neighbouring Bisley. The party from Henley Park included Lord and Lady Pirbright, Faudel-Phillips relatives and Mrs. Dunn, who appeared as the dinner was concluding. The Vicar, the Reverend Dunn, was not present on medical grounds. Sports for the children came after dinner, and at 6 p.m. Lady Pirbright unveiled the drinking fountain. A display of fireworks concluded the festivities.[17]

This fountain was formally given to the parish council on 21 July 1897. The Halsey family assumed that it had been erected on a portion of the wastes of the Manor of Pirbright without the licence of the Lord of the Manor, and immediately sent a letter of objection to the parish council. To this, Lord Pirbright tartly replied that 'the fountain is built on a piece of the garden of Collyer's cottage which belongs to me', and the correspondence was closed.[18]

Two Village Priests

When the Halsey family bought the Manor of Pirbright they also acquired the advowson of the parish church, making the Lord of the Manor solely responsible for paying the stipend and choosing the priest, who was then appointed for life by the Bishop of Winchester; the Halseys retained this right until 1910.[19] Henry Dunn (1846–1898), rector 1889–1898, was much respected by his parishioners and became a good friend of Lord Pirbright. When he was unable to continue through ill health, Lord Pirbright himself paid the stipend of a replacement clergyman until Dunn died. Alfred Krauss (1849–1925) was then appointed for life. Krauss was born in Manchester to English parents; his grandfather had migrated there from Germany because of the cotton trade and stayed. Alfred's father was active in St Saviour's Church in Chorlton-upon-Medlock and married a girl from Manchester. Alfred was educated in the north of England and entered the theological college in Birkenhead, becoming ordained in 1875. He served in Canada during 1890–91, then returned to England and after a period in Dorset, was inducted on 20 October 1898 as vicar of Pirbright. Very few of the villagers had travelled far in those days, so with his Lancashire accent he must have seemed to them a foreigner. Very soon there was friction between him and his parishioners, and also between him and Lord Pirbright.[20]

Henry de Worms began a custom at Christmas of treating the Pirbright schoolchildren to games followed by a good tea. Henry Halsey had built the school in 1871. It continued as a voluntary school under Church control until 1885, when the Halsey family withdrew financial support. Administration of the school buildings, which belonged to the Church, was then transferred to a management board, while control of staff and teaching was in the hands of the Pirbright School Board, elected under the provisions of the 1870 Education Act. The school board could raise funds through the rates, it received a per capita income from the state, and it controlled the curriculum. By agreement, a school management board owned the buildings and had use of them outside school hours, but had no source of income. Henry Dunn was chairman of the school board, and as vicar he was ex officio chairman of the management board.

Henry de Worms' Christmas party for schoolchildren was open to all children of any denomination residing in the village. The villagers regarded it as Lord Pirbright's Party and it passed off well until December 1898. During that year Alfred Krauss had been appointed as vicar, but he did not replace Dunn on the school board. When Lord Pirbright applied ahead of time for use of the school buildings on Thursday 29 December, in the same fashion as for previous years, the board granted permission on 19 December. No one thought to inform Alfred Krauss, who as chairman of the management board had control of the buildings after school hours. There must have been very little spontaneous communication between the vicar and his congregation.

When Krauss became aware of the intended party he wrote to Lord Pirbright on 22 December, saying that 'in view of the Agreement for the Transfer of Schools in 1885, the Board have no permission which can only be granted by the Managers'. It was impossible, he said, to convene a meeting of the management board at such short notice. Of the six managers, five resided in Pirbright and the sixth was Edward Halsey, now chairman of Surrey County Council. When Krauss did agree on 27 December for this party on one occasion only, the arrangements had already been cancelled. Newspapers reported the affair all over England with headlines of 'Vicar censured by his flock', commenting that Mr Krauss was making himself and the Church of England cordially disliked by his parishioners. Krauss had only been in post for six weeks and acted hastily without looking into village customs, but once he had acted against Lord Pirbright he found it difficult to retreat.[21]

The school board was incensed at this strict application of the old agreement. If carried to the extreme, the ruling implied that they would have to ask permission to clean the school after hours, and for access to carry out repairs and rebuilding works, for all of which they had to pay. A strong letter was forwarded to the government requesting renegotiation of the agreement. The villagers were informed by the school board that 'through what we consider his [Reverend Krauss's] ill-advised and extraordinary action we are unable to grant the use of the schools, and thus the children of Pirbright will be prevented from enjoying the hospitality and amusement which Lord and Lady Pirbright have for many years so generously provided for them'. This row over the agreement continued until April 1899, when the board insisted on use of the school on three evenings a week and during holidays and vacation time. Surrey Education Committee eventually overturned the old agreement and took over the school in 1903. Villagers' resentment over the high-handed actions of the vicar continued over years. Lord Pirbright and Arthur Krauss never became friends; instead, a friendship developed between him and the vicar of the neighbouring parish of Wyke. Henley Park straddles both parishes, and the house is in Wyke and Normandy, while part of the grounds is in Pirbright.[22]

After this quarrel over a tea party Lord Pirbright determined to build a new village hall on his land, in the area known as Green House, which he had acquired from Mrs Collyer. He employed the Henley Park estate builder and the job was completed in four months. The new hall had oak panelling with oak floors and was lit by acetylene lamps. A kitchen, an office for Lord Pirbright and an office for the parish council abutted the hall. The rear wall facing the green had a clock and a stained-glass window bearing the arms of Lord Pirbright. The main body of the hall stands today but the stained-glass window was removed to allow the building of an extension, which holds the stage. The abutting offices have been enlarged and the acetylene lamps replaced by electric lighting.

Reverend Krauss began to show a more kindly face to the village by giving a tea party to the Sunday School children of the parish on 11 May 1899. Over one hundred children were present. After a church service the children moved to the recently completed school extension paid for through a mortgage for which the school board, not the management board, was responsible. After tea a professional magician from London entertained them with conjuring tricks.[23]

Princess Christian, daughter of Queen Victoria, opened Lord Pirbright's hall on 31 May 1899. Decorative arches were erected across the approach road, which was lined with flagpoles. The princess lunched at Henley Park and then drove with her hosts in an electric car to open the hall. In his address to the company, Lord Pirbright encouraged children both to play and to read, like the little girl whose statue was outside the hall, and he noted that there was a small library in the hall. The Bishop of Winchester was unable to be present, so the Archdeacon dedicated the building. Races for the children followed, with prizes given by Lady Pirbright. Her speech at the prize-giving shows the depth of feeling she held against the vicar, as she said that 'a sacred calling should never denigrate a holy office by attributing wrongful motives to those who only seek the good of others, from personal spite dictated by envy and malice'. After tea on the hall terrace Princess Christian left by special train from Brookwood station in the late afternoon.[24]

The electrically driven landau must have been a sensation at the time. It was powered from accumulators, which could be recharged using the steam-driven dynamo which operated the electric lighting installation at Henley Park. After 1895 any self-propelled vehicle was allowed to travel without the requirement for it to be preceded by a man with a red flag – but no faster than 14 mph.

The quarrels with Krauss extended to include the Church's right to decide when the church bells should be rung. Visitors to Henley Park usually came from London by train to Brookwood and then drove in Lord Pirbright's carriage through the village to the house. When Dunn was vicar, the church bells pealed to greet important visitors, including the Duke of Cambridge and the Lord Mayor of London. They also pealed on Queen Victoria's birthday (24 May). After Krauss became vicar the bell ringers pealed as usual for the Queen's birthday, to be told in no uncertain terms that 'in future you must ask my permission'. Princess Christian arrived shortly after this spat and Krauss tied up the bell ropes, locking the church so the bells did not peal. The villagers were so incensed at this act that the bell ringers refused to act on Sundays for some time. On a further occasion when Krauss refused to allow a peal, there was a riot outside his vicarage.[25]

Lord and Lady Pirbright continued their customary Christmas treat for the schoolchildren of the village in the new Lord Pirbright's Hall. On 2 January 1901 a Christmas tree, tall enough to reach the roof, was erected in front of the stage and a party of some 430 children of all denominations under the age of fourteen assembled for tea and entertainment. The tables were cleared for songs and games and Lord and Lady Pirbright presented gifts appropriate to the age of each child. In his address, Lord Pirbright extolled the value of education and said he had given land so that a new infants' school could be constructed. Lady Pirbright in her speech recalled how Martin Luther, when a small child, had been taken from the streets of a small German town by a lady and educated so that, in time, he 'presented us with the Protestant faith which we now enjoy'.[26]

Pirbright's school was successful in attracting pupils from outside the parish, and by 1899 the infants' department had become overcrowded. The board attempted without success to acquire more land from the War Office adjacent to the school buildings and then began to look for alternative sites. Lord Pirbright offered freehold land across the road from the school, while the School Management Committee, under Krauss, offered part of the grounds of the master's house adjacent to the school. The committee's offer was subject to the same terms of agreement as applied to the school buildings, offering a lease for 21 years, whereas Lord Pirbright's offer was freehold and without restrictions. The board refused to spend ratepayers' money on buildings they did not own, so the School Management Committee's offer was rejected and Lord Pirbright's proposal accepted. Lord Pirbright also offered sufficient freehold land for the construction of new school buildings adjacent to the proposed infants' department. Lady Pirbright opened the new infant's school on Wednesday 2 April 1902. She spoke of the value of education, saying that 'the character of a man or a woman is largely dependent on the education imparted to them in their infancy'. The offer of further land lapsed with the death of Lord Pirbright in January 1903, but many years later a replacement school was built on the site he had proposed. The infants' school, now greatly altered, is used as a school for children with special needs.[27]

Apology for Empire

Towards the end of the nineteenth century there was great public unease over the lack of accommodation for discharged and wounded soldiers. No system of social welfare existed to help the man who was disabled or otherwise unable to work, so he was driven into the workhouse. That this might happen to old soldiers was considered a disgrace to the nation, and Lord Pirbright was at the forefront of rich people who devised schemes to improve this dishonourable state of affairs. During his career in Parliament he had witnessed, criticised and sometimes applauded the wars in Afghanistan, Egypt and South Africa. Only a trickle of wounded soldiers returned from the many colonial wars in which Britain had then been involved. Sadly, however, the succession of small conflicts in South Africa led up to the full-scale Second Boer War of 1899–1902, and the flood of casualties from this fighting precipitated a crisis over accommodation for the disabled.

The discovery of gold in the Transvaal in 1886 had led to a large influx of non-Boers into that country so that ten years later Boers were in a minority. The republic under Paul Kruger (1825–1904), president from 1883 to 1900, remained ultra-Conservative, denied civil rights to the Uitlanders, mostly British and German, and used the wealth created through taxation to build up railways and to arm a guerrilla force with modern weapons. The private army of the British South Africa Company raided the Transvaal from the north hoping to encourage a rising of the Uitlanders and provoke a change in the government. Its effort was a total fiasco: the immigrants were more interested in making money and then returning to their own countries than in modernising the outlook of the Transvaal government. Alarmed by the expansionist plans of the Boer Republics, Britain began to dispatch large numbers of troops to Cape Colony, where it feared that the substantial Boer minority might cause instability. In reply to this move Kruger issued an ultimatum on 9 October 1899 demanding the evacuation of all British troops who had landed in South Africa since 1 June 1899 and the immediate recall of all reinforcements on the high seas. Britain did not comply and hostilities began on 11 October, when the ultimatum expired. British troops were not facing unsophisticated tribesmen, but a force armed with modern weapons, and for this they were ill prepared, suffering several defeats in the first few weeks, with many casualties. Soon there was expected to be a flood of the disabled returning to Britain and resources had to be expanded in order to cope. The War Office mobilised its efforts around the Soldiers' Help Society.

The Soldiers' Help Society had existed for some years and aimed at having in every parish one member, a soldier's friend, to whom discharged soldiers could be referred for help. In May 1899 two of Queen Victoria's daughters, Princess Christian of Schleswig-Holstein and Princess Henry of Battenberg, galvanised this society with further schemes to meet the expected situation. They proposed to organise a network of cottage homes where, with care and nursing, invalids discharged from service might be restored to health. Homes of rest were proposed for the incurably disabled where they could be sheltered and cared for and instructed in industries suitable to their strength and capabilities.[28] Princess Christian became president of the society, and the secretary of state for war, Lord Lansdowne, gave his approval for the scheme.[29]

In May 1899 the Army commanders, including Major-General Trotter for the Army, as well as others, favoured this scheme for cottage homes set out by Princess Christian, because it was based on the connection between a regiment and the districts from which its members had been recruited. It was envisaged that these homes would be scattered around the country supported by thousands of employers of labour who consented to enrol themselves as a soldier's friend. Counties were divided into districts, each with a head whose duty was to find a helper or soldier's friend for each town or group of villages in his district. These helpers were ready to see and help discharged soldiers commended to them. Many wealthy people supported the Army scheme and also placed seaside hotels and country houses at the disposal of the society for it to organise as hospital accommodation. Contributions of money helped equip these buildings and soon the accommodation was on standby. These provisions were of course temporary and after the emergency it was expected that the buildings would revert to their original use. The whole scheme was at first supported by small voluntary subscriptions. In a short time it also involved the Navy, and under Princess Christian the society became the Soldiers' and Sailors' Help Society (SSHS).[30]

During a train journey from Brookwood to London in June 1899, Lord Pirbright discussed with Lord Wolseley, Commander-in-Chief, a scheme of his own for building homes for discharged soldiers. This scheme was later crystallised in a letter to Wolseley dated 5 June 1899 offering the freehold of a 5–6-acre site at Bisley for the erection of homes of rest to be called 'Convalescent Homes for Disabled Soldiers and Sailors at Bisley'. Bisley is the adjacent parish on the north side of Pirbright. The War Office did not wish to be directly involved in such a venture, so Wolseley contacted Princess Christian, who brought the SSHS to Lord Pirbright's notice.[31]

At first glance these two schemes, one from Lord Pirbright and the other from the Soldiers' Help Society, appear to be the same. The difference is that the War Office, through the Soldiers' Help Society, wished to develop small cottage homes in the territorial bases of Army regiments, whereas Lord Pirbright envisaged a large establishment occupied by disabled soldiers from different regiments. The War Office scheme was to be run by mentors recruited from the territorial bases while Lord Pirbright's scheme required a central administration supported by an endowment, and in the eyes of some, it began to resemble the Chelsea Pensioners' establishment.

After 4 July 1899, arrangements were begun to transfer the piece of land at Bisley in perpetuity to trustees. Lord Pirbright planned an independent trust, and pending the establishment of a full rulebook and Constitution, the immediate steps were to be carried out under the umbrella of the SSHS. Lord Pirbright was invited to join the executive committee of the SSHS, and construction of accommodation began in August 1899, with completion of the first home, capable of accommodating 16 men, expected by January 1900. Lord Pirbright expected that the working institution would form the subject of a separate trust for which rules and regulations were to be devised.[32] The land was transferred directly to the trust without reference to the SSHS and that Society nominated the Duke of Connaught, the 16th Earl of Derby and Lord Pirbright as the three trustees. A committee of management was set up, with Lord Pirbright as chairman and a superintendent appointed for one year. The Duke of Connaught was an unfortunate choice as trustee since in January 1900 he was sworn in at Dublin Castle as Commander-in-Chief in Ireland. During the year he made tours of inspection in Ireland and planned Queen Victoria's visit to that country, and he was barely in England at all. Princess Christian attended the Queen during this visit to Ireland in April 1900. Lord Derby was another unfortunate choice for the management committee since he had a reputation for indecision.[33]

The war began in earnest during October 1899 with a three-pronged attack by the Boers, who laid siege to Kimberley, Mafeking and Ladysmith, all outside the territory of the Boer Republics. British forces suffered defeats, so the government moved the experienced General Kitchener from Khartoum to Cape Town and placed him together with General Roberts in command of the Army. Roberts had been in charge of the Army in Afghanistan during 1880. Kitchener left Khartoum on 18 December, travelling by liner from Alexandria to Gibraltar and then on, to arrive in Cape Town on 10 January 1900. The Army under his leadership moved north to relieve Kimberley on 15 February, Ladysmith on 26 February and Mafeking on 17 May. President Kruger resigned as the Army approached Pretoria, travelled to the Portuguese port of Lourenço Marques (now Maputo in Mosambique) and went into exile, leaving on a Dutch warship. The campaign then descended into a vicious guerrilla war.[34]

Funds for Lord Pirbright's scheme were quickly forthcoming. He solicited subscriptions from friends, one of whom, Sir Theodore Martin (1816–1909), a parliamentary draughtsman and well-known literary figure, gave £500. Martin figured strongly in subsequent acrimonious disputes over the misuse of funds. The Allied Building Trades (an artisans' association) under its president, Edwin O. Sachs (1870–1919), a theatre architect, made a very generous offer during January 1900, when the war situation was dire, to build and equip at its expense six homes on the site at Bisley.[35] This became known as the Building Trades Gift to the Nation and it was an essential help towards completion of the scheme. It was organised by circulating lists of requirements and co-ordinating the responses. The gifts were in kind, bricks, plaster, etc., together with cash from workers' associations, and impressive lists of material donations were reported in the press. A second phase of construction commenced in April 1900, by which time £20,000 had been collected in contributions from building workers along with most of the materials required to build accommodation for 100 men. Materials were transported by rail to Bisley Camp via the branch line from Brookwood and then by a specially constructed light railway to the building site, now called Stafford Lake.[36]

Construction of the buildings proceeded rapidly, and a grand architect's drawing of the site was unveiled envisaging homes each for sixteen men grouped around the superintendent's house, a workshop and a common room to hold 300 men. Electric lighting was to be supplied from a local generating station.[37] Princess Christian, in a letter to the Lord Mayor of London, outlined the progress made at Bisley and requested funds from the mayor's relief fund 'for the endowment of the only permanent homes in Great Britain for her Majesty's disabled heroes' before she left on the tour of Ireland.[38]

Bazaars and charity concerts were organised to raise funds for the Bisley Homes during the first months of 1900, and in Princess Christian's letters of appeal it was envisaged that the scheme would cater for about 250 men.[38] Donations were solicited and to be marked 'Princess Christian's Homes, Bisley' and designated either 'Building Fund' or 'Endowment Fund'. Further schemes for raising money included the Children's Penny Fund advertised across the country, where donations of 1d and upwards to £1 were solicited from children between the ages of 2 and 16 to be applied to the building of convalescent homes on the ground at Bisley.[39] The children of Pirbright village raised 2,400 pence.[40] There was also a 'Jubilee Children's Silver Donation Fund' from children born in the Jubilee years of 1887 and 1897. The silver coin this collected was to be used to endow a bed in the Princess Christian Homes for wounded and disabled soldiers and sailors at Bisley, and the collection from the Children's Penny Fund would be added to this.[41]

Independently and alongside these efforts were schemes for sending comforts for the troops. Lady Pirbright enthusiastically organised one such venture beginning in January 1900. A large quantity of khaki woollen material was made into garments for the East and West Surrey regiments by members of her guild of needlework recruited from the Henley Park household and the tenants on the Pirbright estate. These and other contributions received by parcel post at Brookwood station were dispatched in relays to South Africa. By March more than 12,000 articles had been dispatched. The shirts, which her team made and dispatched to South Africa, were designed by Lord Pirbright himself.[42,43]

The relief of Mafeking caused great celebrations in Pirbright and the schoolchildren were given a holiday on the following Monday (21 May). Ross Mangles and the deputy chairman of the council gave out refreshments and the children paraded through the village. Lord Pirbright was in London and attended the reception given by the Duke of Devonshire.[44] The fall of Pretoria, capital of the Transvaal, soon followed on 5 June 1900, causing a huge and enthusiastic demonstration in the village. Lord Pirbright heard the news at Henley Park by telephone from London and immediately drove to the village to spread the glad tidings, when a demonstration was immediately decided upon.

Lord Pirbright proceeded to the Army camp at Bisley to obtain the Commander's consent to allow the brass and bugle bands to play in Pirbright. Church bells began to ring out, probably with the permission of Reverend Krauss, and a public meeting in Lord Pirbright's Hall was fixed for 9 p.m. Soon a large crowd of villagers, regular soldiers and volunteers assembled, with the brass band playing patriotic songs. The hall was decorated with flags and Chinese lanterns and Lord and Lady Pirbright arrived accompanied by some of Lady Pirbright's relatives. Lord Pirbright gave a long patriotic speech noting that he was one of the first volunteers, having been a private in the Victoria Rifles in 1858 and a captain in the King's College Company in 1859.[43] His interest in rifle shooting was well known, and he was president of the Guildford District Rifle and Pistol Club from its foundation in April 1900 until his death. Lady Pirbright was the club's first lady member.[45]

Lady Pirbright thanked all those who had assisted in the dispatching of garments from Henley Park.[43] Earlier in March, a contingent of the Surrey volunteers had embarked for South Africa and were given a farewell dinner in Guildford beforehand. On that occasion Edward Halsey, chairman of the District Council, included in his toast to the Houses of Parliament a reference to Lord Pirbright, 'the present inhabitant of his old home, who with Lady Pirbright is doing so much for our soldiers and sailors at the present time'.[46]

Although the land at Bisley was transferred, the separate trust that had been envisaged in February 1900 was never fully established. The sub-committee that was then set up met rarely, if at all, and Lord Pirbright complained of the difficulty in obtaining a quorum. By August 1900 all was not well with the scheme and a ferocious argument erupted in the columns of *The Times*. Lord Pirbright believed that donations to the Bisley homes of rest were made independently of all the other schemes brought forward by the SSHS. His solicitor, Richard Dawes, maintained in the strongest terms that Lord Pirbright had intended from the outset for the homes to form a stand-alone permanent and endowed institution to serve the men disabled in the service of their country.[47] Sir Theodore Martin, Lord Pirbright and other subscribers maintained that their donations had been for construction of the Bisley homes, not for other schemes. They had a point, for the concerts and bazaars organised in London were advertised as expressly to collect funds for the Bisley homes. The SSHS had assumed that the Bisley Homes Trust was to be under its control and so it refused to consider a separate institution. Officials of the SSHS maintained that the gifts were to the SSHS in general and not to a separate trust. When this fundamental disagreement surfaced Lord Pirbright resigned from the executive committee of the SSHS in protest.[48]

Major-General H. Trotter, on behalf of the SSHS, tried to smooth the argument and put forward a compromise proposal. It was suggested that the future of the Bisley homes be decided by a committee of five: two appointed by the Society, two appointed by Lord Pirbright and an independent chairman. This committee was to consider the best means of constituting the homes and would prepare rules and regulations for management of the institution, subject to the approval of the executive committee, the SSHS remaining in charge.[49] Finally, the money received for the specific purpose of the Bisley homes should be separated from the general account. A letter from another society official confirmed that 'all sums received specifically for convalescent homes (Bisley homes included) are entered [in the ledgers] under the heading of Convalescent Homes while sums sent for Bisley homes only are earmarked B'.⁵⁰ Pirbright rejected these proposals since they inevitably placed the Bisley homes under the society's management committee.⁵¹

Major-General Herbert Eaton (1845–1925; from 1902 Lord Chesylemore), who had joined the SSHS after the time of Lord Pirbright's gift, expressed the views held by the Army in a letter to *The Times*. It was considered a great mistake to build as large an institution as the Bisley homes, which would become like a miniature Chelsea Hospital. It would be better, he concluded, to develop small cottage homes where invalids could live with their families in their community. Herbert Eaton wrote: 'In my belief such an institution as is contemplated at Bisley is little better than a workhouse, and certainly would not be appreciated by the men for whom it is intended.'⁵²

The official view of the SSHS was set out by its chairman, Major-General Trotter (1844–1905). The society considered the trustees set up for the Bisley establishment to be trustees for the society and not the nucleus of a separate unit for Bisley homes. Lord Pirbright was informed that Princess Christian 'would never have accepted your gift of land if she had for one moment understood that you contemplated forming a separate society'.⁵³ Progress on the homes had reached an impasse. Lord Pirbright's solicitor was able to state positively that the name of the SSHS was never mentioned to him in the context of the gift of land at Bisley and that his client always intended the homes to be an absolutely independent institution. He felt that because of the business of the Bisley homes and of the SSHS 'being managed for the sake of economy by the same secretary and staff, the society, without any warrant, came instinctively to identify itself with the homes'. He proposed to the chairman of the SSHS the appointment of accountants to examine the books, after which any balance due could be paid into 'The Bisley Homes Account' and a declaration of trust be prepared, after which work could continue.

In reply to the statement by Major-General Trotter giving the official view of the SHSS, Lord Pirbright wrote that the SSHS wished to imply that 'I for some occult reason of my own, prevented the execution of the deed of trust. This suggestion is false and without the slightest foundation. I executed the conveyance in October last year.' A simple conveyance was indeed approved by the society's solicitor, who suggested that the rules and regulations should form the subject of a separate trust. The sum of money brought in by the appeals on behalf of the Bisley homes was estimated at £23,000, which should, when invested, have been enough to support an independent institution.⁵⁴

The matter was closed when the honorary solicitor of the SHSS wrote to Lord Pirbright's solicitor on 4 October 1900 that the society considered that Lord Pirbright had signed a deed of gift of the land. Therefore 'the SSHS will accordingly proceed to carry out their original scheme for building homes of rest at Bisley, on land given by Lord Pirbright, and will employ for this purpose the funds subscribed for the Bisley Homes, and which funds are so largely due to the appeal of her Royal Highness Princess Christian, the president of the society'.[55] Lord Pirbright in reply gave up his demand for a separate institution, saying he now realised the real reason behind the objections of the SSHS – namely, 'to retain the money belonging to the Bisley Homes but improperly paid into the general account of the SSHS.' He resigned as a trustee of the society in October.[56]

After more than a year of wrangling amongst the working officials Lord Pirbright's original scheme fell through, but by then the homes had been partly built with the co-operation of the Allied Building Trades. They declined to help the scheme further on 23 October 1900, expressing exasperation at the wrangling between Lord Pirbright, Theodore Martin and the SSHS, as well as the poor business procedures.[57] Cash, however, continued to trickle in up to December.[58] In the happier times of *la belle époque* Lord Pirbright's antagonist from the SSHS, Major-General Trotter, had been entertained at Henley Park. Trotter followed the views of his committee without, it appears, wholehearted agreement. In the course of these arguments Herbert Eaton, who was strongly opposed to the Bisley homes scheme, followed Henry Trotter as chairman of the SSHS, and the scheme then had negligible chance of success.

A New Sovereign

Queen Victoria died on 22 January 1901. Lord Pirbright commemorated the accession of Edward VII by presenting his hall to Pirbright Parish Council together with the surrounding grounds, which had formed the original Green House estate. He undertook to lay out the grounds and furnish them with seats. A granite memorial in honour of the King was to be erected in the grounds and engraved stone plaques commemorating his gift were erected over the two entrances to the hall. The deed of conveyance was completed at a meeting of the council on 24 May 1901. Lord Pirbright not being present, the council resolved to give him an address of thanks, expressing its gratitude in warm terms: 'We feel assured that it [this gift] will also be regarded as a standing monument of the deep interest that both your

Lordship and Lady Pirbright have ever taken in the parish and of your attachment to the parishioners.'[59] The building of the hall and its later transfer to the village are recorded on the plaque placed over the entrance door:

> DIE MERCURII XXXI MAII ANNO DOMINI MDCCCXCIX
> PRESENTED TO THE VILLAGE OF PIRBRIGHT MAY 27TH 1901
> TO COMMEMORATE THE ACCESSION OF HIS MAJESTY
> KING EDWARD VII

The Boer War was now in its final stages, and the peace signed on 31 May 1902 in a small town south of Pretoria provided for the Boers to hand over all their arms and to recognise Edward VII as their lawful sovereign. On Wednesday, 6 August 1902 Lord Pirbright gave a reception for the villagers to commemorate the King's coronation. The weather was unfortunately very inclement so a marquee capable of holding 800 diners had been erected in the grounds of Lord Pirbright's Hall. Lord and Lady Pirbright, accompanied by their niece Mrs Henriques and her husband, drove up shortly after 2 p.m. in the electrically driven landau. The children, altogether about 470, were marshalled in the tent and presented with medals to commemorate the occasion. On their behalf the headmaster thanked Lady Pirbright for sending toys to the children during the recent attack of measles and then presented her with a silver-mounted diary with a perpetual calendar paid for by donations from the children. The children were provided with a tea of bread and butter and cakes, after which the tables were set for dinner. The dinner was for everyone over the age of sixteen, and about 700 sat down. Roast and boiled meats were provided, together with salad bread and cheese, accompanied by beer and mineral waters. Lord Pirbright used the occasion to give a patriotic speech and the villagers presented him with an illuminated address. Dinner was followed by vocal entertainment from the villagers, after which Lord and Lady Pirbright left for Henley Park. A bonfire was lit at about 10 p.m. and the committee and friends remained in the hall for a dance.[60] A second fête was held at Henley Park for the inhabitants of Wyke and Normandy.

Clearly, when the SSHS took over control of the Bisley homes in October 1900, it had little idea what to do with them. It required a further year to complete proper re-conveyance of the land. Theodore Martin inspected the homes in April 1902 and saw them derelict, with no caretaker, no furniture and partly vandalised. The forecourt displayed the following notice: 'The Princess Christian's homes for disabled soldiers and sailors erected by voluntary contributions on land given by Lord Pirbright'.[61] Lord Pirbright visited the homes on 3 August 1902 and for the first time in two years found a caretaker in residence, together with his wife and children. The homes themselves were in a disgraceful state. Windows were smashed, pipes broken, rooms full of refuse left by the builders and the wallpaper discoloured from damp. The gardens were a mass of weeds and the gravel paths overgrown.[62] Lord Pirbright acquiesced to a proposal from the SSHS that the homes should be used for the reception of orphans of men who had given their lives for their country, but this scheme was never carried out.[63] Another suggestion from Lord Pirbright was for the homes to be used for widows and orphans of soldiers, but this also was not taken up.[64]

Troops began to return to Britain from South Africa in the autumn of 1902 and Lord Pirbright welcomed the detachment of the Queen's West Surrey Regiment when it reached Guildford.[65] The soldiers were entertained to a dinner over which he presided. When the 1st battalion of the Coldstream Guards arrived in Farnborough, Lord Pirbright was among those to greet the men at the railway station.[66]

Lord Pirbright died before the Bisley complex was put to use. Eventually the five homes were restored and put to the use he had originally intended. Beds for the use of totally disabled soldiers were endowed in memory of Queen Victoria in 1904 and the balance of the Jubilee Children's Silver Donation fund was used to equip a library.[67] The buildings became the Princess Christian Homes and Training Centre. With the passage of time the SSHS became the Soldiers, Sailors, Airmen and Families Association, while the buildings at Bisley were less used and fell into disrepair. In 2005 they were sold for £2.5 million to a commercial residential and care home company that completely refurbished the interiors.[68]

9

Epilogue

> *O quam cito transit gloria mundi*
> [How quickly the glory of the world passes away]
>
> Thomas à Kempis, *The Imitation of Christ*, Book I, Chapter III (1418)

Lord Pirbright died at his London home on Friday, 9 January 1903 after a short confinement. When the news was broken by telegram in Pirbright a group of parishioners set out to toll the Church bell. They tried to give the appropriate fee but Reverend Krauss maintained that he had had no personal communication with anyone over the death and refused to give permission even though he had been seen in the post office reading the telegram. Even now he frustrated the villagers by locking the church and leaving the village. In response to a flurry of telegrams the churchwarden attempted to ring the bells and found the church locked. Resentment broke out among the villagers at this unfeeling behaviour and they rioted all the evening outside the vicarage, smashing gates, pulling up shrubs and breaking the wooden stile over the back fence which the vicar used as a shorter way to the church. The police had to be called to restore order. Finally a compromise was reached with Reverend Krauss, who announced in the Sunday service that the bell would be tolled for one hour on the following Tuesday during the funeral service.[1]

Mr H.M. Briant, later confirmed as the new chairman of the parish council, convened a village meeting in the hall (erected by Lord Pirbright) on the Monday (19 January) after the funeral and some 400 arrived to express their indignation. There were several strong speeches expressing disapproval of the vicar's actions towards both Lord Pirbright and the village, and during this time the vicarage was under police protection. Lady Pirbright acted to calm tempers by sending a letter which was read at the meeting. She protested against any acts of aggression or personal violence, adding, 'that which man failed to avenge God was sure to punish – Believe me'. A resolution calling on the vicar to resign was carried unanimously. However, he had been appointed for life and so remained in post.[2]

Lord Pirbright's daughters were provided for in his will, and after other small bequests, the remainder of his estate was transferred to Lady Pirbright, including the paintings and china inherited from his uncle. He made no provision for his first wife. Many years before his death, Lord Pirbright had reserved a plot in the Jewish cemetery at Willesden,[3] but over the period from his eldest daughter's Christian wedding, his religious views gradually changed and in his will he desired a Christian burial. It is thought that he hoped to be buried at St. Michael and All Angels in Pirbright, but this presented a problem. He owned much property in the village but his place of residence at Henley Park House was just outside the parish. From ancient times the boundary passed between the house with its immediate grounds and the adjacent common, which later formed part of the Henley Park estate. The house itself is situated in the parish of Normandy and Wyke. It was unlikely that either Henry Joseph Tenison Halsey or the Reverend Arthur Krauss would agree to his burial in Pirbright.

There were probably negotiations before the death, and in his will, dated 4 December 1902, Lord Pirbright specified that he wished to be buried in Normandy parish churchyard. Planning for this ceremony must have been ongoing during his last illness. The faculty that granted permission for construction of the brick-lined tomb was seen attached to the church notice board at the time of his funeral which, for a small parish church, was a grand affair. Of his two adversaries in this matter, Henry J.T. Halsey, the last Lord of the Manor of Pirbright, died in Monte Carlo in 1937 and is buried in Pirbright churchyard. Arthur Krauss changed his surname to Neild, after his mother, during the 1914–18 period, and he also is buried in Pirbright churchyard.[4]

Arthur Krauss went to extraordinarily petty lengths to thwart Lord Pirbright's wishes, and in so doing he outraged the villagers. He can only be said to have acted at first on impulse and then to have felt unable to retreat. There seems also to have been little informal contact between him and the village. He may also have been acting on advice from Henry Halsey, who resented Lord Pirbright's entry to the village. Arthur Krauss was born in Chorlton-upon-Medlock near Manchester, where his father, Adolphus (1806–1872), was associated with St. Saviour's Church. His grandfather had immigrated to the district from Germany during the late eighteenth century, a time when there was strong anti-Semitic feeling among Protestants, and these feelings could have been transmitted to the grandson, who never had any informal contact with Lord Pirbright. This anti-Semitism surfaces in letters written by Bismarck in the mid-nineteenth century. He remarks that if he did not enter politics he could become an 'officer with a moustache, who curses and swears a justifiable hated of Frenchmen and Jews'.[5]

EPILOGUE

Lord Pirbright's remains were transported by special train to Wanborough station accompanied by Lady Pirbright and then conveyed on a bier by the tenantry of both Henley Park and Pirbright to Wyke parish church, where a short service was held by the vicar, Reverend C. Page Wood. The coffin rested in the church overnight covered with his peer's robes and coronet, and the funeral service, taken by the sub-dean of the Chapels Royal, was held on 13 January. A special train from London conveyed the mourners to Wanborough, from where a fleet of coaches transferred them to the church.[6]

Lady Pirbright was accompanied by her Faudel-Phillips relatives, including Philip Henriques, who was married to her niece. Lord Pirbright's eldest daughter Alice, accompanied by her husband, was the only blood relative attending. Close friends who were present included the Duke of Argyll, Lord Arthur Hill (MP for Down West until 1898) and the actor Sir Charles Wyndham. King Edward VII, the Duke and Duchess of Connaught, Baroness Leonine de Rothschild, the National Rifle Association and the Colonial Office sent representatives. Also present were representatives of Pirbright Parish Council, the School Board and the Fire Brigade, together with Ash Parish Council, Guildford Rifle Club and Guildford Athletic Association. Wreaths were sent from Lord Pirbright's daughter Alice and her two children, from his youngest daughter Connie and her husband Count Maximillian of Löwenstein, living in Munich, from the three children of his elder brother, living at Milton Place, Egham, and also from Sir Edward Lawson and Alfred de Rothschild. The elder brother himself, George Baron de Worms, sent no acknowledgement. Edward VII and Queen Alexandria, the King of the Belgians, the Empress Eugénie, the Duke and Duchess of Connaught, Prince and Princess Christian, Princess Henry of Battenberg, Princess Louise Duchess of Argyll, the Duke of Cambridge, Princess Edward of Saxe-Weimar, the Grand Duke of Mecklenburg-Strelitz, the Duke of Abercorn and the Archbishop-designate of Canterbury sent letters and telegrams of sympathy. The list of people who either attended the service or sent flowers or a telegram is most impressive. It includes all the living children of Queen Victoria, together with her cousin, the Duke of Cambridge. The Archbishop-designate of Canterbury was Randall Davidson, Bishop of Winchester, who had agreed to Lord Pirbright's request to construct the vault in Wyke churchyard.

Wyke church choir was augmented for the occasion with nearby choirs. A traditional Hebrew tune, 'A Memorial to the Departed', began the service, and 'Abide with Me' and 'The Lord is My Shepherd' were sung. The coffin was taken out to Beethoven's funeral march and interred in the cemetery. A large chest tomb bearing the Pirbright coat of arms surmounts the grave and the south side bears the following inscription:

Here lies all that is mortal of a man whose rare gifts of intellect cultivated to the highest were combined with a warmth and largeness of heart that delighted in doing good in thinking for others and in ministering bountifully of his means towards lightening the trials of the poor. He was endeared to his friends not more by the brilliancy of his gifts than by the breadth of his sympathies and the largeness of his views. All that devoted love could do he did to make life happy to her who consecrates this tablet to his memory.

Sarah Pirbright

Lord Pirbright's considerable intellect was recognised even by a Jewish author who described him as the Admirable Crichton of the Conservative Party.[7] This sobriquet Admirable was originally applied to James Crichton (1560–1572), a Scottish polymath noted for his extraordinary accomplishments in languages, the arts and the sciences. Lord Pirbright was described in *The Jewish World* as 'a remarkable linguist and a man of singularly cultivated mind and many-sided interests. His company was in much request at exalted gatherings'.[8] The villagers paid for a handsome engraved brass memorial plaque to be erected in Lord Pirbright's Hall, and it was unveiled by Sir Theodore Martin in June 1904. A large congregation, including schoolchildren and members of Lady Pirbright's needlework guild, attended the ceremony. Reverend Page Wood, vicar of Normandy and Wyke, was present, but the vicar of Pirbright, Reverend Krauss, was absent. Fate ensured that this memorial was not placed in Pirbright church, for the chancel had already been decorated with a large plaque listing the members of the Halsey family buried in vaults underneath. Lady Pirbright subsequently donated a framed portrait of her husband to the hall, a copy of the Fildes portrait which had been exhibited in the Academy and which had been overseen by the artist himself.[9]

During his life Henry Worms had two obstacles to surmount for a successful career in politics: he was Jewish, and he was educated at King's College London where he met very few who were destined to enter the political establishment. He used his time at the Anglo-Jewish Association to gain the acquaintance of politicians, and later his performance in Parliament led to a government post, though not to full Cabinet rank, in Salisbury's first administration. The step up to Cabinet rank proved elusive, most probably because of his Jewish background, and he was eventually relegated to the House of Lords.

EPILOGUE

A quip, commonly applied to Conservative MPs, is crystallised in the character of Sir Joseph Porter, First Lord of the Admiralty, in Gilbert and Sullivan's operetta *HMS Pinafore*. In the first act he remarks, 'I always voted at my party's call and never thought of thinking for myself at all', attributing his rise to the position of First Lord to this behaviour. The operetta was written in 1878, and W.H. Smith (1825–1891), Leader of the House when Henry de Worms was in government, is thought to be the model for the character of Joseph Porter. As a Tory, Henry voted at the party call over Church legislation and on the home rule bills. As an intelligent Tory he struck out and sought a fairer deal for workers in his constituencies of Greenwich and Liverpool, as well as for Jews in Europe, even when most of his party was indifferent to these matters. This quip from *Pinafore* could not therefore be applied to him.

Opinion has been expressed that Lord Pirbright was a bore, and some letters of his are indeed written in a flowery style. In his youth, however, he was noted for rowdy behaviour in the Inner Temple dining room and his participation in shooting, fencing, boxing and student societies indicates some companionable behaviour. Sir Theodore Martin, when he unveiled the memorial tablet, touched on Henry's intellect and 'the delightful humour with which he could illuminate a narrative or an argument'.[9] A more surprising view of his character comes from an independent source, Prince Bismarck, with whom he had political discussions during 1888. Henry's intellect must have impressed Bismarck, who presented him with a signed portrait, something he very rarely did.[10] The address given by Sir Theodore Martin gives a better assessment of his character: 'a good man ... setting an example of true Christian charity' given for all, not just to one specific community.[9]

When Henry de Worms took the oath as a member of the House of Commons on the last occasion (1895), he did so in the Jewish manner, wearing his hat. It came as a great shock to the Jewish community in London to learn, when the will was opened, that Lord Pirbright had specified a Christian burial in the churchyard at Normandy and Wyke. He was a close relative of the Chief Rabbi and had been active in Jewish affairs before he entered Parliament. A day after his illness was announced, the sub-dean of the Chapels Royal and the Archdeacon of Westminster made urgent inquiries on his condition. The Chief Rabbi also made enquiries, along with members of the British royal family and the Empress Eugénie.[11]

In taking the final step of a Christian burial, Henry seems to have been influenced by the many Faudel-Phillips relatives, noted on the genealogy, who later received Christian burials. One of these was Sarah's brother, Samuel Henry. Sarah's younger brother George remained Jewish and ran the family firm of Faudel-Phillips, with premises in Newgate Street, London. George oversaw a £1,000 restoration scheme for the nearby Christ's Church, and on his death he was buried in the Jewish cemetery, while Christ's Church gave a memorial service. The most important influence, however, was probably that of Sarah herself.[12]

Sarah seems already to have contemplated Christian views at the time of the marriage of Henry's daughter Alice several years before her own marriage to Henry. She gave a present to Alice of a finely jewelled cross, and when Alice's first husband died young a few years later, Sarah sent an elaborate floral tribute, again in the form of a cross. A further indicator of Sarah's views is seen in an address she gave to the children of Pirbright in 1899 on the occasion of the dedication of Lord Pirbright's Hall; she began with the quotation 'suffer the little children to come unto me' from Mark's Gospel.[13] Her address to the children during the Christmas party given in Lord Pirbright's Hall in January 1901 gives a firm indication of Christian views. She recalled how 'Martin Luther when a small child had been taken from the streets of a small German town by a lady and educated so that in time he presented us with the Protestant faith which we now enjoy'.[14] Lord Pirbright was present at this ceremony, so was he included, along with the children, in his wife's speech?

The last sentence in Sarah's tribute, inscribed on Henry's tomb, strongly suggests her major influence on his final change of views: 'All that devoted love could do he did to make life happy to her who consecrates this tablet to his memory.' Henry in his will requested Christian burial and expressed the wish that his wife would rest beside him, which would be made most certain if they both adopted Christianity.

It appears that Lord Pirbright's change in religious views took place some time before May 1901 and was probably known to some members of the Anglo-Jewish Association. Queen Victoria died in January 1901, and at the beginning of May Edward VII gave an audience in London for the reception of loyal and congratulatory addresses. Representatives of the Board of Deputies of British Jews and the Anglo-Jewish Association tendered the address from the Jews of the United Kingdom. About twenty delegates were chosen for this task, including Claude Montefiore as president of the Anglo-Jewish Association. Lord Pirbright was the only living past president of that organisation and he was not invited. The late Julian Goldsmid (1838–1896) had followed him as president.[15]

On 5 March 1903, shortly after Lord Pirbright's funeral, Edward VII sanctioned the appointment of Lady Pirbright as Dame of Grace of the Order of the Hospital of St John of Jerusalem.[16] Members of the order (male and female) are appointed by the sovereign upon recommendation, having been involved in charitable works to aid those in sickness. On ceremonial occasions they wear a black cassock and a black mantle bearing a white Maltese cross. They have to declare 'always to uphold the aims of this Christian order.' Queen Victoria granted a royal charter in 1888, making the sovereign the head of the order. The St John's Ambulance Association was established by this order.

Lady Pirbright gave up the lease on Henley Park and moved back to London. She spent most of the year following her husband's death on the Riviera, in France and Italy. From 1906 she took a lease on apartments at 11 avenue d'Iéna in Paris, previously occupied by Grand Duke Paul of Russia (1860–1919).[17] Paul was in a difficult financial situation since he had married a commoner in 1902 and the Tzar had dismissed him from all appointments, exiling him to France. In her new establishment, Lady Pirbright continued the Pirbrights' tradition of at-homes and elaborate dinner parties. The French press described her as 'a great English lady'. The Infanta Eulalia was a frequent guest and the Empress Eugénie was also entertained in Paris. There were parties for British residents in Paris, on the Riviera, in Venice and in Rome when she stayed in those cities. Edward VII did not forget her and received her in 1907 while on a visit to Paris.[18]

She perpetuated her husband's memory through a number of charitable bequests, the largest, of £1,000, being given to the Lord Mayor of London's new home for crippled children to endow a bed. Smaller sums were given to the Transvaal War Fund to support widows and orphans of those who fell in the war and to the Union Jack Club for refurbishment.[19] She offered to make a large donation of paintings to the newly created Gallery of Modern Art in Ireland but this gift never materialised. The gallery was the child of the art critic Hugh Lane (1875–1915), who himself made a large donation of paintings, and other works were purchased. The venue, supported by the City of Dublin, was small and the gallery committee considered that there was not enough room for the pictures Lady Pirbright offered. The gallery moved to its present spacious site in 1933, by which time the executors had disposed of Lady Pirbright's collection elsewhere.[20]

Lady Pirbright died in late November 1914 at Claridges Hotel, London and is buried next to her husband in Wyke churchyard. The will, dated 20 April 1914, lists a number of sacred objects in her possession when she died. Sarah stated that she wished to be buried wearing the small diamond and blue cross which she habitually wore, and she had no objection to floral tributes because she considered 'offerings on such occasions are tributes of affection and respect'.

The coffin was brought by motor hearse from London, and the vicar, Reverend Pickford, conducted the simple funeral. She had a keen lifelong interest in the arts and included many prominent actors among her friends. After the death of her husband she had continued to give an annual summer fête for Pirbright schoolchildren. When she was not in England her nephew-in-law, Philip Henriques, who lived near Henley Park, presided. She attended in person in the July before her death, and afterwards Philip and Beatrice Henriques continued the practice into the 1940s.[21,22] The epitaph on the east side of the Pirbright tomb reads:

SEXU FEMINA INGENIO VIR
(A woman by sex, a man by spirit)

Through her will Sarah continued to perpetuate her husband's memory. There was the gift of a Turner oil painting, *The Estuary of the Thames and the Medway*, to the Louvre in Paris, and gifts to the National Gallery in London of three Italian pictures, all to be distinctly labelled in memory of the late Lord Pirbright. The valuable china and paintings she inherited from her husband, together with her jewels, including the famous pearl necklaces, were divided between her Faudel-Phillips relatives. Property outside the village of Pirbright was given to the Henriques family, while property in the village itself was sold by auction to provide the funds for annuities she gave to her servants. Religious objects, paintings and crucifixes, were given to her secretary, Peter McGinn, and his sister, Mary McGinn.

The marriage between Sarah Phillips and Henry de Worms was ideal. Sarah reintegrated herself into society after divorcing her first husband and married Henry in a civil ceremony. She planned all the entertainment they gave and hosted fashionable tea parties during the season. He lavished jewels on her, took leases on two fine houses in England and organised over-winter excursions to the Mediterranean. The circle of friends they entertained grew to include foreign princes and kings, until in the last years the Prince of Wales and other members of the British royal family visited them at home.

Fanny von Todesco's marriage to Henry Worms was not successful; after the divorce, she was supported from a trust fund set up by her parents. She lived in Austria and continued to use her title as Franziska Freifrau (Baroness) von Worms.[23] She is buried in the Todesco family grave in Vienna's Döblinger Friedhof as Fanny Freifrau von Worms-Todesco. The marriage of her sister Gabriella to Ludwig von Oppenheimer also ended in divorce, after which Gabriella continued to live in the Palais Todesco. Both husbands had high political ambitions, which did not appeal to the wives, who preferred the delights of Viennese society. In spite of psychological problems, the third sister, Anna, had a successful marriage with the Viennese stockbroker, Leopold von Lieben. She wrote poetry, in German, which was published after her death.[24]

Lord Pirbright's eldest daughter, Alice, lived in England with her husband after he had retired from business in Calcutta. David McLaren Morrison died in 1924 whilst on a visit to his daughter and was buried in Dorset. Alice outlived him by many years; she died in London in 1952 and was buried close to her husband.

Lord Pirbright's youngest daughter, Constance, and her children continued to live for some time in Austria and Germany but, aware of their Jewish connections, they left during the rise of National Socialism. Felix von Oppenheimer (1874–1938), a cousin of Constance on her mother's side, became a politician and administrator for the arts in post-1918 Vienna. He remained in the city during the National Socialist era and died on the way to a Nazi interrogation centre.

Constance died in England in 1963 and is buried at Wyke; she had divorced her first husband and married Volrath von Alvensleben (1869–1914). Their son, Baron Werner von Alvensleben, was born in France in 1912 one month after the marriage. He was brought up in Austria and from 1938 lived and worked in England. He is better known as Michael Werner, painter and sculptor, who died in 1989, and he is also buried at Wyke. Volrath von Alvensleben died in Graz. By her first marriage, Constance had two daughters, Sophie (1896–1978) and Franziska (1899–1992), and three sons, Johann (1901–1952), born in Vienna, Leopold (1903–1974), born in Salzburg, and Hubert (1906–1984). Hubert, strongly Catholic, became a staunch opponent of Hitler and after 1945 embarked on a political career in Germany.[25] Leopold, who died at Ventimiglia in the south of France, is buried at Wyke along with his second wife, Diane (1921–1967), a daughter of the publisher Victor Gollancz, she converted to the Anglican faith shortly before her death. Henrietta née Jost (1908–1986), second wife of Johann, is also buried in the Pirbright family plot.

Genealogical Tables
THE WORMS FAMILY

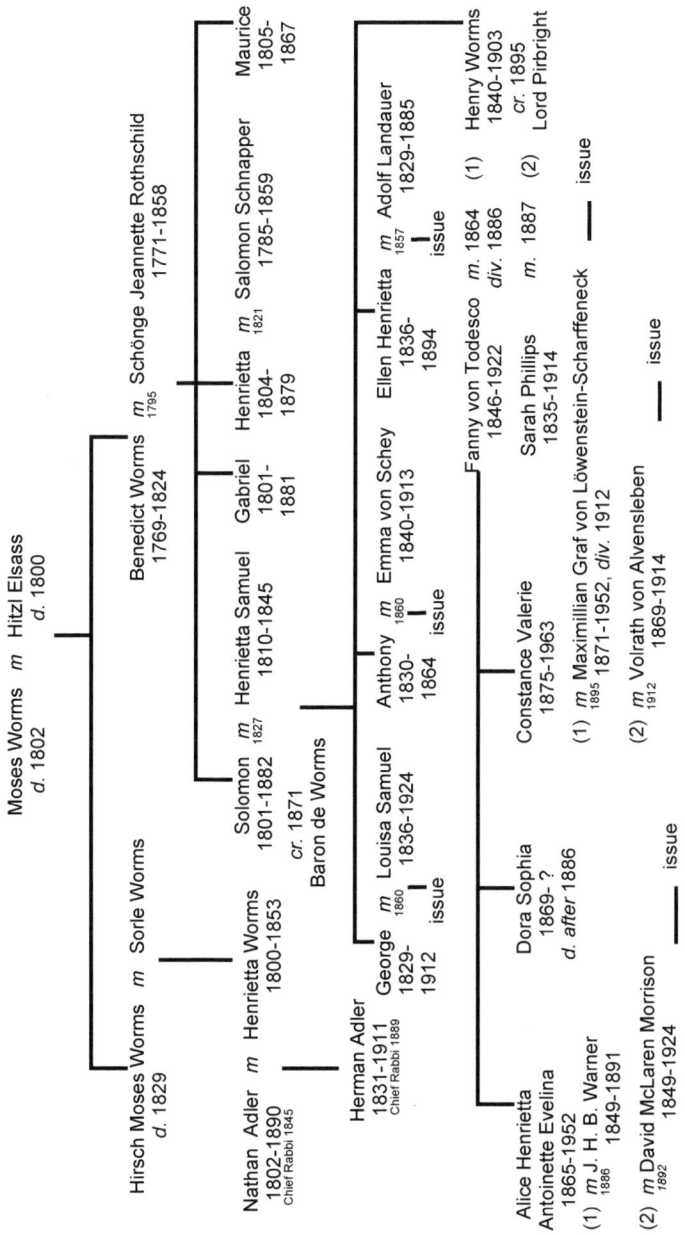

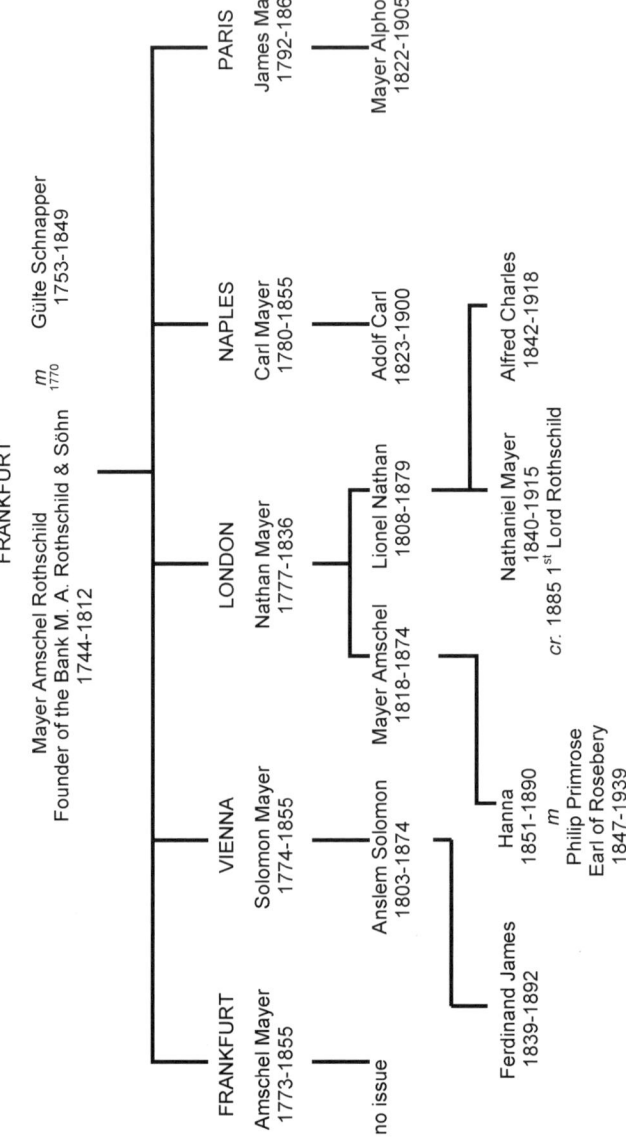

GENEALOGICAL TABLES

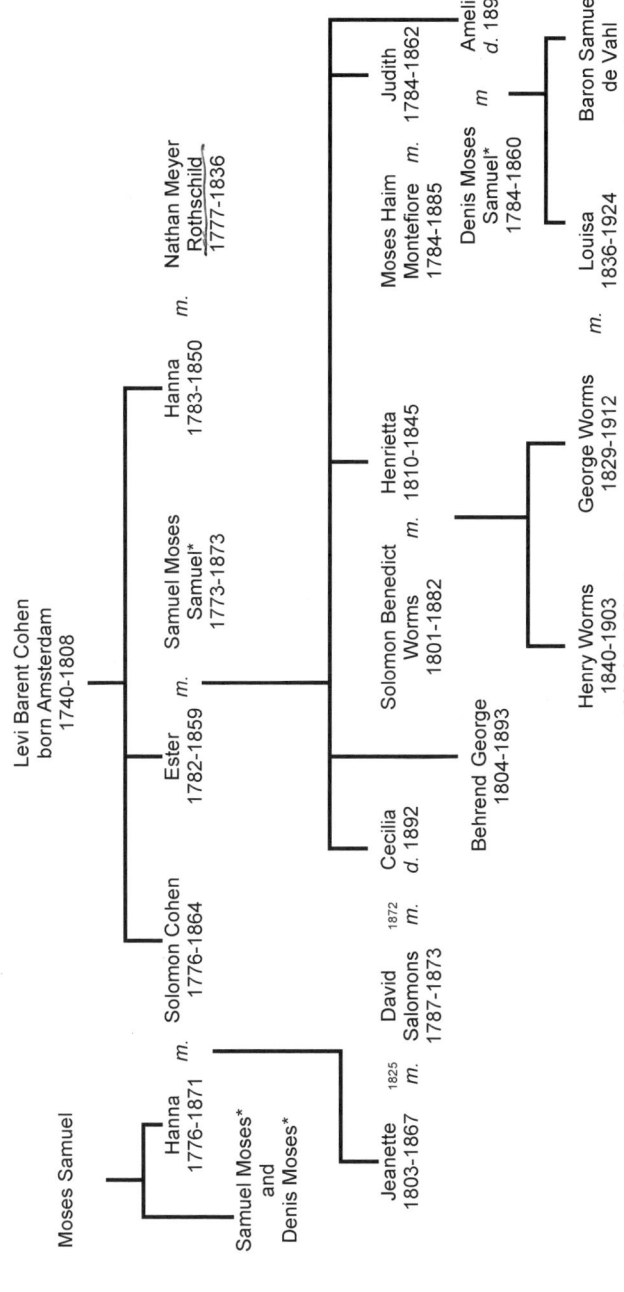

TODESCO GOMPERZ OPPENHEIMER FAMILIES OF VIENNA

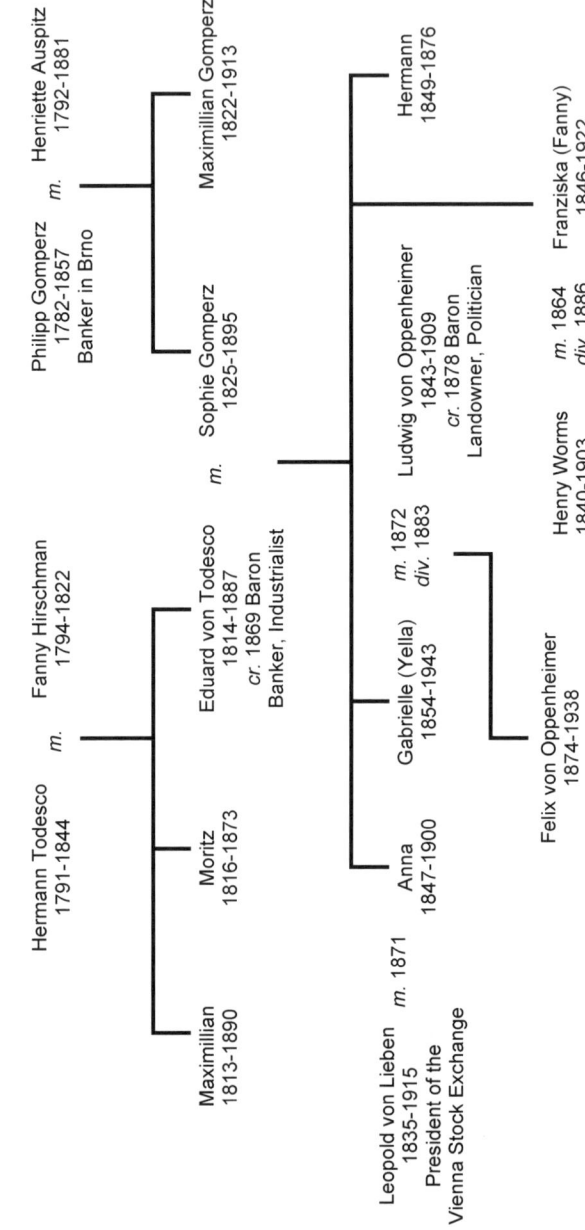

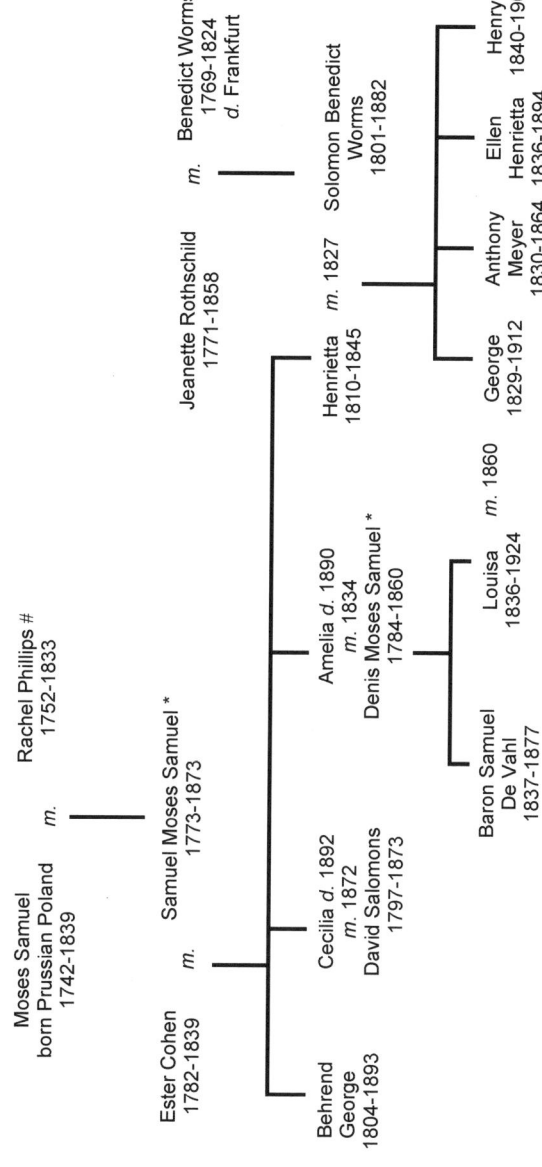

SAMUEL – PHILLIPS FAMILY RELATIONSHIPS

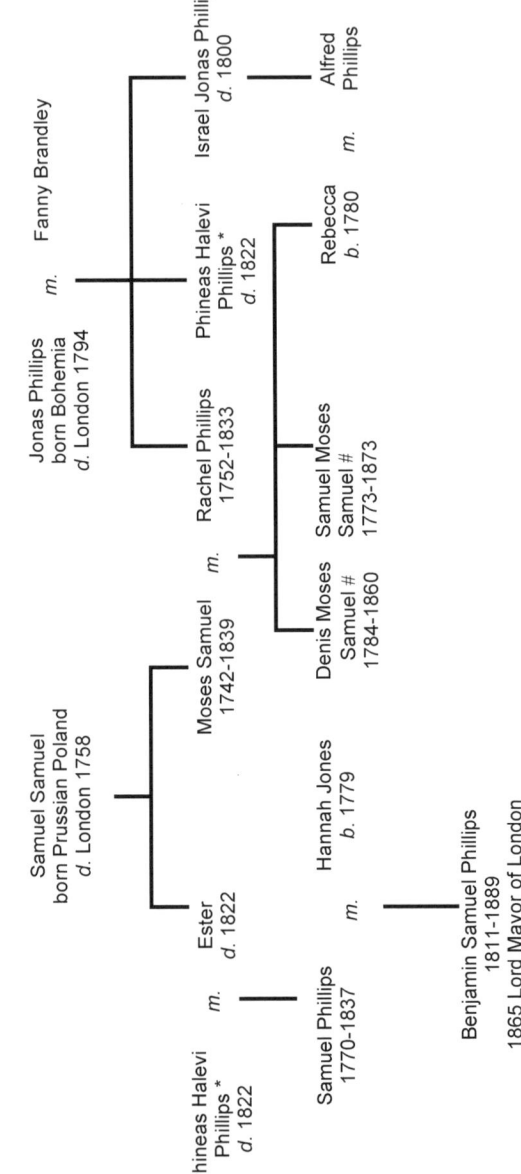

* Appears elsewhere in this diagram
# These and other Samuel brothers operated with Alfred Phillips in Brazil for Samuel & Phillips.

GENEALOGICAL TABLES

WORMS – PHILLIPS - LEVY RELATIONSHIPS

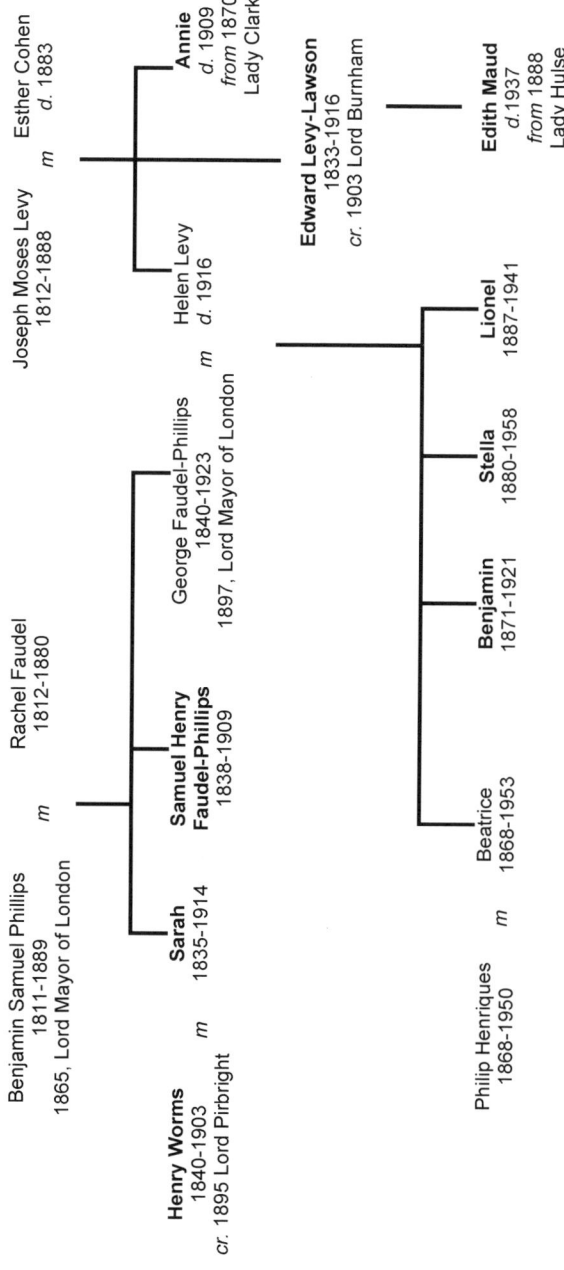

Those in bold type had a Christian burial.

Bibliography

Publications of Henry Worms, Lord Pirbright

The Earth and its Mechanism, being an account of the various proofs of the rotation of the earth. With a description of the instruments used in the experimental demonstrations, to which is added the theory of Foucault's pendulum and gyroscope. With numerous wood cuts and diagrams. London: Longman Roberts and Green, 1862, xiv, 296 pp.

Die Oesterreichisch – Ungarische Monarchie und die Politik des Grafen Beust (von einem Engländer), Leipzig: J.J. Weber, 1870, xviii, 273 pp., 4 maps.

The Austro-Hungarian Empire. A political sketch of men and events since 1866. 2nd edition. London: Chapman and Hall, 1877, v, 324 pp. 4 maps.

England's Policy in the East. London: Chapman and Hall, 1877, vii, 181 pp.

(Translator of) Freidrich Ferdinand Count von Beust, *Memoirs of Freidrich Ferdinand Count von Beust. Written by himself. With introduction and personal reminiscences of Count Beust's career as Prime Minister of Austria and Austrian Ambassador in London, by Baron Henry de Worms.* London: Remington, 1887, vol. 1, xcv, 398 pp.; vol. 2, xv, 391 pp. (Original: *Aus drei Viertel-Jarhunderten. Erinnerungen und Aufzeichnungen*, Stuttgart, 1887).

Public Speeches and Pamphlets

National education. A speech delivered at the literary and mechanics institute, Egham. London, 1868, 9 pp.

Two speeches addressed to the freemen and electors of the united borough of Sandwich, Deal and Walmer, on 16–17 July 1868. London, 1868, 22 pp.

The eastern question. Speech delivered at Manchester by Baron Henry de Worms, on the occasion of the inauguration of the Junior Conservative Club, Monday, 29 January 1877. Manchester: Charles Smith, 1877, 18 pp.

Home and foreign policy of the Conservative government. Three speeches delivered by Baron Henry de Worms to the electors of Greenwich. Greenwich and London: Kentish Mercury, 1880, 70 pp.

The government policy at home and abroad. A speech delivered by Baron Henry de Worms, MP, at the Free Trade Hall, Manchester, on 14 February 1883. London: National Union of Conservative and Constitutional Associations, 1883, 15 pp.

The Sugar Bounties. Speech reprinted from the Glasgow Herald of 2 November 1888. Glasgow: McNaughton and Sinclair, 1888.

The Ruin of the West Indies. *The National Review*, 1897, vol. 30, pp. 519–534.

Archives

Bildarchiv, Österreichische Nationalbibliothek
Gloucester Regional Archives
Inner Temple, London
King's College London, Archive: King's College Engineering Society Minute Books (one volume of the Transactions is in the British Library)
National Archives, Kew
Newspaper Library, Colindale
Pirbright Parish Council [*PPC*]: Minute Books, deeds and letters
Sigmund Freud Museum, London
Surrey History Centre [*SHS*], Woking.
The Armstrong Browning Library: Lady Layard's Journal.
University of Southampton, Parkes Library: Anglo-Jewish Association Minute Books.

General Bibliography

Adler, Marcus M. *The Adler Family*. Reprinted from the *Jewish Chronicle*, London, 1909.
Adler, Michael. *History of the Central Synagogue 1855–1905*. Reprinted from the *Jewish Chronicle*, London, 1905.
Allfrey, Anthony. *Edward VII and his Jewish Court*. London: Weidenfeld and Nicholson, 1991.
Argyll, Duke of. *The Eastern Question from the Treaty of Paris 1836 to the Treaty of Berlin 1878 and to the Second Afghan War*. London: Strahan, 1879.
Arthur, G. (ed.) *The Letters of Lord and Lady Wolseley, 1870–1911*. London: Heinemann, 1922.
Beerbohm, Max. *Fifty Caricatures by Max Beerbohm*. London: William Heinemann, 1913.
Beesen, E.W. *Port Sunlight: The Model Village of England, a Collection of Photographs*. Architectural Book Publishing Company, 1911.
Berghöffer, C.W. *Mayer Amschel Rothschild: Der Gründer des Rothschilder Bankhauses*. Frankfurt am Main, 1924.
Bermant, Chaim. *Cousinhood: The Anglo-Jewish Gentry*. London: Eyre and Spottiswood, 1971.
Cambacérès, M. *Funérailles de Napoléon III*. Paris, 1873.
Cawthorne, Miss. *Collections for a History of Pirbright*. Typescript published 1931 with Henry Curtis.
Chambers, G.F. *Eastbourne Memories of the Victorian Period 1845–1901*. Eastbourne: V.T. Sumfield, 1910.
Chromet, Seweryn. *Helena – Princess Reclaimed: The Life and Times of Queen Victoria's 3rd Daughter*. Newman – Hemisphere, 2000.
Clarke, Edward. *The Story of my Life*. London, John Murray, 1918.
Commission on Tea Cultivation in Assam, 1868–9.
Cooke, A.B. and Vincent, J. *The Governing Passion: Cabinet Government and Party Politics in Britain 1885–86*. Brighton: Harvester Press, 1974.

BIBLIOGRAPHY

Corti, Egon Count *The Rise of the House of Rothschild* (translated by Brian and Beatrix Lunn). London: Gollancz, 1928.

Corti, Egon Count. *The Reign of the House of Rothschild* (translated by Brian and Beatrix Lunn). London: Gollancz, 1928.

Cowles, V. *Edward VII and His Circle*. London: Hamish Hamilton, 1956.

Curtis, Henry. *A List of the Curates and Vicars of Pirbright, Surrey*. Typescript, published 1924.

Deane, P. and Cole, W.A. *British Economic Growth 1688–1959. Trends and Structure*, 2nd edition. Cambridge: Cambridge University Press, 1967.

Dennison, Mathew. *The Lost Princess. The Devoted Life of Queen Victoria's Youngest Daughter*. London: Weidenfeld and Nicolson, 2007.

Doraiswami, S.V. *Indian Finance Currency and Banking*. Madras: Doraiswami, 1915.

Emden, Paul H. *Jews of Britain: A Series of Biographies*. London: S. Low, Marston & Co. Ltd., 1944.

Endelman, T.M. *The Jews of Britain, 1656 to 2000 (Jewish Communities in the Modern World)*. Berkeley and Los Angeles: University of California Press, 2002.

Ferguson, N. *The World's Banker. A History of the House of Rothschild*. London: Weidenfeld and Nicolson, 1998.

Frankland, Noble. *Witness of a Century: The Life and Times of Prince Arthur Duke of Connaught 1850–1942*. London: Shepheard-Walwyn, 1993.

Gow, Wilson and Stanton, Ltd. *Tea Companies of India and Ceylon*. London: A. Southey and Co. 1897.

Green, Abigail. *Moses Montefiore, Jewish Liberator – Imperial Hero*. Cambridge, MA and London: Belknap Press, 2010.

Halsey, Katherine D. *Remembrances of Pirbright, 1875–1912*. Manuscript [SHC] 2791/1.

Harvey, A.D. *Collisions of Empires: Britain in Three World Wars, 1793–1945*. Cambridge: Cambridge University Press, 1992.

Harvey, W.A. *The Model Village and its Cottages: Bournville*. London: B.T. Batsford, 1906.

Hazan, Thayer and Lord. *Three Peace Congresses of the Nineteenth Century*. Cambridge, MA: Harvard University Press, 1917.

Homes, Oliver Wendell. *Our Hundred Days in Europe*. Boston: Houghton Mifflin & Co., 1887.

Ireland, George, *Plutocrats A Rothschild Inheritance*. London: John Murray, 2007.

Jackson, S. *The Sassoons*. London: Heinemann, 1968.

Janik, Allan and Veigh, Hans. *Wittgenstein in Vienna: A Biographical Excursion through the City and its History*. Vienna and New York: Springer, 1998.

Jathar, G.B. and Beri, S.G. *India Economics: A Comprehensive and Critical Survey*, vol. I. Indian Branch, Oxford University Press, 1942.

Kindleberger, Charles P. *Manias, Panics and Crashes, A History of Financial Crises*, 3rd edition. London: John Wiley & Sons, 1996.

King, W. *History of the London Discount Market*. London: Routledge, 1936.

Lane, C.H. *Dog Shows and Doggy People*. London: Hutchinson, 1902.

Leven, N. *Cinquante Ans d' Histoire: L'Alliance Israélite Universelle (1860–1910)*, vol. I. Paris: Librairie Félix Alcan, 1911.

Levy, Benas. *Die Juden in Worms: ein Vortrag gehalten von Benas Levy Berlin im verein für Jüdische Geschichte und Literatur*. Berlin: M. Poppelauer, 1914.

Lieben, Anne von. *Gedichte. Ihren Freunden zur Erinnerung*. Vienna: Carl Fromme, 1901.

Loewenstein, Leopold. *A Time to Love – A Time to Die*. London: W.H. Allen, 1970.
Lyons, F.S.L. *Charles Stewart Parnell*. Dublin: Gill & McMillan, 2005 (1st edition 1977).
Mahajan, Sneh. *British Foreign Policy 1874–1914*. London and New York: Routledge, 2002.
Malden, H.E. (ed.) *A History of the County of Surrey*, vol. 3. Victoria County History, 1911.
Matthew, H.C.G. *Gladstone 1809–1898*. Oxford: Oxford University Press 1997.
Mégroz, Phyllis. *Memoirs of H.R.H. Infanta Eulalia* (translated). London: Hutchinson & Co., 1936.
Meith, S., Rohrer, J. and Rosani, T. *Trauttmansdorff, Geschichte eines Schlosses*. Tourismuseum, Schloss Trauttmansdorff.
Mintz, Sidney W. *Sweetness and Power: Place of Sugar in Modern History*. New York: Viking, 1985.
Molineux, Nellie Z.R. *History Genealogical and Biographical of the Molyneux Families*. Syracuse, NY: C.W. Bardeen, 1904.
Morais, H.S. *Eminent Israelites of the Nineteenth Century*. Philadelphia: Edward Stern & Co., 1880.
Morris, Marc. *Edward I and the Forging of Britain*. London: Hutchinson, 2008.
Morton, Frederic. *The Rothschilds, A Family Portrait*. Philadelphia: Curtis Publishing Co., 1961.
Müller, Reinhard. *Marienthal Das Dorf – Die Arbeitslosen – Die Studie*. Innsbruck and Vienna: StudienVerlag, 2008.
Norgate, Kate. *John Lackland*. London: Macmillan, 1902.
Parker, Matthew. *The Sugar Barons*. London: Hutchinson, 2011.
Philipson, David. *Old European Jewries*. Philadelphia: Jewish Publication Society of America, 1894.
Pryor, Francis. *The Making of the British Landscape*. London: Allen Lane, 2010.
Röhl, J.C.G. *Wilhelm II – The Kaiser's Personal Monarchy 1888–1900* (translated by S. de Bellaigne). Cambridge: Cambridge University Press 2004.
Romeike, H. *The Wife Beaters' Manual, a Guide to Husbands' Connubial Corrections* (C.W. Barker, editor). London: Artistic & Literary Correspondence Offices, 1884.
Rosebery, Lord. *Lord Randolph Churchill*. London: A.L. Humphreys, 1906.
Rungta, Shyan, *Rise of Business Corporations in India, 1851–1900*. Cambridge: Cambridge University Press, 1970.
Salbstein M.C.N. *The Emancipation of the Jews in Britain: The Question of the Admission of the Jews to Parliament, 1828–1860*. East Brunswick, NJ: Associated University Presses, 1982.
Salomons, D.L. *The Management of Accumulators; a Practical Handbook*. London: Whittaker & Co., 1888, in many editions.
Simmons, P.L. *Coffee and Chicory: Culture, Chemical Composition, Preparation for Market and Consumption*. London: E. & F.N. Spoon, 1864.
Sinclair, Tollemanche. *A Defence of Russia and the Christians of Turkey*. London: Chapman & Hall, 1877.
Squier, John. *Henley Park in Surrey: The History of a Royal Manor*. Normandy Historians, 2012.
Steinberg, Jonathan. *Bismarck – A Life*. Oxford: Oxford University Press, 2011.
Stepansky, Paul F. (ed.) *Freud Appraisals and Reappraisals*, vol. I. London: Analytical Press, 1986.

Stern, Fritz. *Gold and Iron: Bismarck, Bleichröder and the Building of the German Empire.* London: Allen and Unwin, 1977.
Strong, George V. *Seedtime for Fascism: The Disintegration of Austrian Political Culture, 1867–1918.* New York: M.E. Sharpe, 1998.
Treasures of Jewish Heritage. London: The Jewish Museum, 2006.
Vervaeke, P. *Dieu, la Couronne et l'Empire: La Primrose League 1883–2000.* Doctoral thesis, University of Lille, 2003.
Vitzthum, Charles Count *St. Petersburg and London in the Years 1852–1864* (translated by E.F. Taylor). London: Longmans, 1887.
Wechsberg, J. *The Merchant Bankers.* London: Weidenfeld and Nicolson, 1967.
Williams, Montague. *Leaves of a Life.* London: Macmillan & Co., 1890, 2 vols.
Wilmore, David. *Edwin O. Sachs: Architect, Stagehand, Engineer and Fireman.* London: Theatresearch, 1999.
Wright, Arnold, *Twentieth Century Impression of Ceylon: Its History, People, Commerce, Industries and Resources.* India: Asian Education Services, 1999.
Wurzbach, Constant von. *Biographisches Lexikon des Kaisertums Österreich*, part 45. Vienna: State Press, 1882.
Yool, Helen. *The Day Before Yesterday: The Story of Pirbright.* Pirbright Church, 1973.

Notes

Introduction

1. Cawthorn and Curtis, *Pirbright*. Yool, *Pirbright*.
2. Parliamentary Research Paper 12/31 (29 May 2012).

Chapter One: Frankfurt to London

1. Philipson, *Old European Jewries,* pp. 5–18.
2. Levy, *Die Juden von Worms,* pp. 15–16.
3. Philipson, *Old European Jewries*, pp. 46–67; Adler, *The Adler Family*, pp. 18–19.
4. Gulden – sterling exchange rates gleaned from Rothschild correspondence, Ferguson, *World's Banker*, pp. 1037–08.
5. Berghöffer, *Mayer Amschel Rothschild,* p. 146 and 201ff; Ferguson, *The World's Banker*, p. 48; Emden, *Jews of Britain*, p. 283; Corti, *Rise*, pp. 5–9, 22, 31.
6. Deane and Cole, *British Economic Growth*, pp. 28–31 and 185–281; Phillipson, *Old European Jewries*, pp. 73–4.
7. Norgate, *John Lackland*, p. 137.
8. Morris, *Edward I*, pp. 87, 125, 226–7.
9. Lucien Wolf, in Wolf and Roth, *Essays*, p. 225.
10. Corti, *Rise*, p. 26; Margrit Schulte Beerbühl, Crossing the channel: Nathan Mayer Rothschild and his trade with the Continent during the early years of the blockades (1803–1808), *Rothschild Review of the Year 2007–8*, pp. 41–8; Harvey, *Collisions*, pp. 103–09.
11. Corti, *Rise*, p. 193 quoting from the Prussian State Archives.
12. Bermant, *Cousinhood*.
13. Ferguson, *The World's Banker*, p. 203.
14. Pryor, *British Landscape*, pp. 559–61.
15. Roderick J. Barman, Nathan Mayer Rothschild and Brazil: the role of Samuel Phillips & Co., *Rothschild Review of the Year 2002–3*, pp. 38–45.
16. *Treasures of Jewish Heritage.*
17. *Hansard,* HL Deb 21 April 1828, vol. 18, c1586.
18. Ireland, *Plutocrats*; Geoffrey Alderman, Lionel de Rothschild in *DNB*; The Late Baron Lionel de Rothschild, *The Times*, 4 June 1879.
19. Wolf and Roth, *Essays*, pp. 329–38.

20. Quoted in *The Times*, 28 June 1887.
21. Kindleberger, *Manias*, pp. 51–4.

Chapter Two: Tea and Coffee

1. For Maurice and Gabriel, see Victor Gray and Ismeth Raheem, *Rothschild review of the year April 2003 to March 2004*, p. 52.
2. Letter 19/6/1874, Count Beust, Austrian ambassador London to Lord Derby, Foreign Office, National Archives FO 83/468 section 16.
3. George de Worms writing in restrospect, *The Times*, 23 August 1886.
4. Wills and bequests, *The Times*, 25 November 1881; will proved on 2nd November, personal estate of £70,000.
5. Deeds, sale of Milton Park, *SHC*, 185/10/30 (Dec. 1871) and 185/11/203 (1872). Sale by auction of the contents, *The Times*, 21 September 1948. Report ref. MJP/KMJ/02A303252 from G.V.A. Grimley, London, International Property Advisors, 19 February 2003.
6. Advertisements appeared in the larger newspapers of Britain and Ireland e.g. *Daily News*, 7 October 1863, *Birmingham Post*, 10 October 1863.
7. *Birmingham Daily Post*, 7 October 1863.
8. *Daily News*, 30 November 1864 and advertisement for the Bank in *Daily News*, 16 January 1866.
9. Report of the 5th ordinary general meeting, *The Standard*, 31 July 1868, p. 2.
10. Advertisement in *Daily News*, 28 January 1864.
11. Gilbert and Sullivan, *Trial by Jury*, 1875. The Gurneys were a byword for riches.
12. 4th annual report, *Daily News*, 27 April 1867.
13. Albert Simpson, Silver vs. Cotton, *The National Review*, 1897, vol. 30, p. 244. Chapter 1 in S. V. Doraiswami, *Indian Finance Currency and Banking*.
14. Oscar Wilde in *The Importance of Being Earnest* (1895).
15. He was Mr Bainbridge, a thoroughly practical tea-planter, *Daily News*, 10 December 1875.
16. Report of the 17th Ordinary General Meeting, *The Bullionist*, 3 July 1880, copy in Gloucester Regional Archives, D6163/2/13.
17. Notice of liquidation meeting, *London Gazette*, 23 July 1897, p. 4152; *The Times*, 31 August 1897.
18. *Morning Post*, 22 July 1896. Gow, Wilson and Stanton, *Tea Companies of India and Ceylon*.
19. *The Morning Post*, 1 September 1897, p. 2.

Chapter Three: Science, Law or Politics?

1. Epitaph to Lord Pirbright, St. Mark's churchyard, Wyke, Surrey.
2. Worms, *Reminiscences*, in Beust, *Memoirs*, vol. I, p. xxix.

3. Skeat, *King's College London Engineering Society*, 1957. Worms 'promising to assist' in *Engineering Society Minute Book*, 19 November 1857.
4. Peter Johnston, George F. Chambers 1841–1915, in *J. British Astronomical Association*, 1990, vol. 100, pp. 13–16.
5. *Engineering Society Minute Book*, 11 June 1858, 6 December 1858, 5 April, 14 June and 6 December 1859, 22 March and 11 December 1860, 19 March and 11 June 1861.
6. Obituary, *The Times*, 10 January 1903; Chambers, *Memories*, pp. 279–80.
7. Committee Minute Book, 2 February 1860; Society Minute Book, 7 February 1860.
8. Society Minute Book, 30 April 1861.
9. The Leviathan, *Transactions*, p. 8; progress of engineering science, ibid., pp. 14–16.
10. The manufacture of iron, Society Minute Book, 29 March 1859; the Suez Canal, Society Minute Book, 21 February 1860; drainage, Society Minute Book, 5 June 1860; presidential address, Society Minute Book, 9 October 1860.
11. Society Minute Book, 15 November 1859. Experiment reported in *The Standard*, 1 December 1859; *Morning Chronicle*, 2 December 1859; *Daily News*, 3 December 1859.
12. Provisional patent 1081, *London Gazette*, 22 May 1860, 2693.
13. Sporting prowess, *Jewish World*, 16 January 1903; promotion to captain, *London Gazette*, 20 March 1860, 1139.
14. War Office announcement on Volunteer Corps, *The Times*, 13 May 1859; G. Sheffield, British Army in *The Oxford Companion of Military History*, Richard Holmes (ed.), OUP, 2001.
15. *Daily News*, 24 January 1868.
16. W.E. Gladstone, *Bulgarian Horrors and the Question of the East*, John Murray, London, 1876.
17. Sir Tollemanche Sinclair, M.P. *A Defence of Russia*, appendix, pp. 98–107.
18. *The Standard*, 30 April 1867; *Nottinghamshire Guardian*, 19 July 1878; *The Standard*, 27 October 1879.

Chapter Four: The Anglo-Jewish Association – Apprenticeship to Politics

1. Obituary, *The Times*, 22 January 1890.
2. Obituary, *The Times*, 19 July 1911.
3. Michael Adler, *History*; Jewish United Synagogue Act 1870, 33&34 Vict. c116.
4. N. Leven, *Cinquante Ans d'Histoire*, chapter 2.
5. AJA Minute Book, 30 May 1871.
6. *Pall Mall Gazette*, 5 July 1871, AJA Minute Book, 2 July 1871.
7. AJA Minute Book, 10 October 1872
8. Annual Report of the AJA for 1872–3, MS137/AJ95/150/1, pp. 6–7.
9. Record of the Shah's audience, *The Times*, 25 June 1873; content of the address, *The Times*, letter to the editor, 29 July 1873.
10. On the state grant, *The English Independent and Free Church Advocate*, 15 February

1872. Prize-giving ceremony in *Lloyd's Weekly Newspaper*, 3 May 1874. The Patriotism of the Jews in *The Morning Post*, 7 June 1878, p. 6.
11. AJA Minute Book, 10 October 1872, 2 June 1873, 8 July 1878, 3 April 1879 and 4 May 1882.
12. Reported in *The Times*, 5 August 1876 and 15 August 1877.
13. W.R. Thayer, *The Congress of Paris*, in Hazen, Thayer and Lord, *Three Peace Congresses*, pp. 23–45.
14. Report of the council meeting, *The Times*, 18 November 1876; AJA Minute Book, 21 December 1876.
15. Roberts, *Salisbury*, pp. 149–168.
16. Reports of the conference in *The Hampshire Advertiser*, 16 December 1876 and *The Morning Post*, 20 December 1876, p. 5.
17. AJA Minute Book, 21 December 1876, reported in *The Times*, 22 December 1876.
18. For diplomatic manoeuvres towards the treaty, Argyll *The Eastern Question*, pp. 134–214; Roberts, *Salisbury*, pp. 189–204.
19. The full text of the memorial is given in *The Morning Post*, 21 June 1878, p. 3.
20. Stern, *Gold and Iron*, pp. 376–77. R.H. Lord, *The Congress of Berlin*, in Hazan, Thayer and Lord, *Three Peace Congresses*, pp. 47–68.
21. *The Standard*, 17 July 1878.
22. On the Jews in Romania, A. Löwy, *The Times*, 28 November and 21 December 1878; Ion Ghica, member of Romanian senate, *The Times*, 20 January 1879, p. 4C, Henry de Worms, *The Times*, 23 January 1879, p. 10F.
23. Letter 2/3/1879, Salisbury to Worms (copy), *The Times*, 4 March 1879.
24. Position of the Jews in Romania, *The Morning Post*, 26 July 1879, p. 3.
25. Letter, Henry de Worms to the editor, *The Times*, 16 August 1884.
26. Jews in Russia, *The Times*, 25 May 1881; AJA Minutes, 24 May 1881.
27. Meeting in Manchester, *The Times*, 3 February 1882; in Liverpool, *Manchester Evening News*, 4 February 1882.
28. *The Times*, 10 February 1882. Persecution of the Jews in Russia – resolution and debate, *Hansard*, HC Deb 03 March 1882 cc30-70. The conduct of Prince Lobanoff, the Russian Ambassador, and the text of the memorial are noted in *The Times*, 25 January 1882, p. 7E.
29. Letter 7/3/1882, H. de Worms to Mr. Löwy, secretary of the AJA (copy) AJA Minutes for 2 April 1882.
30. *Liverpool Mercury*, 4 February 1882. AJA Minute Book 5 March 1882.
31. Herr Stöcker's notoriety in *Memoirs of Count Beust*, vol. I p. 85, also Green, *Moses Montefiore*, p. 410. Letter 21/12/1883, H. de Worms, Palais Todesco, Vienna to Montagu Scott, Brighton (copy), *The Morning Post*, 31 December 1883, p. 3.
32. AJA Minute Book 6 June 1884; letter 12/8/1884, H. de Worms to the editor, *The Times*, 16 August 1884, p. 8.
33. Letter 3/7/1885, H. de Worms to Rev. A. Löwy, (copy) AJA Minute book, 5 July 1885; see *Hansard*, HC Deb 07 July 1885 vol 298 cc1939-40
34. Marriage of Cyril Flower, *Leeds Mercury*, 23 November 1877; Marriage of Lord Rosebery *Hampshire Telegraph & Sussex Chronicle*, 23 March 1878. Editorial, *Jewish World*, 20 October 1882.
35. Letter 2/5/1886, H. de Worms to Dr. Löwy (copy) AJA Minute Book, 2 May 1886.

NOTES

36. AJA Minute Book, 6 June and 19 July 1886.
37. *The Standard*, 20 October 1893, p. 5, *The Star*, 24 October 1893, p. 1
38. *The Morning Post*, 31 October 1890, p. 3. *The Times*, 30 April 1901, p. 10. *London Gazette*, 25 January 1901.

Chapter Five: Banking and Marriage – the Austrian Connections

1. Lord Byron, *Don Juan Cantos XII-XIII-XIV*, John Hunt, London, 1823. The poem was fully completed in 1837
2. No. 57 in *Fifty Caricatures by Max Beerbohm*.
3. For the cousinhood see Chapter 19 in Chaim Bermant, *The Cousinhood*.
4. F. Morton, *The Rothschilds*, pp. 59–63.
5. Bildarchiv, Österreichische Nationalbibliothek, Cat. No. 1092360
6. Letter, George Worms to the editor, *The Times*, 26 May 1870; obituary, Baron de Worms, in *The Times*, 28 November 1912, p. 9C
7. Bildarchiv, Österreichische Nationalbibliothek, Cat. No. 882123.
8. Todesco anecdotes collected by P.J. Swales in Stepansky (ed.), *Freud*, pp. 3–32.
9. G.V. Strong, *Seed Time for Fascism*, p. 119; A Janik and H Veigh, *Wittgenstein in Vienna*, p. 72.
10. Constant von Wurzbach, *Biographisches Lexikon*, Part 45, pp. 224–227.
11. Ficticious transactions based on, for cotton to Austria, William Rathbone (MP for Caernarvonshire) in *Hansard*, HC Deb 26 July 1882, vol. 272 c 1862; for the sugar trade, Charles Ritchie (MP for Tower Hamlets) in *Hansard*, HC Deb 22 April 1879, vol. 245 c 262.
12. Gulden and Krone currency, Oesterreichische Nationalbank, http://www.oenb.at
13. Notice of dissolution, *London Gazette*, 21 May 1880, p. 3144.
14. Notice of sale, *The Times*, 11 June 1887.
15. Forgery of £10,000, *The Whitehaven News*, 7 October 1869.
16. Will and Bequests, *Daily News*, 1 December 1882; will proved on 16 November, personal estate £429, 271.
17. Worms, *Reminiscences*, in Beust, *Memoirs*, vol. I, p. xxviii.
18. *Musical World*, 5 May 1849.
19. Information from Gerstner Beletage im Palais Todesco, Kärntner Straße 51, Wien.
20. Tagesneuigkeiten, *Der Botschafter*, 5 May 1864 [trans. by the author].
21. Wedding certificate in the National Archives J/77/358/808.
22. John Greencombe (general editor), *Survey of London*, 2000, vol. 45, pp. 19–21.
23. Anna von Lieben, *Gedichte* , p. 54 *Krankenzimmer (1867)*, p. 76 *Frühling 1861* [must be a typographical error for 1867]. On the identification of Cäcilie M, Peter J. Swales in P.F. Stepansky (ed.), *Freud*, pp. 3–32.
24. Worms, *Reminiscences*, in Beust, *Memoirs*, pp. i and xvi.
25. Report 11–12/5/1866 Benary to Bleichröder, Bleichröder archive quoted in Stern, *Gold and Iron*, p. 79.
26. Ferguson, *The World's Banker*.
27. Corti, *Rise*, ch. XX; Corti, *Reign*, ch. V and VIII.

28. Vitzthum, *St. Petersburg and London*, p. 266.
29. The Augustenburg line had branched off from the Danish royal house in the sixteenth century.
30. Frequently quoted, e.g. *Wall Street Journal*, 25 February 2000; a historical account of the problem is given by Count Vitzthum, Saxon Ambassador, in *The Times*, 2 December 1863.
31. L.D. Steefel, 'The Rothschilds and the Austrian Loan of 1865', *J. Modern History*, 1936, 8: 27–39.
32. Stern, *Gold and Iron*, pp. 43–46.
33. Quoted from the *Neue Freie Presse* in *Daily News*, 10 May 1866.
34. *Mon Dieu! Il me donne son linge sale à laver*, a quotation by Beust from Voltaire, Worms, *Reminiscences*, in Beust, *Memoirs*, vol. I, p. vi. Beust, *Memoirs*, vol. I, chap. XXXII, vol. II, chap. I.
35. Worms, *Reminiscences*, in Beust, *Memoirs*, vol. I, p. ii–iii.
36. Worms, *Reminiscences*, in Beust, *Memoirs*, vol. I, p. xvii.
37. Letter 28/5/1868, Beust to James Rothschild in State Archives Vienna, quoted in Corti, *Reign*, p. 407.
38. Letter 9/6/1868, Beust, Vienna to Count Apponyi, London, quoted in Worms, *Austro-Hungarian Empire*, pp. 46–52.
39. Letter 24/5/1870, Chairman Committee of Anglo-Austrian Bondholders to the Stock Exchange, London (copy). *The Times*, 25 May 1870 summarises the situation.
40. Telegram 12 /7/1870 Count Apponyi, Austrian Ambassador in London, to Beust, Vienna, State Archives Vienna, quoted in Corti, *Reign*, p. 414.
41. Letter 2/5/1870, George Worms to editor *The Times*, 26 May 1870.
42. Letter 13/6/1870, Apponyi to G. Worms (copy), *The Times*, 16 June 1870.
43. Vienna 23/4/1871, Letters Patent for the Austrian title (certified translation). National Archives FO 83/486 section 16.
44. Certificate of Naturalization, National Archives, HO 334/5/1305.
45. Letter 19/6/1874, Beust, London to Lord Derby, Foreign Office: '*La maison de Worms ne vous est pas inconnue, vous avez été son hôte pendent votre séjour aux Indes et a meme de juger de son activité que l'on me dit avoir donné une grande impulsion au commerce entre l'isle de Ceylon et l'Europe.*' Letter 13/8/1874, Home Office to Beust, London. National Archives FO 83/468 section 16.
46. The revocation of royal licences for holders of Austrian and German titles (1920), National Archives HO 45/10964/363538.
47. Reprinted in *The Times*, 9 January 1872.
48. *The Times*, 17 January 1873.
49. Stern, *Gold and Iron*, p. 430.
50. Rutland Gardens and South Place: South Place and South Lodge, *Survey of London* vol. 45, pp. 128–134; for the memorial on Knightsbridge barracks, see *The Standard*, 15 July 1874.
51. Letter 30/8/1871, from Nathaniel Mayer Rothschild to Lionel Rothschild, quoted in Ireland *Plutocrats*, p. 334.
52. Ambassadorial dinner, *The Times*, 6 May 1872.
53. For the visit of the Archduke, *Hampshire Advertiser*, 28 August 1872.

NOTES

54. Worms, *Reminiscences*, in Beust, *Memoirs*, vol. I, p. lxv; the Worms family took Grantham House in Cowes, *Hampshire Advertiser*, 24 July 1872, p. 4.
55. M. Cambacérès, *Funérailles de Napoléon III*, p. 76.
56. Address of condolence, *Daily News*, 13 July 1879; Details of Henry's funeral, *The Times*, 5 June 1903.
57. Advertisement, *Pall Mall Gazette*, 16 July 1874. The Institute, *Morning Post*, 17 July 1874.
58. Advertisement for the bank, *Pall Mall Gazette*, 14 June 1872.
59. Report of the meeting, *Morning Post*, 3 March 1874, p. 2.
60. Police, *The Times*, 12 March 1874; Law and Police, *Pall Mall Gazette*, 11 March 1874.
61. *Archives commerciales de la France*, December 1875, p. 72. Report of the general meeting in *The Standard*, 1 April 1876, p. 6.
62. Letter February 1876, Beust, London to Worms, Egypt (copy); Worms, *Reminiscences*, in Beust, *Memoirs*, vol. I, p. lxxxi.
63. Baroness Henry de Worms has left town for Carlsbad, *Morning Post*, 10 June 1876.
64. S. Mieth, J. Rohter and T. Rosani, *Trautmannsdorff*, pp. 57–65.
65. Ibid., pp. 67–78.
66. A brief biography of new MPs gives this address, *The Times*, 3 April 1880 p. 6D.
67. See subsequent divorce proceedings, *The Times*, 15 July 1886, p. 3.
68. He is recorded as living here in the 1881 census.
69. Letters concerning the Stöcker affair at the Carlton Club were posted from these addresses.
70. Arrivals and departures from the Lord Warden Hotel, Dover, *Morning Post*, 17 August 1883; Baron de Worms at Edinburgh, *Morning Post*, 1 February 1884.
71. *New York Times*, 13 July 1886.
72. *New York Times*, 13 February 1887.
73. Notice in *Morning Post*, 23 May 1884, p. 5.
74. London gossip in the *Hampshire Telegraph & Sussex Chronicle*, 14 June 1884.
75. See reports of the divorce in *The Times*, *Birmingham Daily Post* and *Freeman's Journal*, all of 15 July 1886. The trial papers are preserved in the National Archives J/77/358/808.
76. Letter 3/7/1885, H. Worms to Rev. A. Löwy (copy), AJA Minute Book, 5 July 1885.
77. S. Mieth, J. Rohter and T. Rosani, *Trautmannsdorff*, pp. 67–75.
78. The bequests are outlined in the will of Lord Pirbright dated 4 December 1902, probate London 27 February 1903.
79. S. Mieth, J. Rohter and T. Rosani, *Trautmannsdorff*, pp. 76–140.
80. Marriage at St. James's, Piccadilly, *Morning Post*, 9 April 1886, p. 5; *Pall Mall Gazette*, 18 April 1886; *Nottinghamshire Guardian*, 30 April 1886, p. 6. J. Jacobs and V.R. Emanuel, later criticism in *Jewish Chronicle*, 16 January 1903.
81. For the honeymoon trip see *York Herald*, 7 December 1888; on New Zealand see *Evening Post (Wellington)*, 22 April 1891, p. 2; An account of the State Ball appears in *The Times*, 4 July 1889.
82. *Quorndon Magazine*, summer 1996; Bulmer's *History and Directory of North Yorkshire*, 1890.

83. Obituary, *Leeds Mercury*, 14 April 1891. Will given in *The Times*, 25 September 1891, p. 5F.
84. C.H. Lane, *Dog Shows*, pp. 186–88.
85. Alice Morrison, article in www.navigare.de/hofmannsthal derived from *Kritische Ausgabe Sämtlicher Werke Hugo von Hofmannsthal* and conversations with her great-nephew and -niece John and Evamarie Kallir.
86. Announcement of marriage, *The Standard*, 5 November 1895, p. 5. Leopold of Loewenstein, *A Time to Love*, p. 13.
87. Williams, *Leaves of a Life*, p. 268.
88. Thought reading, *Morning Post*, 10 July 1882, p. 2, 4 June 1884, p. 5; a thought-reader's thoughts, *Leeds Mercury*, 8 September 1888. Change of address, *Morning Post*, 31 March 1885, p. 5. The Primrose League, *Belfast News-Letter*, 28 September 1885, *Morning Post*, 2 October 1885, p. 2, 30 October 1885, p. 2, 23 September 1885, p. 2.
89. Williams, *Leaves of a Life*, p. 146.

Chapter Six: House of Commons: House of Lords

1. Vanity Fair, 22 May 1880.
2. Representation of the Peoples Act, 1867, 30 & 31 Vict. I c102.
3. Worms, *Reminiscences*, in Beust, *Memoirs*, vol. I, p. xxx.
4. Manifesto printed in *Pall Mall Gazette*, 11 July 1868.
5. *Guardian*, 23 September 1868.
6. F.W. Newman, *The Permissive Bill, more urgent than any extension of the franchise*, 17 February 1865, Pamphlet printed in London by E. Pitman.
7. Ranger in *Illustrated Sporting and Dramatic News*, quoted in *Newcastle Weekly Courant*, 20 June 1896.
8. *Hansard*, HC Deb 23 March 1868, vol. 191, c 32.
9. P.P. 1881, xlv. 15; this affair was so notorious that it was summarised in the *New York World*, 28 November 1880.
10. O'Leary, *Corrupt Practices*, pp. 8–11, 25, 152; the returns for this borough have been exhaustively studied, F.W.G. Andrews, 'The Poll Books of Sandwich, Kent 1831–68', *Historical Research*, 2002, 71: 75–107.
11. *Freeman's Journal*, 27 March 1874.
12. Letter 22/7/1878 Henry de Worms, London to E. Hughes, secretary City Conservative Association (copy), *The Times*, 23 July 1878.
13. The manifesto was published in *The Times*, 22 March 1880.
14. Full electoral results, *The Times*, 29 April 1880.
15. *The Times*, 31 March 1880.
16. The West Calder speech of 27 November, *The Times*, 28 November 1879, p. 10A.
17. O'Leary, *Corrupt Practices*, pp. 112–113 and 119–124; The Ballot Act, 35 & 36 Vict. I c33; Corrupt and Illegal Practices Act, 43 Vict. c18; Commentary in *Daily News*, 18 March 1880.
18. O'Leary, *Corrupt Practices*, pp. 174–175.
19. *Hansard*, HC Deb 29 June 1883, vol. 280 c. 1883.
20. For a list of all Jewish candidates in 1874 and 1880, see *Daily News*, 12 April 1880;

ejection of Bradlaugh from the Commons, *Trewman's Exeter Flying Post*, 10 August 1881.
21. Baron Henry de Worms, *Hansard*, HC Deb 24 May 1880, vol. 252 cc 333–422.
22. Osborne Morgan (Judge Advocate general), *Hansard*, HC Deb 26 April 1883, vol. 278 c 1220
23. Congregationalists, *Sheffield & Rotherham Independent*, 12 May 1883, p. 7
24. Speech 16 May to Greenwich Conservatives, *Morning Post*, 17 May 1883, p. 2.
25. The Oaths Act, 51&52 Vict. c46; for the AJA, see chapter 3.
26. Roberts, *Salisbury*, chap. 15; statistics from *North Wales Chronicle*, 2 July 1881.
27. R. Power and William Harcourt on the Christian and Jew in *Hansard*, HC Deb 20 February 1882, vol. 266 cc 1098–9.
28. Seating arrangement, *Leicester Chronicle & Leicestershire Mercury*, 28 October 1882; this description of his manner was quoted frequently, e.g. in *Belfast News-Letter*, 15 June 1882; his looks are recorded in *Dundee Chronicle & Argus*, 8 July 1885.
29. London correspondence from *Nottinghamshire Guardian*, 24 February 1882, p. 6; debates on *clôture*, *Hansard*, HC Deb 20 March 1882, vol. 267, cc 1138–44, HC Deb 11 November 1882, vol. 274 c 1635: Conservatism in North Wilts. *Hampshire Advertiser*, 15 April 1882, p. 7; Gravesend meeting in *Birmingham Daily Post*, 19 December 1882, p. 8; The new Rules of Procedure are given in *The Times*, 2 December 1882, p. 5F.
30. Baron Henry de Worms in *Hansard*, HC Deb 28 June 1880, vol. 253, cc 991–2.
31. Statement on the Royal Patriotic Fund by Mr. Childers in *Hansard* HC Deb.18 March 1881, vol. 259, c 1360; gazetting, *Morning Post*, 12 October 1881, p. 5.
32. Annual meetings are reported in: *Bristol Mercury & Daily Post*, 1 March 1880; *Essex Standard*, 25 March 1882, p. 3; Cartoon in *Vanity Fair*, 5 March 1887.
33. Deputation to the Metropolitan Board of Works, *The Standard*, 9 June 1883, p. 3.
34. Letter, 2/5/1881, E.A. Cattar, West Kent coroner to Baron Henry de Worms (copy), *The Times*, 3 May 1881; proposed bill, *Morning Post*, 7 May 1881, p. 4; William Vernon-Harcourt in *Hansard*, HC Deb 11 August 1881, vol. 264, c 1522.
35. Baron Henry de Worms in *Hansard*, HC Deb 30 May 1883, vol. 279, cc 1223.
36. Henry de Worms, *Hansard*, HC Deb 20 January 1881, vol. 257, c 1025
37. Henry Romeike, *The Wife Beaters' Manual*, pp. 8-9.
38. *Pall Mall Gazette*, 22 April 1884.
39. Extension of franchise to women, *Hansard*, HC Deb 06 July 1883, vol. 281, cc 664–724; commentary in *Glasgow Herald*, 7 July 1883
40. *Trewman's Exeter Flying Post*, 10 August 1881; *Hampshire Telegraph & Sussex Chronicle*, 13 August 1881.
41. West Kent Club, *Morning Post*, 31 December 1881, p. 3; Dover Club, *Morning Post*, 27 January 1882; Greenwich Conservative Club, *Morning Post*, 16 June 1882, p. 3.
42. The British Museum has a set of these cards, Reg. No. 1896.0501.1070.
43. Letters to the editor: A Tory, *The Times*, 29 March 1883; Churchill, *The Times*, 2 April, 1883; MP, *The Times*, 5 April 1883; Worms, *The Times*, 3 April 1883 and 6 April 1883.
44. Churchill and the Conservative Party, *Pall Mall Gazette*, 10 July 1883; *The Times*, 6 May 1884, p. 10C. Rosebery in *Lord Randolph Churchill*.
45. Vervaeke, *La Primrose League*, première partie 3.2 on H. Worms; annex 2 les

fondateurs; annex 4 grand maîtres. The Grosvenor habitation, *Belfast News-Letter*, 28 September 1885. Marylebone district, *The Times*, 10 March 1887, p. 7E.

46. For an overview of The Great Game, see Sneh Mahajan *British Foreign Policy*.
47. The Second Afghan War, Mahajan, *British Foreign Policy*, pp. 60–1.
48. Henry Romeike, *The New York Times*, 4 June 1903.
49. Baron Henry de Worms, *Hansard*, HC Deb 25 July 1881, vol. 263, c 1778.
50. Transvaal debate, *Hansard*, HC Deb 25 July 1881, vol. 263, cc 1756–880.
51. L. Wolf, The Story of the Khedive's Shares, *The Times*, 26 December 1905, p. 11.
52. Egypt (Political Affairs), *Hansard*, HC Deb 25 May 1882, vol 269, cc 1603–4, 12 June 1882, vol. 271, cc 834–6, 26 June 1882, vol. 271, cc 412–4; Supply Debate, *Hansard*, HC Deb, 26 July 1882, vol. 271, cc 1829–902.
53. *Hansard*, HC Deb 11 June 1883, vol. 280, cc 229–80; Mahajan, *British Foreign Policy*, pp. 63–73.
54. *Hansard*, HC Deb 5 February 1884, vol. 284, cc 40–94.
55. Votes of censure, *Hansard*, HC Deb 14 February 1884, vol. 284, cc 930–6; 12 May 1884, vol. 288, cc 88–93; 23 February 1885, vol. 294, cc 1100–10. The quotation of Napoleon comes from his dispatch to the French Directory, 7 October 1798. Salisbury in *Hansard*, HL Deb 26 February 1885, vol. 294, cc 1311–28. Remark of Gladstone in *Hansard*, HC Deb 22 May 1884, vol. 288, c 1027.
56. *Hansard*, HC Deb 21 May 1885, vol. 298, c 1035; Mahajan, *British Foreign Policy*, pp. 75–9.
57. Roberts, *Salisbury*, pp. 94-5.
58. Reported in *Guardian*, 6 August 1884.
59. Representation of the People Act 1884, 48 & 49 Vic c3; Redistribution of Seats Act 1885, 48 & 49 Vic c23.
60. House of Commons for 8 June 1885, reported in *The Times*, 9 June 1885 p. 10.
61. Sir Edward Clarke, *Life*. p. 240.
62. Commentary from *Punch*, 4 July 1885, p. 10.
63. The ministerial crisis, *Birmingham Daily Post*, 13 June 1885.
64. Election Intelligence – Greenwich, *The Times*, 19 December 1884, p. 5F; Letter 15/12/1884, H de Worms to the editor; letter 15/12/1884, H.L. de Montmorency to the editor; *The Standard*, 16 December 1884, p. 2. Election Intelligence – Greenwich, *The Times*, 8 January 1885, p. 6B.
65. Election Intelligence – Liverpool, *The Times*, 22 October 1885, p. 10F; – Greenwich, *The Times*, 24 October 1885, p. 6E; Presentation to Baron H. de Worms, *The Morning Post*, 17 June 1886, p. 2.
66. The political libel case, *The Standard*, 20 June and 24 June 1885, *Morning Post*, 23, June 1885.
67. The political libel case, *The Standard*, 4 March 1886 p. 3, 5 March p. 3 and 6 March p. 2.
68. Baron de Worms v. Hughes, *The Standard*, 11 March 1886
69. General Election, *Liverpool Mercury*, 26 November 1885.
70. Lyons, *Charles Stewart Parnell*, pp. 206–9, 343–5.
71. A first-hand account of the affray by Oliver Wendell Homes, *Our Hundred Days in Europe*
72. Lord Rosebery, *Lord Randolph Churchill*, p. 71.

NOTES

73. The Liverpool Vacancy, *Leeds Mercury*, 4 January 1887. *The Penny Illustrated Paper*, 19 February 1887.
74. Queen's speech, *Hansard*, HL Deb 27 January 1887, vol. 310, c 5; 2nd reading, *Hansard*, HL Deb 26 July 1887, vol. 318, cc 12–6; The watch trade, *Liverpool Mercury*, 30 April 1887; Merchandise Marks Act 1887 50&51 Vict. c15.
75. T.H. Farrer, Equalization of Railway Rates, *Fortnightly Review*, 1882 vol. 32 (*n.s.*) pp. 174–190.
76. 2nd reading, *Hansard*, HC Deb 10 May 1888, vol. 325, cc 1831–92; Railway and Canal Traffic Act 1888 51&52 Vict. c25.
77. The West India Docks, Parker, *The Sugar Barons*, p. 346–7.
78. Statistics in *Times* leader column, *The Times*, 19 September 1887, p. 9D, and the executive of the London Trades Council, *The Times*, 30 November 1887, p. 4F. The history of sugar conventions is summarised in *Receuil Des Cours de l'Academie de Droit international de la Haye*, vol. 78, pp. 162–5 (1951). Letter (undated), Baron Henry de Worms, Paris, to Joseph Arch, London (copy), *The Times*, 9 August 1888, p. 12D.
79. Full protocol, *The Times*, 20 December 1887, p. 8B; Baron Henry de Worms: '*nous avons contribué à un grand acte de justice à l'égard du commerce international*'; Count Küfstein: '*nos plus chaleureux remerceiments pour la manière courtoise dont il a dirigé les travaux*' from *The Times*, 23 December 1887, p. 3F. On Salisbury's linguistic skill, Roberts, *Salisbury*, p. 197.
80. The journey is noted in *The Times*, 18, 21 and 23 January, 11 and 13 February 1888; *Birmingham Daily Post*, 17 January 1888, p. 5E; *Glasgow Herald*, 24 January 1888, p. 4A.
81. L. Wolf, Old times in New Court, Wolf and Roth, *Essays*, p. 273.
82. Lady Guendoline Cecil (Salisbury's daughter), diary 15 February 1888, quoted in Roberts, *Salisbury*, p. 482.
83. Debate on Zululand, *Hansard*, HC Deb 23 July 1888, vol. 329, cc 215–41.
84. Mr. Biggar in *Hansard*, HC Deb 28 February 1888, vol. 322, c 1654. Sugar Bounties Conference, *The Times*, 6 August 1888, p. 12D, 17 August 1888, p. 6D. Text of the Convention, *The Times*, 31 August 1888, p. 6A. Salisbury's speech at Bristol, *The Times*, 24 April 1889, p. 6.
85. Thomas Farrer, *The Times*, 5 September 1888, p. 11F. The Brighton election, letter 14/11/1889, Gladstone to Sir R. Peel (copy), *Daily News*, 16 October 1889; campaign slogans, *Pall Mall Gazette*, 18 October 1889, p. 1.
86. Baron H. de Worms on Sugar Bounties, *The Times*, 2 November 1888, p. 7E.
87. *Morning Post*, 30 August 1888, p. 4; *The Standard*, 17 April 1889, p. 5; *Liverpool Mercury*, 4 May 1889, p. 5.
88. Baron Henry de Worms, *Hansard*, HC Deb 11 April 1889, vol. 335, cc 303–26. Dinner at Grosvenor Place, *Daily News*, 20 May 1889 p. 3.
89. Lord Pirbright, 'The Ruin of the West Indies', *National Review*, 1897, vol. 30, pp. 519–534.
90. Commentary on opposition to the Bill, *Liverpool Mercury*, 4 May 1889, p. 5.
91. Lord Pirbright, *Hansard*, HL Deb 10 March 1902, vol 104, cc 850–9.
92. *Hansard*, HC Deb 1 June 1888, vol. 326, cc 988–9.
93. *Huddersfield Chronicle*, 14 July 1888, p. 7.
94. *Belfast News-Letter*, 19 July 1889, *The Times* leader, 5 August 1889, p. 7C. Regulation

of Railways Act 1889, Vict. 52&52 c57. *Iron*, 19 November 1886. Hicks Beach, *Hansard* HC Deb 23 January 1891, vol. 349, c 994.
95. HC Deb 11 March 1890, vol. 342, c 510; HC Deb 12 March 1890, vol. 342, c 618; HC Deb 12 March 1891, vol. 351, c 777.
96. Aims of the conference, *The Times*, 1 March 1890, p. 7A.
97. Röhl, *Wilhelm II*, pp. 133–4.
98. British delegation, *The Standard*, 14 March 1890, p. 3.
99. Speeches on the Labour Question, *The Times*, 26 February 1891, p. 10B; 23 October 1891, p. 3F. Hansard, HC Deb 24 February 1890, vol. 341, cc 1088–1127.
100. Reported in *Liverpool Mercury*, 13 May 1891, p. 8I.
101. HC Deb 24 April 1888, vol. 325, cc 411-412.
102. HC Deb 28 February 1888, vol. 322, cc 1637–8 and 27 February 1890, vol. 341, cc 1353–97. Western Australia Constitution Act, 1890, Vict. 53&54 c123.
103. Henry de Worms, *Hansard*, HC Deb 3 March 1890, vol. 341, c 1642; 12 August 1890, vol. 348, cc 801–802.
104. Telegram quoted in *Daily News*, 8 April 1891.
105. HC Deb 11 February 1890, vol. 341, cc 279–283.
106. Reply to Sir G. Campbell, *Hansard*, HC Deb 2 June 1890, vol. 344, cc 1764–1765. Zanzibar and Heligoland, *The Times*, 21 June 1890, p. 13F.
107. Swaziland, *Hansard*, HC Deb 04 August 1890, vol. 347, cc 1736–8.
108. Another Boer Treck, *Manchester Guardian*, 21 April 1891, p. 9. Baron H. de Worms in *Hansard*, 23 April 1891, vol. 352, c 1167.
109. Worms, *Hansard*, HC Deb 09 March 1891, vol. 351, cc 519–524.
110. *Freeman's Journal*, 8 September 1891, *Belfast News-Letter*, 25 September 1891, *Yorkshire Herald*, 13 October 1891, p. 4.
111. Countrywide election results in *Reynolds's Newspaper*, 10 July 1892. On taking the oath, *Aberdeen Weekly Journal*, 6 August 1892.
112. Roberts, *Salisbury*, p. 577. Queen's Speech, *Hansard*, HL Deb 08 August 1892, vol. 7, cc 21–2. Herbert Asquith, *Hansard*, HC Deb 08 August 1892, vol. 7, cc 94–105.
113. *Aberdeen Weekly Journal*, 6 November 1893.
114. History of the agreements, *The Times*, 8 August 1893, p. 3, 14 April 1894, p. 7A and 21 April 1894, p. 7D.
115. Sydney Buxton (under-sec. for the colonies) and others, *Hansard*, HC Deb 31 July 1894, vol. 27, cc 1461–92.
116. Baron de Worms on Home Rule, *Liverpool Mercury*, 8 November 1892.
117. The Local Government Act, 1894, Vict. 56&57 c73. Address to the Worplesdon Agricultural Association, *The Standard*, 17 October 1891, p. 3; to Liverpool constituents, *Morning Post*, 13 December 1893, p. 3.
118. H. Asquith, *Hansard*, HC Deb 23 February 1893, vol. 9, cc 204–87.
119. Baron Henry de Worms at a Conservative meeting in Liverpool, *Liverpool Mercury*, 7 March 1893.
120. Baron de Worms at the Toxteth Conservative club, *Liverpool Mercury*, 24 October 1891.
121. *Hansard*, HC Deb 28 April 1893, vol. 11, cc 1447–1964; HC Deb 24 May 1897, vol. 49, cc 1117–1126.
122. The royal wedding at Kingston, *The Times*, 26 June 1895, p. 8.

NOTES

123. *Birmingham Daily Post*, 21 September 1895.
124. Roberts, *Salisbury*, pp. 668–676. Gossip from the World, *Birmingham Daily Post*, 23 October 1895, p. 3. Article on Samson Gideon (Lord Eardley's father) by E. Samuel in *DNB*.
125. *Liverpool Mercury*, 19 December 1895.
126. *Hansard*, HL Deb 02 July 1896, vol. 42, cc 515–6; HL Deb 25 May 1897, vol. 49, c 1241. *Liverpool Mercury*, 2 June 1897, *Morning Post*, 17 March 1898, *Glasgow Herald*, 16 March 1898, 25 March 1899.
127. Lord Pirbright, 'The Ruin of the West Indies', *National Review (London)*, December 1897.
128. The destruction of the British sugar trade, *Huddersfield Daily Chronicle*, 28 June 1894, p. 4. Benjamin Taylor, 'The Brussels Sugar Convention', *North American Review*, 1909, 190: 347–354. S.M. Mintz, *Sweetness and Power*.
129. *Hansard*, HL Deb 10 March 1902, vol. 104, cc 850–9.
130. Parliamentary report in *The Echo*, 11 March 1902.

Chapter Seven: *La Belle Époque*

1. Worms, *Reminiscences*, in Beust, *Memoirs*, vol. I, pp. l-lxv.
2. Beust, *Memoirs*, vol. I, p. 38.
3. Roderick J. Barman, 'Nathan Mayer Rothschild and Brazil: The Role of Samuel Phillips & Co.', in *The Rothschild Archive Trust*, 2003, pp. 38–45.
4. Williams, *Leaves of a Life*, p. 268. Obituary, *Jewish World*, 18 October 1889.
5. Marriage Barnet and Phillips, Marylebone 1853 April–June, vol. 1A, p. 902; Stillborn daughter, *Morning Chronicle*, 14 June 1854; Divorce Court File, National Archives, J 77/2/3359.
6. Change of name, *The Standard*, 4 March 1875. Marriage Worms and Phillips, Westminster 1887 January–March, vol. 1A, p. 740.
7. Presentation at court, *The Times*, 11 May 1887.
8. Advertisement by Messrs. Trollope, *The Times*, 24 May 1886.
9. Baron de Worms's new house, *The New York Times*, 13 February 1887.
10. Article in *British Journal of Nursing*, February 1918, p. 76.
11. Hamilton, *Edward VII*, pp. 128–37 and 216.
12. State Ball, *The Times*, 4 July 1889, p. 9E; visit to Hatfield, *The Times*, 9 July 1889, p. 9F.
13. Dr. Clark and Mr. Conybeare in *Hansard*, HC Deb 22 February 1887, vol. 311, c 302. The cartoon, *Punch*, 5 March 1887, p. 113.
14. On the reception, *The Times*, 5 December 1887, p. 9E. Letter 2/9/1896, Lord Wolseley to his wife (copy), in Arthur (ed.), *Letters*.
15. New Zealand meat at home in *Marlborough Express* 20 November 1891, p. 3.
16. Royal Society of London, Fellowship elections, EC/1889/01.
17. Information from the Folkestone Historical Society.
18. The textbook on electric light was Salomons, *The Management of Accumulators*.
19. For decorations, see Royal visit to Pirbright, *Surrey Advertiser*, 3 June 1899. Sale brochure of 1922, Henley Park Estate – Surrey, describes the house.

20. The Chiddingfold hunt, *Lloyd's Weekly Newspaper*, 2 November 1890, *Surrey Advertiser*, 4 April 1891, p. 5.
21. Leases of shooting rights SHC 1320/8/15/26–27. Guildford and District Rifle and Pistol Club, Minute Book 19/2/1200 to 20/2/1903 SHC 7721/1/1. Opening of the range, *Surrey Advertiser*, 26 July 1902.
22. *Morning Post*, 21 March 1891.
23. Mégroz, *Memoirs of Infanta Eulalia*, pp. 26, 68–70, 102–110. *Surrey Advertiser*, 14 & 21 December 1895.
24. H.M. Stanley, *Morning Post*, 19 May 1890; Sir Arthur Sulivan, *Morning Post*, 12 May 1891.
25. *The Times*, 4 September 1896. Letters 4/9/1896 and 26/6/1898, Lord Wolseley to his wife (copies), in Arthur (ed.), *Letters*.
26. On the jewellery, see *Pall Mall Gazette*, 3 April 1889; *Star (NZ)*, 26 April 1889, p. 2, 'The Opening of Parliament in Full State', *The Queenslander (AUS)*, 6 April 1901, *Lady Layard's Journal* for 7 October 1909. *Le Matin*, 10 March 1897, p. 3: *Lady Pirbright qui est une des femmes les plus distinguées de Royaume-Uni, sera, sans contredit, une des mieux habillers.*
27. *The Times*, 3 May 1902 and 11 August 1902.
28. Allfrey, *Edward VII*, p. 62.
29. Pierre-Camile Cartier, http://fondationpierrecartier.org/web%20pages/history.html
30. For Duke of Cambridge, *Surrey Advertiser*, 18 November 1895; for Princess Christian, *Surrey Advertiser*, 3 June 1899; for Prince of Wales, *Surrey Advertiser*, 8 December 1900.
31. *Surrey Advertiser*, 3 June 1899, p. 2. *Déjeuner*: trout, grilled sole, spring chicken, lamb cutlets with peas, quail with watercress, cold roast beef, salad, asparagus, strawberries on a bed of whipped cream, frozen egg and cream custard coated with apricot ice.
32. Inflation: The Value of the Pound 1750–2011, *House of Commons Research Report 12/35* (29 May 2012).

Chapter Eight: Baron Pirbright of Pirbright

1. Worms, *Reminiscences*, in Beust, *Memoirs*, vol. I, p. xi.
2. Information from monuments in Pirbright church and churchyard. Faculty for burial ground, 1879, SHC 1794/Box 3.
3. Squier, *Henley Park*, pp. 71–99. Cawthorne, *History*, pp 13–14, Katherine Halsey, *Remembrances*, with Musical Society concert programme for 1880, *SHC*, 2791/3
4. Land purchases, *Morning Post*, 2 May 1895, p. 5.
5. Letter Nov. 1894 Baron Henry de Worms to Normandy parish Council (copy), *The Morning Post*, 13 November 1894, p. 7.
6. Pirbright Parish Council Minute Book January 1895; Local Government Act 1894, 56& 57 Vict. c73.
7. For the note from Mr H. Halsey, see *Daily News*, 16 October 1895. The decision of the Attorney General is printed in the *Liverpool Mercury*, 19 October 1895.
8. Presentation to Lord Pirbright and announcement of donation of the organ, *Surrey*

NOTES

Advertiser, 21 December 1895, p. 7; 7 November, application for faculty re: the organ, Parish of Pirbright Minute Book 1883–1921, *SHC*, PSH/Pi/71. Christmas decorations, *Surrey Advertiser*, 23 December 1895. Dedication ceremony, *Daily Mail*, 9 June 1896.

9. *Burk's Peerage and Baronetage*, 1897 p. 1162.
10. Letter 23/1/1897, Pirbright Parish Council to the Local Government Board copied into the PPC Minute Book. Information culled from the Pirbright Poor Rate Books 1891–1900 and deeds in the possession of some Pirbright residents.
11. *Surrey Advertiser*, 5 and 12 December 1896. Henrietta Anne Molineux in Molineux, *History*, p. 247.
12. Letter Nov. 1894 Baron Henry de Worms to Normandy Parish Council (copy), *Morning Post*, 13 November 1894, p. 7. Reinhard Müller, *Marienthal*.
13. E.W. Beesen, *Port Sunlight*; W.A. Harvey, *Bournville. The Times*, 19 July 1875, p. 13.
14. Letter 6/3/1900, Lord Pirbright, Nice, to the Chairman of the Parish Meeting, Pirbright, *PPC*.
15. Copy of the auctioneer's brochure in the hands of Jonathan Foster, the Pirbright Historians.
16. Indentures relating to Green house, *PPC*.
17. *Surrey Advertiser*, 3 July 1897.
18. 21 July 1897 Deed of Conveyance, *PPC*; letter 3/7/1897, Bircham & Co solicitors to clerk of the parish council and letter 5/7/1897, Lord Pirbright to Bircham & Co. (copies), *PPC* Minute Book, pp. 61–3.
19. Concerning the advowson of Pirbright, *SHS*, 1794/Box 3
20. Curtis, *Vicars of Pirbright*, pp. 32–33.
21. *Lloyd's Weekly Newspaper*, 1 January 1899. *Sheffield & Rotherham Independent (Supplement)*, 3 January 1899, *Leeds Mercury*, 3 January 1899. *The Standard* and *Morning Post*, 2 January 1899.
22. The correspondence is copied into *SHS* 3265/1/2 *Minutes of the Pirbright School Board*, 19 and 27 December 1898 and 9 January 1899 and *SHS* CEM/169/1 *Minutes of the School Board*, 17 April 1899.
23. *Surrey Advertiser*, 27 May 1899.
24. Proposed hall, *Surrey Advertiser*, 21 January 1899, p. 5. Royal visit to Pirbright, *Surrey Advertiser*, 3 June 1899, p. 2, *The Times*, 1 June 1899, *Woking News and Mail*, 2 June 1899.
25. Letter 6/6/1899, Alfred Johnstone, Pirbright, to the editor, *Woking News and Mail*, 9 June 1899; the vicar and the bellringers, *Woking News and Mail*, 16 June 1899.
26. *Surrey Advertiser*, 5 January 1901, p. 7.
27. *SHS* CEM/169/1 *Minutes of the Pirbright School Board* 29 October 1900 and 22 April 1901. Opening ceremony, *Surrey Advertiser*, 7 April 1902.
28. *Morning Post*, 26 May 1899.
29. *Morning Post*, 25 January 1899, p. 4, and 9 June 1899, p. 5.
30. Origins of the SSHS are set out in *Morning Post*, 26 May 1899, p. 4 and *The Times*, 20 August 1900.
31. Letter, 5/6/1899 Pirbright to Wolseley (copy), *Morning Post*, 10 June 1899, p. 7.
32. Extracts from letters published by Lord Pirbright, *The Times*, 15 August 1900.
33. Letter, Maj. Gen. Trotter and Lt. Gen. Greary to *Morning Post*, 29 November 1899, p. 3. Letter, Lord Pirbright to *The Times*, 22 January 1900, p. 4.

34. Magnus, *Kitchener*, chapter 9.
35. *The Standard* and *The Times*, 12 January 1900; subsequently reported at the Annual General Meeting of the SSHS, *Birmingham Daily Post*, 1 June 1900.
36. *Glasgow Herald*, 19 January 1900; 25 January 1900; *The Derby Mercury*, 23 May 1900. Building commenced, *The Builder*, 7 April 1900, vol. lxxviii, p. 342.
37. *Daily Graphic*, 24 March 1900.
38. Letter 9/3/1900, Princess Christian, Windsor to the editor, *Daily News*, 12 March 1900.
39. *Lloyd's Weekly Newspaper*, 4 February 1900
40. *Echo*, 16 February 1900.
41. *Daily Mail* 18 June 1900; *Jackson's Oxford Journal*, 21 July 1900.
42. Comforts for the troops, *The Times*, 17 January and 27 March 1900. *Church Weekly*, 15 June 1900.
43. *Surrey Advertiser*, 9 June 1900.
44. *Surrey Advertiser*, 26 May 1900.
45. Guildford and District Rifle and Pistol Club, Minute Book, *SHC* 7721/1/1
46. *Surrey Advertiser*, 5 March 1900.
47. Letter 18/9/1900, Richard Dawes to the editor, *The Times*, 19 September 1900.
48. *The Times*, 10 August 1900.
49. Letter 3/9/1900, Major-General Trotter to Lord Pirbright (copy), *The Times*, 11 September 1900.
50. Letter 5/9/1900, G.E.W. Malet to the editor, *The Times*, 10 September 1900.
51. Letter 9/9/1900, Pirbright to the editor, *The Times*, 10 September 1900.
52. Letter 12/9/1900, Herbert F. Eaton to the editor, *The Times*, 15 September 1900, p. 8.
53. Letter 11/9/1900, H. Trotter, Chairman SSHS, to the editor, *The Times*, 25 September 1900.
54. Letter 25/9/1900, Pirbright to the editor, *The Times*, 28 September 1900, p. 2.
55. Letter 4/10/1900, Henry White, London to Richard Dawes, London (copy), *The Times* 8 October 1900.
56. Letter 10/10/1900, Pirbright to the editor, *The Times*, 11 October 1900.
57. Building Trade's position was later summarised: letter 18/9/1902, a subscriber to the editor, *The Times*, 19 August 1902.
58. Continued cash flow, *The Builder*, 15 December 1900, vol. lxxix, p. 545.
59. Pirbright Parish Council Minute Book, 17 April 1901, p. 110, 24 May 1901, p. 119.
60. *Surrey Advertiser*, 11 August 1902.
61. Letter 11/4/1902, Theodore Martin to the editor, *The Times*, 14 April 1902, p. 3.
62. Letter 5/8/1902, Pirbright to the editor, *The Times*, 6 August 1902.
63. *The Times*, 16 August 1902, p. 7.
64. Letter 19/8/1902, Pirbright to the editor, *The Times*, 20 August 1902, p. 5.
65. *The Times*, 12 August 1902, p. 10.
66. *The Times*, 6 October 1902, p. 4.
67. Naval and Military intelligence, *The Times*, 20 February 1904.
68. Soldiers, Sailors, Airmen and Families Association Forces Help, Report to the Council December 2004.

NOTES

Chapter Nine: Epilogue

1. *Surrey Advertiser*, 10, 17 and 24 January 1903.
2. Letter 17/1/1903, P. McGinn, secretary for Lady Pirbright, Henley Park to H.M. Briant (copy), *Surrey Advertiser*, 24 January 1903.
3. Emden, *The Jews of England* p. 285.
4. Announcement of Halsey's death, *Surrey Advertiser*, 5 June 1937.
5. On Protestant anti-Semitism, Beust, *Memoirs*, vol. I, p. 85. Letter 7/4/1834, Bismarck to Scharlach quoted in Steinberg, *Bismarck*, p. 43.
6. Funeral of Lord Pirbright, *Surrey Advertiser*, 17 January 1903; *The Times*, 14 January 1903.
7. L. Wolf, 'Old Anglo-Jewish Families', in Wolf and Roth, *Essays*, p. 213.
8. Death of Lord Pirbright, *Jewish World*, 16 January 1903.
9. *The Times*, 10 June 1904; *Surrey Advertiser*, 11 June 1904.
10. *The Times*, 13 February 1888.
11. *The Times*, 2 January 1903, p. 4.
12. Samuel Henry Faudel-Phillips, *The Times*, 5 June 1909; Sir George Faudel-Phillips, *The Times*, 2 January 1923; Christ's Church restoration, *The Times*, 27 February 1896.
13. Gospel according to Mark (King James version), ch. 10, v. 14. Royal visit to Pirbright, *Woking News and Mail*, 2 June 1899.
14. Childrens' treat, *Surrey Advertiser*, 5 January 1901, p. 7.
15. Court Circular, *The Times*, 30 April 1901.
16. *The Times*, 7 March 1903.
17. *The Times*, 8 July 1906; *Le Figaro*, 30 September 1906, p. 2.
18. 'Lady Pirbright une grande dame des anglais qui a fixé à Paris ses pénats', *Les Modes (Paris)*, May 1907, p. 3. Social details from *Le Figaro* 1907–1912. Edward VII, *Le Figaro*, 5 February 1907, p. 2.
19. *The Times*, 12 November 1904, 4 December 1906, 25 July 1904, 6 August 1906.
20. *The Times*, 4 March 1905. Report of the Royal Hibernian Academy, 10 October 1905, p. 12 para. 296.
21. *Surrey Advertiser*, 25 July 1914, p. 5.
22. Lady Pirbright's funeral, *Surrey Advertiser*, 5 December 1914.
23. Used in the announcement of her mother's death, *Neue Freie Presse [Wien]*, 10 July 1895.
24. Anna von Lieben, *zu Erinnerung*.
25. Obituary, *The Times*, 5 December 1984.

Index

Adler, Herman 28
Adler, Nathan 28
Affirmation Bill 72, 73
Afghanistan 25, 81, 86, 140, 142
Alexander II, Czar, assassinated 34
Alliance Israélite Universelle 28, 30, 33
Allied Building Trades 143, 147
Anglo-Jewish Association:
    and the Balkans 31
    and Edward VII 38, 156
    formation 29
    and Henry Worms:
        president 29
        resigns 38, 87
    and Jewish schools 30
    and Russia 34
    and the Shah of Persia 29
Anti Semitism:
    in the Balkan states 31
    of Bismarck 152
    in Germany 36, 152
    and Henry Worms 25, 66
    in Romania 32, 33
    in Russia 34
Argyll, Duchess of 123, 153
Armagh railway disaster 99
Austria:
    Austro-Prussian war (1866) 49
    Finance 44, 48, 52
    land area 43

Baden-Powell, George 107
Barnet, William 117
Beckford, William 9
beet sugar industry 93
    London conference 94, 98
    and subsidies 94
Belcredi, Richard Count, first minister of Austria 49
Berlin conference (1878) 32

Berlin conference (1890) 100
Beust, Friedrich Ferdinand Count von, Chancellor of Austria:
    in Austria and Saxony 50
    on Austrian financial situation 52
    and Disraeli 66, 69
    and the Franco-Prussian war 115
    and Henry Worms 25, 50, 55
    in London 57, 116
    in Salzburg 51
    and the Worms' Austrian title 53
bills of exchange 14
Bisley homes 124, 141, 145,
    see also Princess Christian Homes, Bisley
Bismarck, Prince Otto von, Chancellor of Germany 32, 33, 48, 50, 52, 74, 95, 100,
    on Henry Worms 155
    anti-Semitic views 152
Bleichröder, Gerson, banker 33, 44, 48, 50, 52, 54
Boer War (1880-1881) 83
Boer War (1899-1902) 107, 140
Bombay 17
Boord, Thomas 70, 78, 88
Borough Jewish Schools 29
Bosnia and Herzegovina 33
Bournville 133
Bradlaugh, Charles 71, 72, 74
Briant, H.M. 151
British and Foreign Exchange and Investment Bank 55
British South Africa Company 103, 104, 106
Brussels Sugar Convention 112
Burnand, Francis 24

Calcutta 17, 61, 132, 159
Cambridge, Prince Adolphus 1st Duke of 28
Cambridge, Prince George 2nd Duke of 75, 123, 139, 153
cane sugar industry 93

INDEX

London conference on 94, 98
Capper, Charles 66, 89
Carlsbad 57
Cavendish, Lord Frederick 85
Central Synagogue 28
Cetshwayo, Zulu king 82, 102
Chief Rabbi 3, 28, 30, 155
Christian and Jew, newspaper 73
Churchill, Lord Randolph 72, 84,
  and leadership controversy 79-83
  Chancellor of the Exchequer 91
Clarke, Sir Edward 20
clôture 74
Cohen family 10
Cohen, Arthur 34, 36, 71
Cohen, Lionel Louis 90
Colombo 16
Constantinople conference (1876) 31, 32
Continental System 9
conveyancing of voters 71
Corrupt Practices at Elections Act 67
Cowes 55
Crimean War 20, 31, 75
Cumberland, Stuart, thought reader 62

Danish-German war (1864) 49
Dante, *Divina Commedia* quoted 33
Davidson, Randall, Bishop of Winchester (*later* Archbishop of Canterbury) 126, 131, 136, 138, 153
Derby, Edward George Geoffrey Smith-Stanley, 14th Earl of 65
Derby, Edward Henry Stanley, 15th Earl of 16, 3, 53
Derby, Frederick Arthur Stanley, 16th Earl of 92, 142,
  see also Stanley, Frederick
Dinuzulu, Zulu chief 102
Disraeli, Benjamin (*later* Lord Beaconsfield) 27, 32, 37, 65, 66, 68, 70, 79, 81-83
Drummond Wolff, Henry 63, 72, 73, 80, 84
Dunn, Reverend Henry 125, 131, 135, 136

Eaton, Major-General Herbert, 3rd Baron Chesylemore 146, 147
Edward, Prince of Wales 38, 41, 125, 126, 147, 153, 157
Egham, Surrey 16, 45, 47, 54, 58, 116, 121, 153
Egypt 56, 61, 81, 83-85, 91, 104
electrically driven landau 138, 148
Elizabeth, Empress of Austria 57, 60

Eugénie, Empress of France 55, 123, 153, 157
Eulalia, Infanta of Spain 123, 157

Faggetter, James 132, 135
Farrer, Thomas, permanent secretary to the Board of Trade (*later* 1st Baron Farrer) 93, 97, 99
Faudel-Phillips & Son 62, 117
Fergusson, Sir James, 6th baronet 105
Fort Salisbury, Rhodesia (*now* Harare, Zimbabwe) 103
Foucault's pendulum 23
Fourth Party 80
Franco-Prussian war (1870) 52
Frankfurt 6, 8, 11, 13, 42, 53
Franz Joseph, Emperor of Austria 50, 57
free trade 95, 98, 112

G. & A. Worms 14, 17, 33, 42, 43, 52, 56, 116
Game of Parliament, The 78
Ghica, Prince Ion, Romanian premier (*later* ambassador) 33, 124
Gilbert, W.S. 17, 20, 155
Gladstone, William Ewart 25, 35, 65, 67, 72, 74, 79, 82, 85, 86, 94, 97,
  1st administration 68
  2nd administration 70
  3rd administration 90
  4th administration 106
gold standard for currencies 17, 44
Goldsmid, Julian 29, 38, 110, 156
Gordon, General Charles George 85
Gorst, Sir John 68, 80, 96, 101
Goschen, George (*later* 1st Viscount Goschen) 91
Graham, Cunningham 101
Grammont, Duke of 115
'Great Game', the 81
Great German Synagogue 11, 27, 28
Green House, Pirbright 135, 137, 147
Greenwich 70, 73, 75-78, 86, 88, 155
Guildford Rifle Club 23, 153

Halsey, Edward Joseph 130, 137, 145
Halsey, Henry Joseph Tenison 129, 130, 131, 134, 136, 152
Hartington, Spencer Compton Cavendish, Marquis of (*later* 8th Duke of Devonshire) 90, 99, 119
Heligoland 10, 103
Henley Park 2, 108, 121, 122, 124, 137, 152, 157,

INDEX

visit of the Prince of Wales 127
visit of Princess Christian 126, 138
Henriques, Philip 148, 153, 158
Hermann Todesco und Söhne, private bank 43
Hicks Beach, Sir Michael (*later* 1st Viscount St. Aldwyn) 63, 93, 96, 99-101
Hill, Lord Arthur 107, 153
Hofmannsthal, Hugo von 62
Holy Roman Empire 6, 8
hours of work 101
Hughes, Edwin 68, 69, 77, 88-89
Humboldt, William, Prussian diplomat and Nathan Rothschild, 10
HW ciphers 134

Indian currency depreciation 17
Inner Temple 24
Irish Church Bill (1869) 66, 68
Irish Home Rule Bills (1896 & 1893) 90, 107
Irvine, Henry 61
Isma'il Pasha, Khedive of Egypt and the Sudan 83, 84

Jewish Disabilities Removal Act (1845) 12
Jewish disabilities
  in England 9
  in Frankfurt 6, 8
  in the Holy Roman Empire 6
  in Vienna 6
  in Worms 6
Jewish emancipation
  Austria 43, 45
  England 12
  Frankfurt 8
Jewish peers (England & Ireland) 111
Judengasse 6

Kahn, Prince Michael, Persian ambassador 119, 124
Kandahar 81
Kepwick Hall 61
Khartoum 85
King's College London 19
  engineering society 20-23
Knutsford, Henry Thurstan Holland, 1st Viscount 96, 110, 122
Königgrätz, battle of 50
Krauss, Reverend Alfred 136, 137-139, 144, 151, 152, 154
Kruger, Paul, President of the South African Republic 83, 102, 104, 106, 140, 143

Küfstein, Count 94

Land Mortgage Bank of India 17
land reform bill, Irish (1881) 74
Landauer, Adolf (brother-in-law) 42, 47, 56
Lawson, Sir Edward 41, 153
Lawson, Sir Wilfrid 67, 102
Léon et Dreher of Paris 56
Léon, Count Moritz von 58, 59
Leopold II, King of the Belgians 95, 153
Levy, Edward, (*later* 1st Lord Burnham) 63
Levy, Joseph Moses 63
Liberal Unionist party 90, 91, 99, 105, 109, 110
Lieben, Anna von 48, 159
Liverpool 34, 88, 90, 93, 101, 108, 109, 111, 155
Liverpool Court of Passage Bill (1896) 111
Local Government Act (1894) 108, 130
London conference (1887) 94
London dockers' strike 100
Löwenstein-Scharffeneck, Count Maximillian von 61, 153
Lowther, James William (*later* 1st Viscount Ullswater) 105
Ludwig Victor, Archduke of Austria 55

Mangles, Ross Lowis 132, 144
Marienthal 43, 133
Matabeleland 103, 106
McLaren Morrison, David 61, 159
Meran, Austria (*now* Merano, Italy) 57
Merchandise Marks Act (1887) 92, 100
Mersey Channels Bill (1897) 111
Metropolitan Artisans and Labourers Dwellings Association 133
Metternich, Prince Klemens von 42, 48
Mayer Amschel Rothschild & Sons 7, 9
Midlothian 70, 83, 98
'mixed marriages in high places' 38
Montefiore, Claude 156
Montefiore, Moses (uncle) 10, 32, 39
Mozart Institute, Salzburg 55

Napoleon I 8, 55, 85
Napoleon III 24, 51, 55, 73, 115
Napoleon, Prince Victor, titular Napoleon V 133
Natal 102
National Union of Conservative Associations 25, 79
Normandy Parish Council 130, 133

195

INDEX

Northcote, Stafford Henry, 1st Earl of Iddesleigh 71, 78, 79-81, 85, 87

Oaths Act (1888), 73
Onslow, William Hillier, 4th Earl of Onslow 99, 112, 120, 122
Oppenheimer, Ludwig von 158
Overend, Gurney & Co. 17, 44

Palais Todesco, Vienna 45, 57, 62, 121
Palmerston, Henry, 3rd Viscount 23, 40, 65, 94
Paris conference (1876) 31
Parliamentary expenses scrutinised 97
Parnell, Charles Stuart 90
Patriotic Fund 75, 123
Permissive Bill 67
Phillips, Benjamin Samuel 28, 58, 60, 62, 117
Phillips, Sarah (2nd wife) 60, 62, 81,
   divorce 117
   see also Worms, Sarah, Baroness and Pirbright, Sarah, Lady
Pirbright Parish Council 108, 130, 132, 133, 147, 153
Pirbright village 1, 129, 130
   and army manoeuvres 124
   and manor 131, 136
   and royal visit 126, 138
   and School Board 136, 137
   vicars 136
   and village hall 126
   village improvement 133, 134
Pirbright, Henry, Lord
   a 'great swell' 126
   and Bisley Homes scheme 141-147
   on Brussels sugar convention 112
   buys land in Pirbright 130
   chairman of parish council 130
   character 154, 155
   and Christmas treats 136
   created 110, 131
   disputes
      with Henry Halsey 131, 134
      with Reverend Krauss 137, 139
      with Ross Mangles 132
      with SSHS 145-6
   on entertainment and costs 125
   funeral 153
   and Lord Pirbright's Hall 138, 148
   and Pirbright infants school 139
   and privileges of property 131
   and religion 156
   retired from public speaking 111
   and sanitation 133
   will 152
Pirbright, Sarah, Lady
   comforts for the troops 144
   Dame of Grace 156
   death 157
   dresses 124
   jewellery 125
   and Martin Luther 139
   move to Paris 157
Plunket, David Robert (*later* 1st Baron Rathmore) 110
Plural Voting Bill 109
Port Sunlight 133
Primrose League 63, 79
Primrose, Archibald Philip, 5th Earl of Rosebery *see* Lord Rosebery
Prince Imperial of France 55
Princess Alice disaster 76
Princess Christian Homes, Bisley 143, 147, 148

Queen Victoria
   birthday 139
   diamond jubilee 119, 135
   golden jubilee 13, 123, 130

Raikes, Henry, Postmaster General 105
Railway and Canal Traffic Bill (1887) 93
Redistribution of Seats Act (1885) 86
Reform Bill (1885) 86
Regulation of Railways Bill (1889) 99
Representation of the Peoples Act (1867) 65
Republic of the North 104
Rhodes, Cecil 103
Ritchie, Charles (*later* 1st Baron Ritchie of Dundee) 97
Roberts, General (*later* Lord Roberts of Kandahar) 82, 142
Romeike, Henry 77, 82
Rosebery, Lord 37, 91, 108, 120, 121
Rothschild Estate in Ceylon 15
Rothschild, Alfred de 41, 119, 153
Rothschild, Ferdinand de 110, 119, 121
Rothschild, Jeanette (grandmother) 7, 8, 15
Rothschild, Lionel Nathan 13, 28
Rothschild, Mayer Amschel (great-grandfather) 7
Rothschild, Nathan (granduncle) 9, 10 96
Rothschild, Nathaniel Mayer, 1st Baron Rothschild 13, 55, 71, 111

INDEX

Russell, Lord John (*later* 1st Earl Russell) 12, 65, 94

Salisbury, 3rd Marquis of
  1st administration 87
  2nd administration 91
  3rd administration 110
  against Jewish relief bill 13
  against 2nd reform bill 65, 86
  and the AJA 34
  at Constantinople conference 32
  leader of the Lords 74
  party dual leadership 79
  praise for HW 97
  and Shah of Persia 119
  'the gateway to India' 85
Salomons, David 12, 29
Salzburg 50, 55
Sami, Suliman 84
Samuel family 10
Samuel Phillips & Co., Brazil 11, 117
Samuel, Behrend George (uncle) 10, 38, 122, 130
Samuel, Henrietta (mother) 11
Sandwich, Deal and Walmer elections 68
Schey family of Vienna 42, 46
Schey, Frederick Baron 43, 46
Schleswig-Holstein question 49
Schloss Trauttmansdorff 57, 58, 59
Schmerling, Anton, first minister of Austria 47
Schnapper, Salomon Mayer (uncle) 42
Seamen's Hospital Society 76
Shah of Persia 29, 61, 119, 124
silver standard for currencies 17, 44
Simon, John, Serjeant at Law 30
  and the AJA 34-37
  and Bradlaughism 71, 73
Simpson, Albert 18
Sinclair, Sir Tollemanche 25
South African Republic 106
  see also Transvaal
Stanhope, Edward 88
Stanley, Frederick, president Board of Trade 91, 92, 96
  see also Derby, Frederick Arthur Stanley
Stöcker, Adolf 36, 101
Strauss, Johann 45
Suez Canal 22, 44, 56, 83
Sugar Convention Bill (1889) 99, 112
Swaziland 83, 104, 107

Test and Corporations Acts (1661 & 1673) 12

Todesco, Anna von 47
  see also Lieben, Anna von
Todesco, Eduard Baron von (father-in-law) 42, 43, 46, 133
Todesco, Franzisca (Fanny) von 42
  see also Worms, Franzisca
Todesco, Gabriella von 158
Todesco, Sophie Baroness Eduard von (mother-in-law) 45, 61
Transvaal 74, 82, 102, 104, 107, 140, 144,
  see also South African Republic
Trauttmansdorff, Count Joseph von 57
Treaty of Berlin (1878) 33
Treaty of San Stefano (1877) 32
Trotter, Major General H. 124, 141, 145-147
Twefik Pasha, Khedive of Egypt and the Sudan 84

Uitlanders 107, 140
University College London 19
Urabi, Ahmed 84
Usibepu, Zulu chief 102

Waley, Jacob 29
Warner, John Henry 58, 60, 61
Welsh Suspensory Bill, (proposed 1893) 108
Western Australia 102
Wheatstone, Professor Charles 20
William II, Emperor of Germany 100
Williams, Montague 24
Wolseley, Field Marshal Garnet Joseph (*later* 1st Viscount Wolseley)
  on the Bisley homes 141
  Egypt 84
  on Henry Worms' hospitality 120, 124
Wood, Sir Evelyn 124
Worms, Alice (daughter) 47, 58, 60, 61, 153, 159
Worms, Anthony (brother) 11, 14, 16, 17,
  death 25
  marriage 42
Worms, Benedict Moses (grandfather) 7
Worms, Constance (daughter) 62, 159
Worms, Dora (daughter) 48, 62
Worms, Ellen Henrietta (sister) 11, 42, 45
Worms, Franzisca (Fanny) Baroness Henry de 47, 55,
  appearance 58
  death 158
  divorce 62
  in Meran 57-59
  see also Todesco, Franzisca von

INDEX

Worms, Gabriel (uncle) 15
Worms, George (brother) 11, 13, 60, 63
  attends King's College London 19
  broker 42, 52
  in East India trade 16
  marriage 42
  and Milton Park 16, 116
  retires 44
Worms, Henrietta (aunt) 42
Worms, Henry, (*later* Baron Pirbright of Pirbright)
  appearance and voice 73, 78, 112
  Austrian title 53
  Birth 18
  and Thomas Boord 69, 78, 88
  British title 110
  charity commissions
    Greenwich Hospital charity 75
    London Orphan Asylum 76
    Patriotic Fund 75
    Seamen's Hospital Society 76
  and conservative clubs 78
  conservative Jews 13
  created FRS 120
  divorce 59
  in Egypt 56
  election results
    Greenwich (1880) 70
    Liverpool (Toxteth east) 90, 105, 110
    London (1880) 69
    Sandwich (1868) 68
  financial affairs
    British and Foreign Exchange and Investment Bank 55
    G. & A. Worms 14, 24, 42
    inherited funds 45, 38
    Land Mortgage Bank of India 16
    will 127
  and Gladstone 35, 72, 74, 83, 85, 90, 98, 107
  government positions
    Berlin conference (1890) 101
    Board of Trade 87
    Colonial Office 95
    Privy Councillor 98
    Sugar Bounties Conference 94
  guests
    Chiddingford hunt 122
    Duke of Cambridge 123
    Duke of Connaught 123
    Edward, Prince of Wales 126
    Empress Eugénie 123
    Infanta Eulalia 123
    King of the Belgians 122
    Major-General H. Trotter 124
    Onslow, Lord 120
    Prince Ion Ghica 124
    Prince Malcolm Khan 124
    Prince Victor Napoleon 123
    Princess Christian 126
    Sir Evelyn Wood 124
    Wolseley 120, 124
  and Edwin Hughes 69, 89
  Inner Temple 24
  Jewish associations
    the Anglo-Jewish Association 28
    and Berlin conference (1878) 32
    the Central Synagogue 28
    the Jewish schools' council 29
    and Jews in Russia 34-36
    and Paris conference (1876) 31
    on patriotism of the Jews 30
    presses Salisbury on Berlin treaty 33
    resignation from AJA 38
  King's College London
    enters 19
    political views at King's 20
    president of Engineering Society 20, 24
    public lecture 22
    rifle volunteer corps 24
    sporting life 23, 67
    student lectures 21-22
  libel case 89
  living at
    the Albany 58
    Egham 47,58
    Grosvenor Place 118
    Henley Park 121
    Knightsbridge 47, 54
    Old Burlington Street 58
    Park Crescent 11
  marriage in London 118
  marriage in Vienna 42
  offered Austrian government position 51
  political opinion
    on affirmation 72
    on Afghanistan 86
    on the Boer Convention 83
    on Brussels Sugar Convention 112
    on cheap labour 101
    on *clôture* 74
    on conveyancing 71
    on Egypt 83
    on the Fourth Party 80

INDEX

on Home Rule Bill 107
on hours of work 101, 107
on importance of a religion 30, 67, 73, 109
on Khartoum 85
on payment of MPs 109
on plural voting 109
on the Sami trial 84
on Transvaal 82, 83
on treatment of women 77
Sugar Bounties Convention
 Conference in London 94
 and European trip 95
 T. Farrer criticises 97, 99
 Gladstone criticises 97
 Salisbury praises 97
 Sugar Convention Bill (1889) 98
Tidal Rivers (Interment's) Bill 77
and Vienna 45, 48, 58
see also Pirbright, Henry, Lord

Worms, Maurice (uncle) 15, 57
Worms, Sarah, Baroness Henry de 120-122,
 see also Pirbright, Sarah, Lady and Phillips, Sarah
Worms, Solomon Benedict (father)
 Austrian peerage 53
 a banker and broker 12, 14, 41
 and the Central Synagogue 28
 in Ceylon 15
 Egham home 16, 47
 in England 10
 in Frankfurt 10
 London homes 11, 27
 marriage 11
 naturalisation 53
 and Prince Leopold of Coburg 96
 will 45
Worplesdon Agricultural Association 108

Zulu wars 55, 82, 102